Your
iPad®
at Work

FOURTH EDITION

Jason R. Rich

Que®

800 East 96th Street,
Indianapolis, Indiana 46240 USA

YOUR iPAD® AT WORK
FOURTH EDITION

ISBN-13: 978-0-7897-5103-4

ISBN-10: 0-7897-5103-8

Library of Congress Control Number: 2013951602

Printed in the United States of America

First Printing: November 2013

TRADEMARKS

WARNING AND DISCLAIMER

BULK SALES

Que Publishing offers excellent discounts on this book when ordered in quantity for bulk purchases or special sales. For more information, please contact

U.S. Corporate and Government Sales
1-800-382-3419
corpsales@pearsontechgroup.com

For sales outside of the U.S., please contact

International Sales
international@pearsoned.com

EDITOR-IN-CHIEF
Greg Wiegand

SENIOR ACQUISITIONS EDITOR
Laura Norman

DEVELOPMENT EDITOR
Jennifer Ackerman-Kettell

MANAGING EDITOR
Sandra Schroeder

PROJECT EDITOR
Mandie Frank

SENIOR INDEXER
Cheryl Lenser

PROOFREADER
Megan Wade-Taxter

TECHNICAL EDITOR
Christian Kenyeres

EDITORIAL ASSISTANT
Cindy Teeters

DESIGNER
Mark Shirar

COMPOSITOR
Bumpy Design

CONTENTS AT A GLANCE

TABLE OF CONTENTS

ABOUT THE AUTHOR

Jason R. Rich (www.JasonRich.com) is the bestselling author of more than 55 books, as well as a frequent contributor to a handful of major daily newspapers, national magazines, and popular websites. He's also an accomplished photographer and an avid Apple iPhone, iPad, Apple TV, and Mac user.

Jason R. Rich is the author of the books *Your iPad at Work: 4th Edition*, as well *OS X Mountain Lion Tips and Tricks*, both published by Que Publishing. He's also written *How to Do Everything MacBook Air, How to Do Everything iCloud: 2nd Edition*, and *How to Do Everything iPhone 5* for McGraw-Hill, *iPad and iPhone Tips and Tricks*, Third Edition, and *Ultimate Guide to YouTube For Business* for Entrepreneur Press.

More than 150 feature-length how-to articles by Jason R. Rich, covering the Apple iPhone and iPad, can be read free online at the Que Publishing website. Visit www.iOSArticles.com and click on the Articles tab. You can also follow Jason R. Rich on Twitter (@JasonRich7) or read his blog, called Jason Rich's Featured App Of The Week, to learn about new and useful iPhone and iPad apps (www.FeaturedAppOfTheWeek.com).

DEDICATION

This book is dedicated to the late Steve Jobs, as well as to my niece, Natalie, and to Nick.

ACKNOWLEDGMENTS

Thanks once again to Laura Norman at Que Publishing for inviting me to work on all four editions of this book and for all of her guidance as I've worked on this project. My gratitude also goes out to Jenn Kettell, Greg Wiegand, Kim Scott, Megan Wade-Taxter, Mark Shirar, Cindy Teeters, Todd Brakke, Gregg Kettell, and Paul Boger, as well as everyone else at Que Publishing and Pearson who contributed their expertise, hard work, and creativity to the creation of this *Your iPad at Work* edition (as well as the three previously published editions).

Thanks to my friends and family for their ongoing support. Finally, thanks to you, the reader. I hope this book helps you take full advantage of the power and capabilities of this amazing tablet device so that you're able to fully utilize your iPad in every aspect of your life.

WE WANT TO HEAR FROM YOU!

As the reader of this book, *you* are our most important critic and commentator. We value your opinion and want to know what we're doing right, what we could do better, what areas you'd like to see us publish in, and any other words of wisdom you're willing to pass our way.

We welcome your comments. You can email or write to let us know what you did or didn't like about this book—as well as what we can do to make our books better.

Please note that we cannot help you with technical problems related to the topic of this book.

When you write, please be sure to include this book's title and author as well as your name and email address. We will carefully review your comments and share them with the author and editors who worked on the book.

Email: feedback@quepublishing.com

Mail: Que Publishing
             ATTN: Reader Feedback
             800 East 96th Street
             Indianapolis, IN 46240 USA

READER SERVICES

Visit our website and register this book at quepublishing.com/register for convenient access to any updates, downloads, or errata that might be available for this book.

Introduction

When Apple announced the original iPad back in 2010, the company's iconic CEO, the late Steve Jobs (1955–2011), referred to the tablet device as "magical." That was the start of a technological revolution that has since captured the imaginations of iPad users around the world, and for Apple, it has resulted in tens of millions of iPad units sold each subsequent year.

Just as the iPad itself has evolved a lot in just a few years, so have the ways people are using their tablet on-the-job. Thus, this all-new fourth edition of *Your iPad at Work* is intended to help you quickly get up and running using the iOS 7 operating system, plus introduce you to some of the ways success-driven people are using their tablets as powerful communications, productivity, and organization tools.

NOTE In September 2013, Apple released iOS 7, the newest version of the operating system used exclusively by Apple's mobile devices. As you're about to discover, iOS 7 offers a redesigned user interface and updated look. It also includes a vast selection of new and more-advanced features; better integration with Apple's iCloud service; and enhanced capabilities for sharing app-specific content with others via email, instant message, Facebook, or Twitter. Plus, iOS 7 features an improved version of Siri, which provides an alternative way to interact with the tablet using your voice.

This book covers all of the latest iPad and iPad mini model that are capable of running iOS 7, including the iPad 2, iPad with Retina Display, iPad Air, iPad mini and iPad mini with Retina Display.

In just a few short years, the iPad has gone from being a cool, high-tech gadget to becoming an indispensible business tool used by millions of highly successful people. With each generation of iPad that's been released, more and more business people, entrepreneurs, consultants, freelancers, and other types of professionals have discovered firsthand that the iPad often can replace the need to carry around a larger and heavier notebook computer.

Regardless of what you do for a living, this all-new fourth edition of *Your iPad at Work* can help you quickly learn how to use your iPad and the iOS 7 operating system. When you combine any iPad or iPad mini model with the right collection of apps and accessories, it becomes the perfect tool for anyone who needs advanced computing power while on the go. The iPad can also be used effectively while sitting at a desk, lounging by the pool, in a conference room or classroom, on an airplane, in the car (not while driving), while sitting on a couch at home, or just about anywhere else.

WHAT YOU CAN EXPECT FROM THIS BOOK

Your iPad at Work provides step-by-step instructions, plus hundreds of tips, strategies, and ideas for incorporating the iPad into your personal and professional life with the shortest learning curve possible—even if you don't consider yourself to be technologically savvy or adept at using the latest high-tech gadgets.

TIP As you read *Your iPad at Work*, keep your eye out for the Tips, Notes, and Caution boxes. Each of these boxes has short tidbits of information that are particularly important and directly relevant to the chapter you're reading.

Before we start exploring all the work-related tasks your iPad is capable of, including managing email, web surfing, word processing, managing contacts, scheduling, text messaging, videoconferencing, making voice-over-IP phone calls, sending/receiving faxes, working with databases and spreadsheets, creating and giving digital slide presentations, audio recording (dictation), obtaining business listings and navigation directions, managing to-do lists, facilitating project management, credit card transaction processing, invoicing, time billing, taking and editing pictures, shooting and editing video, tweeting, reading eBooks, online banking, and countless other tasks, you must learn the basics of how to interact with this cutting-edge device.

> **TIP** In addition to what you discover from this book, you can access more than 150 how-to articles by *Your iPad at Work* author Jason R. Rich, which have been published on the quepublishing.com website. Simply visit www.iOSArticles.com and click the Articles tab.
>
> You can also read Jason R. Rich's blog, "Jason Rich's Featured App Of The Week," in order to learn all about new and cutting-edge iPad apps (www.FeaturedAppOfTheWeek.com).

UNBOXING YOUR NEW iPAD

If you've purchased your iPad during or after September 2013, it came with Apple's iOS 7 operating system preinstalled. This operating system includes a robust collection of apps that are designed to handle the core tasks you'll probably be using your tablet for. With a quick visit to the online-based App Store, however, you can greatly enhance the capabilities of your iPad by acquiring optional apps for it.

If you've purchased your iPad prior to September 2013, you need to upgrade it to the iOS 7 operating system. How to do this is explained in Chapter 1, "Activating and Personalizing Your Tablet." Keep in mind, if you're using a first-generation iPad model, it is not compatible with iOS 7.

> **NOTE** Read more about finding, acquiring, and installing apps in Chapter 10, "Finding and Installing Apps from the App Store," and learn more about many popular business-related apps worth checking out in Chapter 15, "Discovering 'Must-Have' Business Apps."

When you take the iPad out of the box for the very first time, its battery should be close to fully charged and be ready for you to activate and set up. Whether the iPad you're about to activate is your first or you're upgrading to a newer model, plan on spending at least 15–30 minutes getting your new tablet up and running. The activation and setup process is described within Chapter 1.

> **NOTE** Just about all of the information within this book relates to all of the latest iPad and iPad mini models, and the term "iPad" refers to all iPad and iPad mini models capable of running iOS 7. However, if an iPad model with cellular data Internet connectivity (using a 3G or 4G LTE Internet connection) is required, as opposed to an iPad model with just Wi-Fi Internet connectivity, this is specified.

CHOOSING THE RIGHT iPAD TO MEET YOUR NEEDS

All current iPad models come in several different system configurations. To begin, you need to choose a color casing. Depending on the iPad model, your options include black, white, "space gray" or silver. You also need to decide how much internal storage space you want or need. Your options include 16GB, 32GB, 64GB, or in some cases 128GB.

Keep in mind that iPads are not upgradable in terms of internal storage space or their microprocessor, so you must anticipate your needs before purchasing a tablet.

Finally, you must choose between a Wi-Fi only and a Wi-Fi + Cellular model. This determines how your tablet connects to the Internet and whether or not you need to pay a monthly fee for Internet access. While a Wi-Fi–only model saves you money over the long term, it limits how and where you can access the Internet.

The iPad itself, as well as many apps you use with the tablet often, relies heavily on Internet access. So, depending on how you plan to use your tablet, you may discover that having a cellular data connection (via a 3G or 4G LTE wireless data service) is essential.

> **NOTE** A Wi-Fi–only iPad can connect to the Internet from any Wi-Fi hotspot or network. However, you must remain within the radius of a Wi-Fi signal to maintain the Internet connection. A Wi-Fi + Cellular iPad model can also connect to the wireless data network offered by a wireless data service provider, such as AT&T Wireless, Verizon Wireless, T-Moblie, or Sprint PCS in the United States.

A cellular data connection requires paying a monthly fee, which includes a pre-determined amount of wireless data usage, such as 2GB per month. If you go beyond your monthly wireless data allocation, you are billed extra (per megabyte or gigabyte, depending on your wireless service provider) for use.

iPAD HARDWARE CONFIGURATIONS

The older iPad 2 models feature a 9.7-inch LED-backlit display that offers 1024-by-768 resolution at 132 pixels per inch. They run using Apple's A5 processor. The iPad 2 measures 9.50 inches by 7.31 inches by .34 inches and weighs between 1.33 and 1.35 pounds (depending on the configuration).

The now outdated iPad with Retina Display models feature a more advanced 9.7-inch LED-backlit display. These displays offer 2048-by-1536 resolution at 264 pixels per inch, so they're capable of showcasing much more detailed graphics and more vibrant colors. These iPad models run using Apple's A6X processor and weigh between 1.44 and 1.46 pounds (depending on the configuration).

The new iPad Air (which became available in November 2013) also features a 9.7-inch Retina display, but is thinner and lighter than any previously released full-size iPad. It weights just one pound and is just 7.5 millimeters thick. What also sets the iPad Air apart from its predecessor is its speed. Using the Apple A7 chip, it runs twice as fast as the iPad with Retina Display and eight times faster than the original iPad.

The iPad mini models feature a 7.9-inch LED backlit display. These displays offer a 1024-by-768 resolution at 163 pixels per inch. The iPad mini measures 7.87 inches by 5.3 inches by 0.28 inches, weighs between 0.68 and 0.69 pounds (depending on the configuration), and runs using Apple's A5 processor.

The newest iPad mini with Retina Display not only dramatically improves upon the clarity and resolution of the Multi-Touch display, like the iPad Air, it runs using Apple's cutting-edge A7 processor.

Some people prefer the iPad mini or iPad mini with Retina Display because it's smaller and lighter but runs all of the same apps as the full-size iPad models.

NOTE   All of the latest iPad models, including the new iPad Air and iPad mini with Retina Display, include Lightning Port, while the iPad second- and third-generation iPad with Retina Display utilizes the older 30-pin connector port. All models have an average battery life of between 9 and 10 hours and have Bluetooth and AirPlay functionality built in.

For a more detailed comparison between iPad and iPad mini models from a technical standpoint, visit www.apple.com/ipad/compare.

NOTE Apple no longer sells most configurations of the iPad 2 and has phased out the iPad with Retina Display in favor of the iPad Air. However, iPad 2 models in several different configurations are still available on the secondary used market or as refurbished iPads. These older models can be purchased on eBay.com, for example, starting around $200.00.

In addition to the price of the tablet itself, you might want to invest in an optional Apple Smart Cover for your tablet ($39.00 for the polyurethane edition or $69.00 for the leather edition) or an Apple Smart Case ($49.00 in polyurethane), as well as the AppleCare+ extended warranty ($99.99 for two years of coverage). A selection of leather and Polyurethane Smart Covers and Smart Cases are available for the iPad Air and iPad mini that come in a different assortment of colors.

PREINSTALLED APPS ON ALL iPADS RUNNING iOS 7.0

Each iPad tablet comes bundled with a handful of preinstalled apps. Here's a quick rundown of each app (listed in alphabetical order) that you can begin using as soon as your iPad is activated (see Figure I.1).

If you're a veteran iPad or iPhone user who is upgrading to iOS 7 for the first time, notice that the Home screen, as well as many of app icons displayed on it, has a new look.

- **App Store:** Find, purchase, download, and install apps directly from your iPad. To learn more, see Chapter 10.
- **Calendar:** Manage your schedule on your iPad and sync data with iCloud and other calendar/scheduling apps on your Mac, PC, and/or iPhone. To learn more, see Chapter 4, "Using the Calendar and Clock Apps to Organize Your Life."
- **Camera:** Take photos or shoot high-definition videos using your iPad's built-in cameras. Learn more about taking, editing, viewing, sharing digital photos, and shooting video using your iPad in Chapter 9, "Digital Photography on the iPad."

FIGURE I.1

The iPad's Home screen with the preinstalled app icons displayed. This is what the Home screen looks like shortly after you activate the iPad.

- **Clock:** This app serves as an alarm clock, world clock, and timer. Learn more about it in Chapter 4.

- **Contacts:** Manage your personal contacts database and sync it with iCloud or other contact management apps on your primary computer and/or iPhone. To learn more, see Chapter 5, "Working with the Contacts App."

- **FaceTime:** Participate in free, real-time video calls from your iPad using a Wi-Fi Internet connection. Depending on your wireless service provider, FaceTime may also now be available using a 3G or 4G (LTE) Internet connection. To learn more, see Chapter 14, "Conducting Videoconferences and Virtual Meetings."

- **Game Center:** This is an interactive, online-based community for participating in multiplayer games via your iPad. You can compete against and communicate with other players from around the world and experience a variety of Game Center–compatible games.

- **Mail:** Send and receive emails, plus manage your message archive. iOS 7 offers a handful of useful new features for effectively managing your email accounts, including your iCloud-related email account. For more information, see Chapter 3, "Staying In Touch Using Email and Instant Messages."

- **Maps:** Use this app to access traditional onscreen maps, satellite maps, and even 3D maps of almost any location on the planet, plus obtain real-time turn-by-turn directions (with related traffic condition information) when your iPad is connected to the Web. You can also look up addresses for companies, restaurants, popular destinations (such as airports), and landmarks. Chapter 8, "Exploring Your World with the Maps App," focuses on how to use this versatile app.

- **Messages:** Send and receive text messages for free using iMessage to communicate with other Mac, iPad, iPhone, or iPod touch users. For more information, see Chapter 3.

- **Multimedia:** Acquire music, TV shows, movies, audiobooks, and other iTunes Store content directly from your iPad.

- **Music:** Listen to music, audiobooks, and other audio content acquired from the iTunes Store and elsewhere.

- **Newsstand:** Acquire and read digital editions of newspapers and magazines. To learn more, see Chapter 16, "Staying Informed Using iBooks and Newsstand."

- **Notes:** Create, organize, share, and print text-based memos with this basic text editor. Learn more about it from Chapter 6, "Managing Information Using the Reminders and Notes Apps."

- **Photo Booth:** Take and share photos on your iPad with whimsical themes.

- **Photos:** View, edit, print, and share photos stored on your iPad. For enhanced photo-editing capabilities, use Apple's optional iPhoto app for the iPad. Learn more about Photos in Chapter 9.

- **Reminders:** Manage detailed to-do lists with this powerful app. Like many other of the iPad's preinstalled apps, it works seamlessly with iCloud for syncing data with Macs or other iOS devices (including your iPhone). To learn more, see Chapter 6.

- **Safari:** Use this app to surf the Web. To learn more, see Chapter 7, "Surfing the Web with Safari."

- **Settings:** Use this app to customize the settings of your iPad and personalize how it functions. More information about Settings is offered within Chapter 1.

- **Videos:** Watch TV shows, movies, and other video content on your iPad that was acquired from the iTunes Store.

NOTE Siri, Control Center, and Notification Center work continuously in the background if activated. These features work in conjunction with most other apps.

OPTIONAL "MUST-HAVE" iPAD APPS DEVELOPED BY APPLE

The following apps developed by Apple (or its partners) do not come preinstalled with iOS 7, but you should seriously consider downloading them from the App Store to enhance the capabilities of your tablet:

NOTE If you purchase a new iPad after September 2013, the iWork apps (Pages, Numbers, and Keynote), along with iPhoto and iMovie, are free to download.

- **Facebook** (Free): The ability to update your Facebook status has been integrated into iOS 7; however, to fully manage your Facebook account and communicate with your Facebook friends, you need to use this free app.

- **Find My iPhone** (Free): Take advantage of iCloud's Find My... feature from this app to pinpoint the exact location of your other compatible Apple equipment, including your Mac(s) and iPhone. This app offers an alternative to visiting www.iCloud.com/#find to locate your lost or stolen equipment. You can also remotely lock down or erase the contents of your tablet if it falls into the wrong hands.

- **Find My Friends** (Free): Discover the location of friends, family, or co-workers who are using an iPhone or iPad, in real time. The other person's permission is required.

- **Garage Band** (Free): Compose and record music using your iPad, and transform the tablet into a multitrack recording studio.

- **iBooks** (Free): Acquire and read eBooks from Apple's iBookstore on your tablet. To learn more, see Chapter 16.

- **iMovie** (Free): Edit professional-quality videos on your iPad using footage shot with the tablet's built-in camera (and the Camera app) or footage transferred into your tablet from other sources.

- **iPhoto** (Free): View, edit, organize, print, and share digital photos on your iPad. This app offers far more advanced image-editing features than the Photos app that comes preinstalled on the tablet. The optional iPhoto app fully integrates with iCloud's My Photo Stream and Shared Photo Stream features, which makes it easy to publish photos online and share them with other people, for free.

- **Keynote** (Free): Part of Apple's iWork trio of apps, Keynote is a feature-packed digital slide presentation tool, similar in functionality (and compatible with) to Microsoft PowerPoint.

- **Numbers** (Free): Also part of Apple's iWork trio of apps, Numbers is a powerful spreadsheet-management application compatible with Microsoft Excel.

- **Pages** (Free): This is a full-featured word processor that is compatible with Microsoft Word. It rounds out the iWork app trio.

- **Twitter** (Free): Manage one or more Twitter accounts from your iPad, and send tweets from within apps such as Photos or Safari.

- **Podcasts** (Free): Download or stream thousands of free audio podcasts which you can listen to on an on-demand basis.

- **iTunes U** (Free): Access thousands of free personal-enrichment programs, college courses, and other interactive and educational multimedia content created by the world's leading educational institutions, museums, and philanthropic organizations.

NOTE   Pages, Keynote, and Numbers all seamlessly integrate with Apple's iCloud service, making it easy to automatically synchronize data, documents, and files between your tablet, Mac, PC and other iOS devices. You can also access online versions of the iWork apps from www.icloud.com, after logging in using your Apple ID and password.

To learn more about Apple's iWork for iPad apps, see Chapter 13, "Getting Work Done On-the-Go Using the iWork Apps."

THE ANATOMY OF THE iPAD MODELS

When you look at the front of the iPad, you see its multitouch display. The front-facing camera is located at the top center of the tablet, and you can find the iPad's Home button at the bottom of the tablet, front and center. Other ports and buttons can be found on the top, bottom, and side of the iPad (shown in Figure I.2).

Aside from these few buttons and ports, you do everything while using your iPad via the tablet's multitouch display. To properly navigate around your tablet via this touch screen, you must utilize several simple finger gestures and movements, as well as the tablet's virtual keyboard.

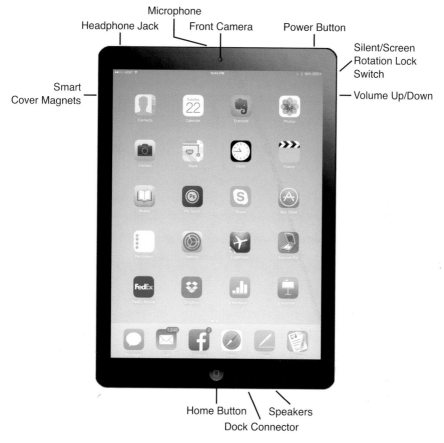

FIGURE I.2

The front of the iPad with Retina Display features a 9.7", full-color, multitouch screen, the Home button, and the device's front-facing camera. On the back of the iPad unit, in the upper-left corner, you see the rear-facing camera. The iPad's power button is located near the top-right corner of the tablet.

USING THE MULTITOUCH DISPLAY

From the moment you turn on your iPad (or take it out of Sleep Mode), aside from pressing the Home button to return to the Home screen at any time, virtually all of your interaction with the tablet is done through the following finger movements and taps on the tablet's highly sensitive multi-touch display:

■ **Tapping:** Tapping an icon or link that's displayed on your iPad's screen serves the same purpose as clicking the mouse when you use your main computer. And, just as when you use a computer, you can single-tap or double-tap, which is equivalent to a single- or double-click of the mouse.

- **Hold:** Instead of a quick tap, in some cases, it is necessary to press and hold your finger on an icon or onscreen command option. When a hold action is required, place your finger on the appropriate icon or command option and hold it there. There's never a need to press down hard on the tablet's screen.

- **Swipe:** A swipe refers to quickly moving a finger along the screen from right to left, left to right, top to bottom, or bottom to top, in order to scroll to the left, right, down, or up.

> **TIP** Regardless of what you're doing on your iPad, as long as it's turned on, to access Notification Center, swipe your finger downward from the very top of the screen. To access the new Control Center, swipe your finger in an upward direction from the very bottom of the screen.
>
> To access iOS 7's Spotlight Search feature from the Home screen in order to quickly find content or data stored on your tablet, swipe your finger downward, starting from the center of the screen (shown in Figure I.3).

FIGURE I.3

To quickly find content stored on your iPad, use the Spotlight Search feature. To access it from the Home screen, swipe your finger downwards, starting near the center of the display.

- **Pinch:** Using your thumb and index finger, perform a pinch motion on the touch screen to zoom out when using certain apps. Or, un-pinch (move your fingers apart quickly) to zoom in on what you're looking at on the screen when using most apps.

- **Grab:** Using all five of your fingers, start with them spread out on the tablet's screen, and then quickly bring them together in a grabbing motion. This immediately returns you to the iPad's Home screen (instead of pressing the Home button).

- **Four-Finger Swipe:** Using all of your fingers on one hand (except your thumb), swipe left or right to switch between apps that are currently running.

> **TIP** To access iOS 7's multitasking bar (shown in Figure I.4), quickly press the Home button twice. When you close an app, in most cases it continues running until it's manually shut down or the tablet is powered off. While it's possible to only use one app at a time, multiple apps can continue to run in the background simultaneously, and you can switch between them with ease.

FIGURE I.4

Use iOS 7's enhanced multitasking bar to quickly switch between apps that are running on your tablet.

> **NOTE** Another way to zoom in or out when looking at the iPad's screen is to double-tap the area of the screen you want to zoom in on.

EXPLORING THE iPAD'S HOME SCREEN

The Home screen on your iPad serves as a central hub from which you can launch individual apps and use the various features and functions of your tablet. Regardless of what you're doing on your tablet, or which app you're using, at any time you can return to the Home screen by pressing the Home button on the front-bottom of the tablet.

See Figure I.5 for a sample Home screen that displays a handful of preinstalled apps, as well as a customized wallpaper in the background.

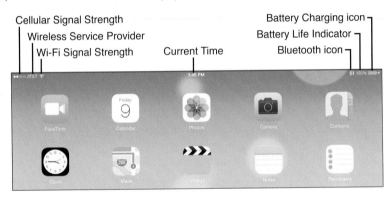

FIGURE I.5

Shown here is the iPad's Home screen and the sampling of the icons displayed along the top of the screen.

Within the main area of the Home screen are all of the icons for apps currently installed on your iPad. On the main iPad Home screen, you can simultaneously display 20 app icons (or folder icons, which are explained shortly), plus an additional 6 app icons on the very bottom of the screen. You also can have multiple Home screens with different app icons displayed on each. From the main Home screen, swipe your finger from right to left (or left to right) to switch between Home screens, if applicable. It's also possible to press the Home button to immediately switch to the main Home screen.

NOTE   You can choose to display up to six app icons at the very bottom of the Home screen. These icons remain constant, regardless of which Home screen you're looking at. Thus, you should select the apps you use the most and place their icons in one of these six locations.

The iPad's wallpaper is displayed behind your app icons. You have the ability to customize this from within the Settings app. Customizing the Home screen's wallpaper is just one way you can personalize your iPad. How to do this is explained in Chapter 1.

ARRANGING ICONS ON THE HOME SCREEN

In addition to selecting your wallpaper graphic, you can determine the position of app icons on your Home screen. To move app icons around, hold down any onscreen app icon for 2 to 3 seconds, until all the icons on the Home screen start to shake.

Next, place your finger on any app icon that you want to move, and slowly drag it to a new position on the Home screen. You can move one app icon at a time, as long as the icons continue shaking. As you move apps around, all neighboring app icons automatically reflow on the Home screen.

During this process (shown in Figure I.6), some of the app icons display a small black-and-white "X" in the upper-left corner of the icon. You can delete the apps displaying the "X" from the iPad by tapping the "X" and then confirming your deletion request. However, you cannot delete the icons for the apps that came preinstalled on your tablet.

When you finish moving the icons around, press the Home button to exit out of this Home screen edit mode and save your changes. The icons stop shaking, and you can return to the normal use of your tablet.

"X" icon

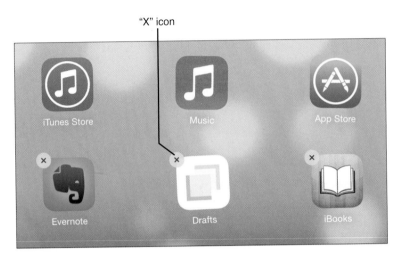

FIGURE I.6

When the app icons are shaking, you can delete the ones with an "X" icon. The icons without the "X" represent the apps that came preinstalled on your tablet.

CREATING FOLDERS TO ORGANIZE APP ICONS

On Your Home screen, it's possible to use folders in order to help organize your Home screen, group together apps based on their category, and remove clutter from your Home screen by consolidating the app icons that are displayed.

To create a folder, from the Home screen, press and hold down any app icon for two to three seconds. When all the app icons start to shake, pick one app icon that you want to place into a new folder. Hold your finger on that app icon, and slowly drag it directly on top of a second app icon that you want to also include within the folder you're creating.

When the two app icons overlap, a folder is automatically created. As soon as this happens, the other app icons on the Home screen fade slightly and a window containing the two apps in the newly created folder appears.

At the top of this window is a text field that contains a default name for the folder based on the category into which the two apps fall. You can keep this name by tapping anywhere on the screen outside the folder window. Alternatively, you can change the name of the folder by tapping the circular "X" icon that's displayed to the extreme right of the folder name field and then use the virtual keyboard to enter a new folder name.

To save your folder, tap anywhere outside the folder window. The newly created folder appears among your app icons on the Home screen. In Figure I.7, the folder is labeled Photography and it contains multiple apps.

FIGURE I.7

When a folder appears on the Home screen, it displays alongside the app icons but looks slightly different. Thumbnails of the apps that are stored in the folder are shown in the folder icon.

After you initially create a folder, it contains two app icons. You can then add more app icons to it whenever all the app icons on the Home screen are shaking. Simply place your finger on the app icon you want to move into the folder and drag that icon on top of the folder icon.

When you're finished adding app icons to the folder, it's possible to move the folder around on the Home screen, just as you would move any app icon. Press the Home button to save your changes and return the Home screen to its normal appearance (causing the app icons to stop shaking).

To launch an app that's stored in a folder, from the Home screen tap the folder icon. When the folder window appears on the iPad's screen (as shown in Figure I.8), it displays all the app icons stored in the folder. Tap the icon for the app you want to use.

To remove an app icon from within a folder, from the Home screen tap the folder icon representing the folder in which the app is stored. When the folder window appears, hold your finger on the app icon that you want to move. When the app icons start to shake, drag the app icon out of the folder window and back onto the main Home screen.

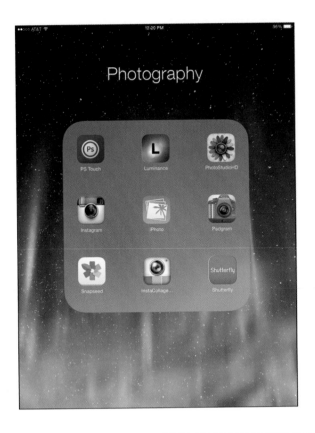

FIGURE I.8

Shown here is an open folder labeled Photography. It contains eight different apps.

If you want to delete an app from a folder and from the iPad altogether, when the icons are shaking, tap the black-and-white "X" icon in the icon's upper-left corner. All apps that you acquire for your iPad from the App Store are automatically stored within your free Apple iCloud online-based account, so they can be reinstalled onto your tablet at any time via the Internet.

1

ACTIVATING AND PERSONALIZING YOUR TABLET

Before you can begin using a new iPad, it must be activated. Then—in addition to choosing your tablet's Lock screen and Home screen wallpaper and rearranging the app icons on your Home screen—you can customize your iPad, as well as individual apps, in a number of ways. The focus of this chapter is activating and personalizing your iPad.

NOTE If you've had your iPad for a while and it's running iOS 6 (or earlier), you need to upgrade the tablet to iOS 7. Directions for how to do this are covered later in this chapter.

TURNING YOUR iPAD ON OR OFF

Like any electronic device, your iPad has a power button. It's located near the top-right corner of the tablet. To turn on the iPad when it's powered off, press the power button for between 1 and 3 seconds. The Apple logo appears as the iPad boots up. Within about 15 seconds, the tablet's Lock screen appears. Once you unlock the iPad, it's ready to use.

To turn off (power down) the iPad, press and hold the power button for between 3 and 5 seconds, until the Slide to Power Off slider appears. Then, swipe your finger from left to right along this slider.

NOTE When your iPad is completely powered off, none of its apps continue to work in the background and the tablet is not able to connect to the Internet.

PLACING YOUR iPAD INTO SLEEP MODE

In addition to being in a powered-on or powered-off state, your iPad can also be placed in Sleep Mode when it's not actively being used. While in Sleep Mode, various apps can continue running in the background. The tablet automatically wakes up if an alert, alarm, or notification is generated by an app that requires your attention. Also while in Sleep Mode, the iPad can automatically access the Internet to check for incoming emails or refresh app-specific data, for example.

To place your iPad into Sleep Mode, press the Power button once quickly (do not hold it down for several seconds as you would when powering it off). Or simply place an Apple Smart Cover or Smart Case cover flap (or compatible cover) over the iPad's screen.

In Sleep Mode, your iPad's screen is turned off. To wake up the iPad from Sleep Mode, quickly press and release either the Power button or the Home button on the tablet. Whenever you wake up the iPad, the Lock screen appears.

TIP If you're using a Smart Cover or Smart Case with your iPad, when you place the cover over the tablet's screen, the tablet automatically goes into Sleep Mode. However, when the Smart Cover or Smart Case is removed, the tablet automatically wakes up and returns you to the Lock screen.

Depending on how the iPad is set up from within Settings, you can adjust the iPad's Auto-Lock feature to place the tablet into Sleep Mode if the tablet is left unattended for a predetermined amount of time. To adjust this, launch Settings, tap on the General option, followed by the Auto-Lock option. Then choose between 2, 5, 10, or 15 minutes, or tap on Never to keep the tablet from shutting down automatically.

ACTIVATING AND SETTING UP YOUR iPAD

When you first purchase your iPad, take it out of the box, and turn it on, you see a black screen that displays the iPad logo, followed by the Hello screen (shown in Figure 1.1). Before you can begin using your tablet, you must activate it. When prompted, swipe your finger along the onscreen slider to begin the activation procedure.

FIGURE 1.1
The Hello screen only appears when the tablet has been turned on for the first time.

> **TIP** The wireless setup procedure that's built in to iOS 7 can be used to initially connect your iPad to the Internet for activation. You may also connect your tablet to your primary computer (PC or Mac) via the supplied USB cable, and then use the iTunes software on your primary computer to initially set up the tablet. This activation procedure is mandatory, but you only need to do it once.

To set up your brand-new iPad running iOS 7, follow these steps:

1. Unpack the iPad and charge its battery.
2. Turn on your iPad by holding down the Power button until the Apple logo appears.
3. When the device is turned on, the Hello screen is displayed (refer to Figure 1.1). Swipe your finger from left to right across the Slide To Set Up slider.
4. Select your Language by tapping on a menu option. English is listed first.
5. From the Select Your Country Or Region screen, tap on the appropriate option (shown in Figure 1.2).

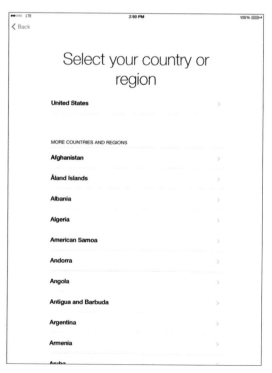

FIGURE 1.2

Select your home country or region.

6. When the Choose a Wi-Fi Network screen appears (shown in Figure 1.3), tap on an available Wi-Fi network (hotspot). If applicable, you can tap on the Use Cellular Connection option in order to allow your device to access a 3G/4G LTE cellular data network and complete the Setup process.

TIP To upgrade to iOS 7, make sure your iOS mobile device is connected to the Internet via a Wi-Fi connection. Also, make sure the battery is fully charged or that your iPad is connected to an external power source. Next, use iCloud Backup or iTunes Sync to back up your device.

When you're ready to upgrade the iOS, launch Settings, tap on the General option, and then tap on the Software Update option. Follow the onscreen prompts to download and install iOS 7. The process will take about 15 minutes.

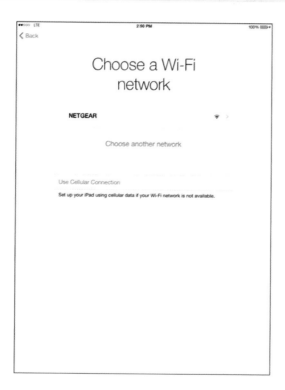

FIGURE 1.3

Choose an available Wi-Fi network so your mobile device can connect to the Internet. If applicable, you also have the option to tap on the Use Cellular Connection option.

7. Your iOS mobile device is now activated. When the Location Services screen appears, tap on Enable Location Services in order to turn on this feature and allow your iPad to pinpoint your location.

8. The Set Up Your iPad menu screen appears next (shown in Figure 1.4). Here, you have three options: Set Up as New iPad, Restore from iCloud Backup, or Restore from iTunes Backup.

FIGURE 1.4

If you are upgrading from an old iPad to a new iPad and want to restore your data from an existing iCloud Backup or iTunes Backup, select one of these options. Otherwise, choose the Set Up as New iPad option.

NOTE When you select the Restore from iCloud Backup or Restore from iTunes Backup option, the Setup process automatically restores your personal settings, apps, files, and documents, for example, to the new iPad using information from your backup files. If you're setting up a new iPad and have no previously created backup files to restore, select the Set Up as New iPad option.

9. From the Apple ID screen, you can either Sign In With Your Apple ID or create a free Apple ID. If you already have another Apple device, use the same Apple ID username and password, so that all of your Macs and iOS mobile devices can sync information via iCloud, as well as share iTunes Store, App Store, iBookstore, and Newsstand purchases. As soon as you enter your Apple ID information, any related content can be transferred from iCloud to your new mobile device, such as your Contacts, Calendar, Reminders, Notes, Mail, and Safari app-specific data, as well as your App Store, iTunes Store, iBookstore, and Newsstand purchases. The information and content that syncs will be based on how you have options within Settings configured.

10. Accept the Terms and Conditions by tapping on the Agree option that's displayed near the bottom-right corner of the screen (shown in Figure 1.5).

FIGURE 1.5

You must accept Apple's terms and conditions before you're allowed to use your new iPhone or iPad.

11. You now have the option to set up and activate the Passcode option. To do this, create and enter a four-digit passcode, and then when prompted, enter the passcode again. To skip this step, tap on the Don't Add Passcode option. (You can always activate or deactivate this feature from within Settings later.)

12. From the Set Up Siri screen, tap on the Use Siri option to activate this fea-
    ture. You can always activate or deactivate it from within Settings later.
    Then, from the Diagnostics screen, tap on either the Automatically Send or
    Don't Send option, based on your personal preference.

13. The Welcome To iPad screen appears next. Tap on the Get Started option
    to begin using your iOS mobile device. The Home screen appears (shown
    in Figure 1.6), and you can now begin using your newly setup and
    activated iPad.

FIGURE 1.6

From the Home screen, you can begin using any of the apps that come pre-installed with iOS 7.

Displayed near the top-left corner of the screen (along the Toolbar) is the Cellular
Data Network and/or Wi-Fi Signal Strength Indicator. As long as one or both of
these options are displayed, your iOS mobile device can freely access the Internet.
Using the App Store app, it's now possible to find, purchase, download, and install
new apps. Or using the iTunes Store app, you can acquire content, such as music,
TV shows, movies, ringtones, music videos, or audiobooks that you can enjoy on
your iPad.

UPGRADING YOUR iPAD FROM iOS 6.X TO iOS 7.X

To upgrade your existing iPad from iOS 6.x (or later) to iOS 7, follow these steps:

1. Make sure your iPad is able to connect to the Internet.
2. Plug in the tablet to an external power source.
3. Back up your iPad using iTunes Sync or iCloud Backup (highly recommended). This ensures that you can save and restore all of your apps, personalized settings, and data.
4. Launch Settings from the Home screen.
5. Tap on the General option that's listed on the left side of the screen.
6. In Settings, on the right side of the screen, tap on the Software Update option.
7. Follow the onscreen prompts. Be patient; it can take up to 15 minutes for the new operating system to download and install itself onto your tablet.

> **NOTE** Upgrading the operating system on your iPad is free of charge. If you don't have access to a Wi-Fi Internet connection, download the iOS upgrade using the iTunes software on your primary computer, connect your iPad to your computer via the supplied USB cable, and then transfer and install iOS 7 via the iTunes Sync connection.

ACTIVATING YOUR iPAD'S DATA SERVICES

Now that you have activated your iPad, if you have an iPad that's a Wi-Fi + Cellular model, you can activate a wireless data service plan. You should see the 3G or 4G (LTE) connection signal dots and the Wireless Service provider's label in the upper-left corner of the screen. Next, tap the Safari app icon from the Home screen.

In the United States, before you can gain access to the Web via a cellular data connection, you must activate an account. In the United States, your wireless data service providers include AT&T Wireless, Verizon Wireless, and Sprint PCS.

> **NOTE** Activating a cellular data plan account takes just a few minutes. A major credit or debit card is required to pay the recurring monthly fee.

When you tap the Safari icon for the first time, follow the onscreen prompts when asked if you want to set up an AT&T Wireless, Verizon Wireless, or Sprint PCS account. Outside of the United States, your service provider options are different. You must choose a monthly service plan that costs between $14.99 and $50.00 per month, depending on the selected plan. This is a month-to-month plan that you can cancel or change any time. No long-term service agreement is required; however, it is auto-renewing until you cancel it.

> **TIP** If you're an AT&T Wireless customer who is upgrading from one iPad model to another, and you have an unlimited wireless data plan that's no longer available and you want to keep it, visit www.att.com/ipadlanding or call (800) 331-0500 to transfer your data plan. Do not cancel your existing data plan and then create a new one on your new iPad. You also have the option to add your new tablet to an existing Family Plan or another service plan that can be shared between multiple devices.

USING NOTIFICATION CENTER ON YOUR iPAD

The iOS 7 version of Notification Center has been redesigned. To access it at any-time when using your tablet, swipe your finger in a downward direction, starting near the top of the screen. Whatever you're doing on your tablet continues running, but the Notification Center screen is displayed.

Near the top-center of the new Notification Center screen are three command tabs, labeled Today, All, and Missed. Depending on how you customize Notification Center within Settings, tap on one of these tabs to display specific information.

NOTIFICATION CENTER'S TODAY VIEW

The Today view of the Notification Center window displays the current day and date, as well as the current temperature where you are and a summary of the day's events and reminders, which it compiles from the Calendar and Reminders apps. A preview of tomorrow's events is also displayed.

NOTIFICATION CENTER'S ALL VIEW

Whenever an alarm from the Calendar or Reminders app, for example, goes off, you can be alerted within the Notification Center screen. Likewise, you can be alerted if you receive a new incoming email; a missed FaceTime call; a new message via iMessage; or other types of alerts, alarms, or notifications that are generated by other apps.

By default, whenever a new alert or alarm goes off signifying activity in an app that requires your attention, Notification Center displays a message about it, and then gives you quick access to the appropriate app and what needs your attention. The Notification Center is always running in the background and works regardless of what apps are currently being used. To customize the Notification Center and determine what alerts, alarms, and messages are displayed, as well as what audible alerts and alarms you hear, launch Settings and select the Notification Center option from the left side of the menu screen.

NOTIFICATION CENTER'S MISSED VIEW

Tap on the Missed tab when the Notification Center screen is visible in order to view a listing of alerts, alarms, notifications, and missed FaceTime calls that occurred while your tablet was in Sleep mode or while you were away from the device.

> TIP   While your iPad is in Sleep Mode, the Notification Center continues to function. From Settings, you can optionally set the Notification Center to display new alerts, alarms, and related content on your tablet's Lock screen. Thus, when you wake up your iPad, you immediately see all new alerts, alarms, and messages. From the Lock screen, you can tap on any of the Notification Center listings to unlock the iPad and access the appropriate app and content.

OPENING CONTROL CENTER FOR QUICK ACCESS TO COMMONLY USED FEATURES

One very useful feature that's new to iOS 7 is Control Center. At anytime the tablet is turned on (including from the Lock screen, if you enable this within Settings), you can access a special control panel on your tablet's screen that gives you quick and convenient access to a handful of commonly used features and functions.

To access Control Center, swipe your finger in an upward direction, starting near the very bottom of the screen. This can be done while holding the tablet in landscape (shown in Figure 1.7) or portrait mode.

Displayed on the left side of the Control Center window are the Music controls and the master volume control slider. The Music controls allow you to play, pause, fast forward, or rewind through the Music app playlist, album, or single that's currently playing on your tablet.

Near the center of the Control Center window are five circular command buttons, which from left to right, allow you to turn on or off Airplane Mode, Wi-Fi, Bluetooth, Do Not Disturb and Rotation Lock. Below these five command icons is the AirPlay icon, which only appears when AirPlay or Bluetooth is active.

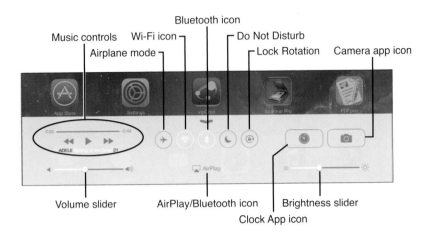

FIGURE 1.7

The new Control Center offers quick and convenient access to a handful of commonly used iPad features and functions.

Tap the AirPlay icon to determine where audio and/or video content will be streamed to wirelessly. AirPlay can be used with a wireless Bluetooth headset (in conjunction with FaceTime), Bluetooth- or AirPlay-compatible speakers, a Bluetooth-compatible keyboard, or a wide range of other iPad accessories. AirPlay can also be used to wirelessly stream content from your tablet to your HD television set via an optional Apple TV device.

On the right side of the Control Center window are app icons to launch the Clock and Camera apps. The screen brightness slider just below these icons is used to manually adjust the iPad's screen brightness based on current lighting conditions.

> TIP To close the Control Center, tap anywhere on the iPad's screen (outside of the Control Center window) or tap on the down-pointing arrow near the top-center of the Control Center window.

CUSTOMIZING iPAD'S SETTINGS

Along with adding optional apps to expand the tablet's features and functionality, use the built-in Settings app to personalize a wide range of options that affect your interaction with the tablet, how it connects to the Internet, and how your apps function.

Regardless of what you use your iPad for, you will occasionally need to access and adjust options within Settings. Think of the Settings app as a centralized place to control the tablet's operating system. Dozens of options are available from the Settings main menu and various submenus.

After you launch the Settings app, you can see the menu screen is divided into two sections. On the left are the main options offered by the Settings app, starting with the virtual Airplane Mode (On/Off) switch that's located near the top-left corner of the screen. In Figure 1.8, the main Settings menu is shown on the left side of the screen and the Control Center option is selected. Thus, the Control Center submenu within Settings is shown on the right.

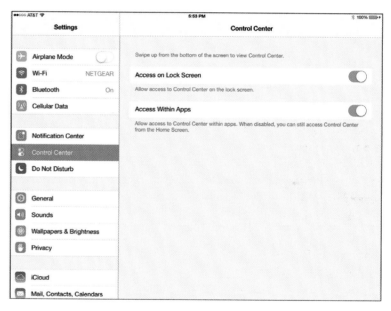

FIGURE 1.8

The left side of the screen displays the main Settings menu. Tap on a menu option to display a relevant submenu on the right side of the iPad's screen.

On the right side of the screen are the various submenu options available to you based on the highlighted selection on the left side of the screen. The Control Center option on the left is highlighted (in blue on your screen), and the specific options you can adjust on your iPad from the Control Center submenu within Settings are displayed on the right side of the screen.

To select a different Settings submenu, tap its menu option in the left column of the Settings screen.

SWITCHING TO AIRPLANE MODE

The first option found under the Settings heading, in the left column of the main Settings menu, is the virtual Airplane Mode on/off switch. This option enables you to turn off the iPad's capability to communicate with the Internet using a cellular data network if you're using a Wi-Fi + Cellular iPad model. To switch Airplane mode to the on or off position, simply tap the virtual switch that's displayed near the upper-left corner of the main settings screen.

> **TIP**   When working with any virtual switch within Settings, when the switch is moved to the right and displays a green background, that feature is turned on. When the switch is turned to the left and shows a white background, that feature is turned off. Simply tap on a virtual switch to turn it on or off.

When Airplane mode is turned off, and you're using an iPad Wi-Fi + Cellular model, the tablet automatically connects to the wireless data network to which you've subscribed (as long as you're not within the signal radius of a known Wi-Fi hotspot). The signal bars for this wireless data connection are displayed in the upper-left corner of the screen.

If you turn on Airplane mode, the tablet's cellular data connection shuts down and your existing Wi-Fi connection also turns off. Everything else on your tablet remains functional. Some apps, however, require an active Internet connection to fully function. When your tablet is in Airplane Mode, a small airplane-shaped icon appears in the upper-left corner of the screen.

> **TIP**   While Airplane Mode is turned on, you have the option to reconnect to a Wi-Fi hotspot from the Wi-Fi Settings option or Control Center. This is useful if you're aboard an airplane that offers Wi-Fi but does not allow you to utilize the 3G/4G (LTE) cellular data connection capabilities of your tablet. You can also turn on Airplane Mode when you travel overseas and want to connect to the Web using only a Wi-Fi hotspot in order to avoid international roaming data charges.

CONNECTING TO A WI-FI HOTSPOT

Located directly below the Airplane Mode option within Settings is the Wi-Fi option. When you tap Wi-Fi in the Settings menu, the right side of the screen immediately displays the various options available to you for choosing and con-necting to a Wi-Fi hotspot.

At the top, the first user-selectable option is labeled Wi-Fi. It's accompanied by a virtual on/off switch to its right. When the Wi-Fi option is turned on, your iPad immediately begins looking for all Wi-Fi hotspots in the vicinity.

The available networks are displayed under the Choose a Network heading on the right side of the screen. A lock icon to the right of any network listed in the Choose a Network section indicates the Wi-Fi hotspot is password protected. The signal strength of each Wi-Fi hotspot in your immediate area is also displayed to the right of the network's name.

Tap any wireless network (that you have a password for, if applicable) or a public hotspot that does not display a lock icon. Keep in mind that the network options you see displayed under the Choose a Network heading are based on the active Wi-Fi hotspots or wireless networks in your immediate vicinity.

When you select a Wi-Fi network that is password protected, an Enter Password window displays on your screen. Using the iPad's virtual keyboard, enter the correct password to connect to the Wi-Fi network you selected. Some Wi-Fi hotspots, particularly at hotels, require a password to connect, which you must obtain from the hotspot provider.

In a few seconds, a checkmark appears to the left of your selected Wi-Fi hotspot, and a Wi-Fi signal indicator displays in the upper-left corner of your iPad's screen to confirm that a Wi-Fi connection has been established.

If you leave the Wi-Fi option turned on, your iPad can automatically find and connect to an available Wi-Fi hotspot, with or without your approval, based on whether you have the Ask to Join Networks option turned on or off. Once you join a network for the first time, your iPad remembers it and automatically joins it when available, even if Ask to Join Networks is enabled.

BENEFITS OF ACCESSING THE WEB VIA A WI-FI HOTSPOT

There are several benefits to connecting to the Internet using a Wi-Fi connection, as opposed to a cellular data connection (if you're using an iPad with Wi-Fi + Cellular capabilities):

- A Wi-Fi connection is often much faster than a 3G or even a 4G (LTE) connection; however, the signal strength and number of people simultaneously accessing the Wi-Fi network affect your connection speed.

- When connected to the Internet via Wi-Fi, you can send and receive as much data as you'd like, stream content from the Web, and upload or download large files without worrying about using up your monthly data allocation that's associated with your cellular plan.

■ Using a Wi-Fi connection, you can use the FaceTime app for video calls, plus download movies and TV show episodes from the iTunes Store directly onto your tablet. With some wireless service providers, you can now use FaceTime with a cellular data Internet connection, but again, this can quickly use up your monthly data allocation.

> **NOTE** The main drawback to using Wi-Fi to connect to the Internet from your iPad is that a Wi-Fi hotspot must be accessible and you must stay within the radius of that Wi-Fi signal to remain connected to the Internet. The signal of most Wi-Fi hotspots only extends for several hundred feet from the wireless Internet router. When you go beyond this signal radius, your Internet connection is lost.

ADJUSTING BLUETOOTH OPTIONS

Tap on the Bluetooth menu option within Settings to turn on your tablet's Bluetooth wireless communication capabilities and then "pair" optional Bluetooth devices to your tablet. Commonly used Bluetooth devices include a wireless keyboard, external speakers, and/or a headset (for use with FaceTime, for example). If you're not using a Bluetooth device, be sure to turn off this feature from within Settings or Control Center in order to conserve battery life.

CONFIGURING CELLULAR DATA OPTIONS

When you select the Cellular Data menu option, a virtual on/off switch appears near the top-right side of the screen (see Figure 1.9). The Enable LTE and Data Roaming options also appear, along with a handful of other options that enable you to customize when and how the cellular data network gets used if you have a Wi-Fi + Cellular iPad model.

> **NOTE** This Cellular Data option only applies to Wi-Fi + Cellular iPad models.

When the Cellular Data option is on, your tablet can access either the 3G or 4G (LTE) cellular data network you subscribe to. When it's off, your iPad can access the Internet using only a Wi-Fi connection, assuming a Wi-Fi hotspot or wireless network is present.

Data Roaming enables your iPad to connect to a cellular data network outside the one you subscribe to. The ability to tap into another cellular data network might be useful if you must connect to the Internet, there's no Wi-Fi hotspot present, and you're outside the coverage area of your own cellular data network (such as when you're traveling abroad).

> **CAUTION** When your iPad is permitted to roam and connect to another cellular data network (such as when you're traveling abroad), you might incur hefty roaming charges, often as high as $20.00 per megabyte (MB). Refrain from using this feature unless you've secured a cellular data roaming plan in advance through your service provider or you're prepared to pay a fortune to access the Web.

FIGURE 1.9

From the Cellular Data option, you can control whether your iPad can connect to a cellular data network. You also can enable your tablet to roam (for an additional fee) to other networks for 3G or 4G LTE Internet access.

You can view or modify your cellular data plan account details by tapping the View Account option. After you log in with the username and password you created when you set up the account, you can do things such as change your billing information or modify your monthly plan.

Depending on your cellular service provider, you may be given the option to use your cellular data (3G / 4G LTE) connection to create a Personal Hotspot from which other Wi-Fi–only devices can use to connect to the Internet. Not all wireless service providers offer this option, and using it will quickly deplete your monthly wireless data allocation, if applicable.

CONFIGURING NOTIFICATION CENTER SETTINGS

The Notification Center settings option enables you to customize a handful of settings related to Notification Center and determine what information the Notification Center displays for each app.

You can decide whether or not information gathered by Notification Center can be displayed within the Lock screen (shown in Figure 1.10) by turning on the virtual switch that's associated with the Notifications View, found under the Access On Lock Screen heading.

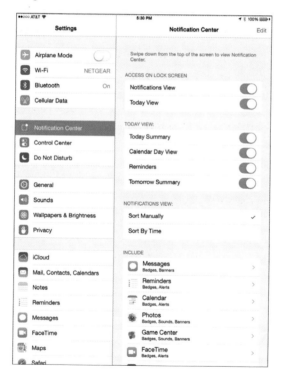

FIGURE 1.10

Decide if Notification Center can be accessed from the Lock screen of your iPad.

Then, if you want to view the new Today's View Notification Center feature from the Lock screen, turn on the virtual switch associated with the Today View option, also found under the Access On Lock Screen heading. When you access the Notification Center window and tap on the Today view, the current date, weather forecast, as well as the day's Calendar and Reminder app entries are displayed. By turning off this feature within Settings, only the All and Missed tabs are available.

> **NOTE** If you turn off the virtual switches associated with Notifications View and Today View, this deactivates the Notification Center feature and it is not viewable at all.

Next, decide how information is organized within the Notification Center screen. Choose between Sort Manually and Sort By Time under the Notifications View heading.

DETERMINING WHICH APPS NOTIFICATION CENTER MONITORS

All Notification Center–compatible apps are listed under either the Include or Do Not Include heading. Apps listed under Include are continuously monitored by Notification Center. Thus, alerts, alarms, or notifications generated by those apps are displayed by Notification Center. Keep in mind that as you add new apps to your iPad, you can return to these settings to configure their appearance in the Notification Center.

Apps listed under the Do Not Include heading are compatible with Notification Center but are not currently being monitored. Thus, the Notification Center screen does not display alerts, alarms, or notifications generated by these apps.

Tap one app listing at a time under the Include heading, starting with Messages. When you do this, the Notification Center customization options for that app display on the right side of the Settings screen, as shown in Figure 1.11.

By turning on the virtual switch that's associated with the Show In Notification Center option, it's possible to determine whether Notification Center pays attention to alerts, alarms, and/or notifications created using the selected app (in this case, the Messages app).

Next, determine how many items (individual alerts, alarms, and so on) display for that app at any given time within Notification Center. Tap on the Include menu option and then select between 1, 5, 10, or 20 Recent Items.

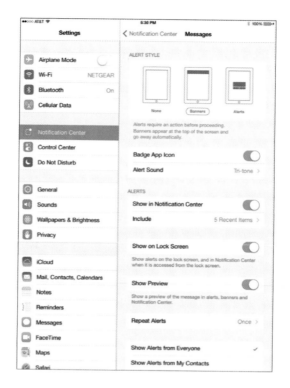

FIGURE 1.11

Shown here is the Messages submenu in the Notification Center settings. It allows you to set Notification Center-related options for the Messages app.

By turning on the Show On Lock Screen option, you can determine whether the alerts and alarms associated with the selected app appear on the iPad's Lock screen when the tablet is woken up from Sleep Mode. You can also adjust the Alert Style and decide whether the visible alert message displays as a Banner at the top of the screen, or as an Alert pop-up window in the middle of the screen.

A banner display appears and then automatically disappears after a few seconds. However, an alert remains on the screen until you tap the appropriate icon in the Alert window to make it disappear. Depending on the app, you can also turn on or off Badge App Icons, which display on the Home screen as part of that app's icon.

When actually viewing the Notification Center screen, tap any item, alert, or alarm listed within it, and the appropriate app automatically launches and shows you the relevant information.

CUSTOMIZING CONTROL CENTER OPTIONS

Control Center is a new iOS 7 feature that allows you to access a special menu at anytime to manage commonly used tablet features, such as Music Controls, Screen Brightness, AirPlay, Airplane Mode, Wi-Fi, Bluetooth, Do Not Disturb, and Rotation Lock. You can also quickly access the Clock and Camera apps.

To determine whether or not Control Center is accessible from the Lock screen, set the Access on Lock Screen switch in the Control Center submenu within the Settings app. If you turn on the Access Within Apps switch, the Control Center is accessible when running individual apps.

SETTING DO NOT DISTURB OPTIONS

The Do Not Disturb options available within iOS 7 allow you to temporarily silence all app-specific alerts, alarms, and notifications and automatically decline incoming FaceTime calls. It's possible to turn on the Do Not Disturb feature manually at anytime (from within Settings or Control Center) or predetermine when the feature automatically activates, such as every night between 10:00 p.m. and 7:00 a.m.

NOTE When the Do Not Disturb feature is turned on, a small, moon-shaped icon appears near the top-right corner of the iPad's screen. All alerts, alarms, and notifications are silenced but collected by Notification Center and promptly displayed when the Do Not Disturb feature is deactivated.

To customize the Do Not Disturb options, launch Settings and tap on Do Not Disturb. Then, from the Do Not Disturb submenu (shown in Figure 1.12), you have the following options:

- **Manual**—Tap on this virtual switch to manually activate the Do Not Disturb feature from within Settings.
- **Scheduled**—After you turn on this virtual switch, you can predetermine exactly when the Do Not Disturb feature will automatically activate by setting the From and To times within the Quiet Hours window (shown in Figure 1.13).
- **Allow Calls From**—Even when the Do Not Disturb feature is turned on, you can override the FaceTime-related settings and allow incoming calls from specific people listed within the FaceTime Favorites list. You can also allow incoming calls from people within a specific Group within your Contacts app.

FIGURE 1.12

From the Do Not Disturb submenu, it's possible to customize this feature and turn off alerts, alarms, notifications, and incoming FaceTime calls at specific times.

FIGURE 1.13

It's possible to specify exactly when you want the Do Not Disturb feature to automatically activate by adjusting the From and To times within this Quiet Hours window.

- **Repeated Calls**—Normally, when the Do Not Disturb feature is on, all incoming FaceTime calls are automatically declined. However, when you turn on the Repeated Calls option, if the same person calls twice within a three-minute period, the second incoming call from that person is not automatically silenced and declined, thus giving you the option to answer it.

- **Silence**—When the Do Not Disturb feature is activated, you have the option to silence incoming FaceTime calls either Always or Only While iPad Is Locked by adjusting the setting found under the Silence option.

WORKING WITH THE GENERAL SUBMENU WITHIN SETTINGS

The General menu of Settings (shown in Figure 1.14) enables you to view and adjust the following options:

FIGURE 1.14

Shown here is the General submenu found within Settings.

■ **About:** Tap the About option to access information about your iPad, including its serial number, which version of the iOS is running, the memory capacity, and how much memory is currently available on the device. This is purely an informative screen with only one option (Diagnostics & Usage) to customize or adjust.

■ **Software Update:** Periodically, when Apple releases a revision to the iOS operating system, you must download and install an update. You can do it wirelessly using the Software Update feature. When you tap Software Update, your iPad checks to see whether a new version of the iOS is available and, if so, prompts you to download and install it.

■ **Siri:** Turn on or off the Siri feature, as well as customize some of the settings associated with it. When turned off, Siri cannot be activated or used.

■ **Spotlight Search:** Select what content stored within your iPad is searched when you use the Spotlight Search feature that's built in to iOS 7. For example, you can opt to search Contacts, Applications, Music, Notes, Events, Mail, Reminders, and/or Messages.

TIP To access the Spotlight Search feature from the Home screen, place your finger near the center of the display and swipe downwards. Use the virtual keyboard to enter what you're seeking, and then tap on one of the search results that are displayed to access that information or content.

■ **Text Size:** Certain apps support what Apple calls Dynamic Type. For these apps, you can universally control the size that text is displayed by using the slider within this submenu.

■ **Accessibility:** The Accessibility options are designed to make the iPad easier to use by people with various sight or hearing difficulties or with some type of physical limitation.

■ **Multitasking Gestures:** When the Multitasking Gestures option is set to On, several additional finger/hand motions are usable when interacting with your tablet's touch-screen. For example, you can start with your fingers spread out and perform a full-hand pinch motion in any app to return to the Home screen. You can also perform a full-hand swipe to switch between apps in the multitasking bar.

■ **Use Side Switch To:** There is a tiny switch located on the right side of your iPad, just above the volume up/down button. You can determine what the primary function of this switch should be. Use it either as a lock rotation switch or a mute switch.

■ **Usage:** Tap the Battery Percentage switch found within the Usage submenu to determine how your tablet's battery life indicator is displayed. Turn the switch on to display a numeric percentage (such as 73%) along with the battery-shaped graphic icon. Turn the switch off to display only the icon. Also from this menu, you can see how the internal storage within your iPad is currently being utilized, plus manage your iCloud online storage space. Displayed under the Time Since Last Full Charge heading, how much time the tablet has been used versus put in Sleep (Standby) mode is displayed.

> **TIP** From the Usage menu within Settings, you can delete apps that are listed under the Storage heading by tapping on the app listing and then tapping on the Delete App option. When you do this, however, you also delete data related to that app.

■ **Background App Refresh:** When turned on, certain apps can automatically access the Internet to refresh content. In the Background App Refresh sub-menu, you can set the master virtual switch for this feature, as well as control the ability of specific apps to make use of it.

> **TIP** If conserving battery life is important, turn off this feature altogether. You always have the option to manually update or refresh app-specific content as you're using various apps.`

■ **Auto-Lock:** Set your iPad to switch into Sleep Mode anytime it is left idle for a predetermined amount of time. This helps conserve battery life. From the Auto-Lock option, you can determine whether Sleep Mode should be acti-vated after 2, 5, 10, or 15 minutes of nonuse. Or you can choose the Never option so the iPad never automatically switches into Sleep Mode, even if you leave it unattended for an extended period.

■ **Passcode Lock:** From the Passcode Lock submenu, you can configure a custom passcode which any user of your tablet will need to enter in order to unlock it. This is a security featured used to prevent unauthorized usage of your iPad. See "Keeping Your iPad Private with the Passcode Lock Feature" later in this chapter for more information.

■ **Restrictions:** Use these features to "childproof" your tablet. You have the option to Enable Restrictions and then manually set those restrictions. For example, you can block certain preinstalled apps from being used, keep the "guest" user from deleting apps from or adding apps to the iPad, or prevent someone from making in-app purchases. You can also keep someone from accessing certain types of iTunes Store or app content (including TV shows, movies, music, and podcasts) or control accessibility based on the rating of the content.

- **Date & Time:** Switch between a 12- or 24-hour clock and determine whether you want your iPad to automatically set the time or date (when it's connected to the Internet).

- **Keyboard:** You can make certain customizations from this submenu that impact how your virtual keyboard responds as you type. The Keyboard submenu includes customizable settings such as Auto-Capitalization, Auto-Correction, and Check Spelling. You also have the option to set the Split Keyboard feature, enable/disable Caps Lock, plus create and edit keyboard shortcuts that are useful when typing text. A keyboard shortcut might include typing "omw," which the iPad translates into "on my way."

- **International:** By default, if you purchased your iPad in the United States, the default language and keyboard options are for English. However, you can adjust these settings by tapping the International option.

> **TIP** If you frequently find yourself needing to enter characters from another language's alphabets, you can enable additional language keyboard layouts and toggle through them by tapping the globe key on the virtual keyboard.

- **iTunes Wi-Fi Sync:** Back up your iPad and sync data with your primary computer by linking the two devices via iTunes and your wireless network. This is an alternative to using the USB cable to connect your tablet directly to your primary computer. These days, most people opt to use iCloud to wirelessly sync and back up their iPads, as opposed to using iTunes Sync or iTunes Wi-Fi Sync, which stores backup files on your primary computer, not "in the cloud."

- **VPN:** Customize virtual private network settings, if applicable, so your tablet can access your wireless network at home or work. Your company's IT department can assist you with this setting, if applicable.

- **Reset:** Every so often, you might run into a problem with your iPad, such as when the system crashes or you need to reset specific settings. In general, you should refrain from using these settings unless you're instructed to use them by an Apple Genius or technical support person.

> **CAUTION** Before using any of the Reset options, which potentially erase important data from your iPad, be sure to perform an iTunes Sync or iCloud Backup to create a reliable backup.

KEEPING YOUR iPAD PRIVATE WITH THE PASSCODE LOCK FEATURE

There are several simple ways to protect the data stored on your iPad and keep it away from unauthorized users. If you want to keep data on your tablet private, the first thing to do is set up and activate the Passcode Lock feature that's built in to iOS 7.

To set up the Passcode Lock feature, enter the Settings app and then tap the General option. Next, tap the Passcode Lock option, and set the Passcode feature to on.

When the Passcode Lock screen appears, tap the Turn Passcode On option to activate this security feature.

When the Set Passcode window appears on the tablet's screen (see Figure 1.15), use the virtual numeric keypad to create a four-digit security passcode for your device. You must enter this code every time you turn on the tablet or wake it from Sleep Mode.

FIGURE 1.15

From the Passcode Lock screen, set and then activate the Passcode Lock. Use it to keep unauthorized people from using your tablet or accessing your sensitive data.

You can enter any four-digit code as your passcode. When prompted, type the same code a second time. The Set Passcode window disappears and the feature becomes active.

From the Passcode Lock submenu (shown in Figure 1.16), it's possible to further customize this feature. For example, tap the Require Passcode option to determine when the iPad prompts the user to enter the passcode. The default option is Immediately, meaning each time the tablet is turned on or woken up.

FIGURE 1.16
The Passcode Lock submenu within Settings.

> **TIP** If you don't believe a four-digit passcode is secure enough, turn off the Simple Passcode option, which makes a Change Passcode window appear along with the iPad's full virtual keyboard. You can now create a more complicated, alphanumeric passcode to protect your device from unauthorized use.

If you enable the Erase Data option, the iPad automatically erases all data stored on your iPad if an unauthorized user enters the wrong passcode 10 consecutive times.

> **CAUTION** Activating the Erase Data feature gives you an added layer of security if your tablet falls into the wrong hands. However, to recover the data later, you must have a reliable backup created using the iTunes Sync process or iCloud Backup feature; otherwise, that data is lost forever.

> **TIP** Another way you can protect your privacy is to adjust the settings in the Restrictions submenu to block others from accessing or using specific apps or content that's stored on your iPad.

CONTROLLING YOUR iPAD'S SOUNDS

Tap the Sounds option in the Settings app to control the master volume of your tablet's built-in speaker. It's also possible to customize the specific sounds various iPad functions and preinstalled apps generate.

ADJUSTING THE WALLPAPERS AND BRIGHTNESS

Tap on the Wallpapers & Brightness option within Settings to manually control the display's brightness, turn on the Auto-Brightness feature, and/or customize the Lock screen and Home screen wallpapers (see Figure 1.17).

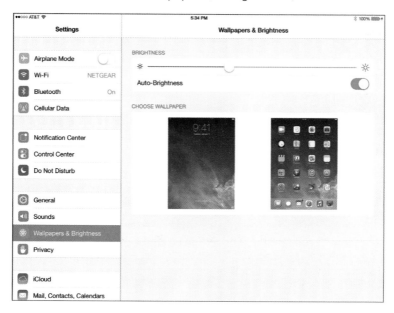

FIGURE 1.17

Use the Brightness slider to control how light or dark your iPad's screen appears. You can change this based on the external lighting conditions where you're using your iPad to make what's displayed on the screen easier to view.

At the top of the screen is a Brightness slider. Place your finger on the white dot on the slider and drag it to the right to make the screen brighter, or drag it to the left to make the screen darker.

The Auto-Brightness option has a virtual on/off switch associated with it. The default setting for this feature is on, which means the iPad uses its built-in ambient light sensor to automatically adjust the brightness of the screen. Manually adjusting the brightness slider resets the "base" brightness of the Auto-Brightness option, making the screen easier to read in certain lighting conditions relative to your chosen base.

CUSTOMIZING THE LOCK SCREEN AND HOME SCREEN WALLPAPERS

One of the ways you can personalize the appearance of your iPad is to change the wallpaper displayed on the device's Lock screen and behind your app icons on the Home screen.

Choosing a Preinstalled Wallpaper

From the Brightness & Wallpaper submenu within Settings, it's possible to quickly change the wallpapers that are displayed on the tablet. Your iPad has many preinstalled wallpaper designs, plus you can use any digital images that's stored within the Photos app on your iPad.

Below the brightness slider is the Wallpaper option. Here, you see a thumbnail graphic of your iPad's current Lock screen on the left and Home screen on the right. Tap the Choose Wallpaper thumbnail images to change your wallpaper (refer to Figure 1.17).

From the Choose submenu, tap on the Dynamic option to select a preinstalled animated wallpaper. Tap the Stills option to view preinstalled static wallpaper graphics (shown in Figure 1.18).

To use your own photo, tap the folder containing the image you want to use as your wallpaper. This might be a photo you've shot using your iPad (found in the Camera Roll folder) or a photo you've imported into the Photos app of your tablet. You could also use a photo you've saved on your iPad from iCloud's My Photo Stream or a Shared Photo Stream.

FIGURE 1.18

Choose between a dynamic or still precreated wallpaper, or select a digital image of your own to use as a wallpaper graphic.

When you find an image you want to use, tap it. The graphic you select is displayed in full-screen mode. In the bottom-right corner of this preview screen are three command buttons. Choose one of these options by tapping its icon:

- **Set Lock Screen:** Tap this icon to change just the wallpaper of your iPad's Lock screen. This is the screen you see when you first turn on your tablet or wake it from Sleep.

- **Set Home Screen:** Tap this icon to change just the wallpaper graphic of your iPad's Home screen. This is the graphic that displays behind your app icons on each of your Home screen pages.

- **Set Both:** Tap this icon to use the same wallpaper graphic as both your Lock screen and your Home screen wallpapers.

After you make your selection, your newly selected wallpaper graphic is displayed when you return to the iPad's Lock screen or Home screen.

ADJUSTING THE PRIVACY SETTINGS

From the Privacy submenu, you can control the Location Services feature of iOS 7. This allows your tablet to determine your exact location and then share it with various apps, which in turn can potentially share it with the public via the Internet through Maps, Facebook, Twitter, Photos, Find My Friends, and other apps.

In addition to turning on or off the main Location Services option, you can leave it on but then limit the access specific apps have to your location information.

The Privacy options also allow you to determine which apps are able to share information and content with other apps (see Figure 1.19). For example, if you tap on the Contacts listing found on the Privacy menu screen, a listing of apps that can access Contacts database data is displayed, along with virtual switches for each. Turning on a virtual switch associated with one of these listed apps allows it to access information from your Contacts database.

By tapping on the Advertising option, you can limit your tablet's ability to track your web surfing activities and sharing that information with advertisers.

FIGURE 1.19

From Settings, it's possible to customize a variety of Privacy options.

> **NOTE** If you don't want the iPad tracking your whereabouts in real time, turn off the Location Services feature. When using Maps, for example, if Location Services is turned off, you must manually enter your location each time you use the app.

CUSTOMIZING iCLOUD SETTINGS

Tap the iCloud option from the main Settings menu to access the iCloud submenu (shown in Figure 1.20) and customize the options associated with Apple's online file-sharing and data backup service.

FIGURE 1.20

The iCloud submenu allows you to determine how your tablet will utilize the iCloud integration that's built in to iOS 7.

It's possible to adjust which app-specific data automatically gets synced with the iCloud service, including Mail, Contacts, Calendars, Reminders, Safari (Bookmarks and related data), Notes, Photo Stream, and Documents & Data. You can also enable or disable the Find My iPad service.

> **TIP** New to iOS 7 is the iCloud Keychain feature. It allows Safari to maintain a centralized database of the usernames, passwords, and related data you enter when visiting individual websites. Your tablet remembers this information, which makes it faster to log into websites you return to later. iCloud Keychain also syncs

this information with all of the Macs and iOS mobile devices that are linked to your iCloud account, so it's accessible anytime you're surfing the Web using the Safari web browser on your iPad, Mac, or iPhone.

Simply turn on the iCloud Keychain feature on each tablet, iPhone, and Mac that's linked to your iCloud account for this feature to work. Each time you activate the feature on one of your computers or devices, you're asked to confirm the activation on one of your other devices for security purposes.

To activate or customize iCloud Keychain, launch Settings, and tap on the iCloud option. Turn on the virtual switch that's associated with the iCloud Keychain option, and then follow the prompts that appear within the pop-up windows. Next, return to the main Settings menu and then tap on the Safari option. Turn on the virtual switch that's associated with the Names and Passwords option, and then turn on or off the Always Allow option. When turned on, Always Allow allows iCloud Keychain to store passwords for websites that this feature isn't automatically compatible with, such as bank or financial institution websites. Next, if you want iCloud Keychain to store credit card information used when you're online shopping, turn on the Credit Cards option that's displayed on the Passwords & Autofill menu and then enter your credit card information once by tapping on the Saved Credit Cards option.

Your free iCloud account comes with 5GB of online storage space. Tap the Storage & Backup option near the bottom of the iCloud screen to manage your existing online storage space or purchase additional online storage space.

From the Storage & Backup screen within Settings, you're able to turn on or off the iCloud Backup feature. This determines whether your iPad automatically and wirelessly backs up your tablet on a daily basis and stores the files "in the cloud."

TIP   Be sure to turn on the Find My iPad feature from the iCloud Control Panel so that you can use iCloud.com or the Find My iPhone app to track the location of your tablet if it gets lost or stolen. The Find My... feature has been enhanced in iOS 7 and now gives you more options to remotely lock down and/or erase the contents of your tablet if it's lost or stolen. For the Find My iPad feature to work, it must be turned on *before* it gets lost or stolen, so it's a good strategy to turn it on as you're setting up your tablet and then leave it on permanently.

ADJUSTING THE SETTINGS FOR MAIL, CONTACTS, CALENDARS, NOTES, AND REMINDERS

If you use your iPad for work, five apps you probably rely heavily on are Mail, Contacts, Calendars, Notes, and Reminders. From Settings, it's possible to customize a handful of options pertaining to each of these apps. Plus, you can set up your existing work and personal email accounts to function with your tablet. To adjust these app-specific options, launch Settings and then tap on the Mail, Contacts, Calendars option, the Notes option, or the Reminders option, respectively.

For directions on how to set up the Mail app to work with your existing personal and work-related email accounts, be sure to read Chapter 3, "Staying In Touch Using Email and Instant Messages."

CUSTOMIZING MESSAGES, FACETIME, MAPS, AND SAFARI FROM SETTINGS

From within Settings, tap on the Messages or FaceTime app to access or modify account-specific settings for these apps. This only needs to be done once from within Settings, or it can be done the first time you use the Messages or FaceTime apps. Learn more about using the Messages app from Chapter 3, while more information about using FaceTime for video calls can be found within Chapter 14, "Conducting Videoconferences and Virtual Meetings."

The options available within Settings pertaining to the Maps app allow you to adjust the master volume of the navigation voice heard when receiving turn-by-turn directions. You can also switch between Miles or Kilometers as the app's default, plus choose your preferred type of directions (driving or walking).

PERSONALIZING YOUR SAFARI WEB SURFING EXPERIENCE

Tap on the Safari option within Settings to access the Safari submenu and be able to personalize a handful of options (shown in Figure 1.21) related to your web surfing capabilities when using your tablet.

For example, tap on the Search Engine option to select your tablet's default search engine (Google, Bing, or Yahoo!). Tap on the Passwords & Autofill option to link your own Contacts entry (within the Contacts app) to Safari, so the web browser can autofill common data fields, like name, address, phone number, email address, and/or credit card details as you visit various websites that require you to complete online forms or when shopping online.

A handful of other options, which are explored in greater detail within Chapter 7, "Surfing the Web with Safari," allow you to adjust privacy options related to your web surfing activities.

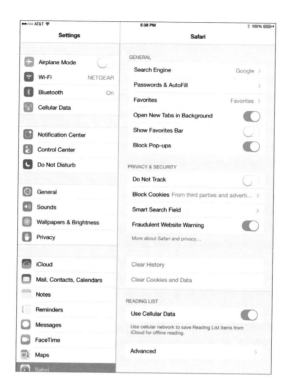

FIGURE 1.21

The Safari submenu within Settings allows you to customize the Safari app.

iTUNES STORE AND APP STORE PURCHASE OPTIONS

Through the iTunes Store, App Store, and iBooks apps, it's possible to access Apple's online-based stores in order to purchase music, movies, TV shows, audiobooks, music videos, ringtones, apps, eBooks, and digital publications for your tablet. These online purchases are paid for using the credit or debit card that's linked to your Apple ID account (or with prepaid iTunes gift cards).

From within Settings, tap on the iTunes & App Store option to adjust settings related to your online purchases. If you turn on Automatic Downloads related to music, apps, books, or app updates, anytime you make a content purchase on any computer or iOS mobile device that's linked to your iCloud account, that purchase is automatically downloaded to your iPad, as well.

PERSONALIZING MUSIC SETTINGS

One of the apps built in to your iPad is the Music app, which transforms your tablet into a full-featured digital music player. It enables you to experience the music and audio files you have stored on your tablet. This includes music and audiobooks acquired from the iTunes Store.

From within Settings, it's possible to customize a handful of options relating to the Music app, including the Sound Check, EQ, Volume Limit, Group By Album Artist, Show All Music, and iTunes Match options.

PERSONALIZING VIDEO SETTINGS

Use the Videos app that comes on your iPad to watch TV show episodes and movies you've purchased or rented from the iTunes Store. From Settings, it's possible to adjust how the Videos app functions by turning on or off various settings.

MANAGING YOUR PHOTO STREAMS

If you opt to use the My Photo Stream or Shared Photo Stream features of Apple's iCloud service in order to back up and share your digital images, you need to enable them from within Settings on your iPad and then customize the functionality of these features. To do this, launch Settings and tap on the Photos & Camera option.

My Photo Stream automatically stores up to 1,000 of your most recently shot digital images online and then makes them available on all your Macs, PCs, and iOS mobile devices that are linked to the same iCloud account. You have the option to share images stored in your Shared Photo Streams with others.

From the Photos and Camera option, there are also several Camera app-related functions that can be customized from within Settings.

iBOOKS AND GAME CENTER CAN BE CUSTOMIZED, TOO

Tap on the iBooks or Game Center options from the main Settings menu to customize options that are directly related to these two apps and how they integrate with Apple's iCloud service, for example.

You'll learn more about the iBooks app and acquiring eBooks from Apple's online-based iBookstore from Chapter 16, "Staying Informed Using iBooks and Newsstand."

SETTING UP THE TWITTER, FACEBOOK, FLICKR, AND VIMEO APPS AND RELATED iOS 7 INTEGRATION

The Twitter, Facebook, Flickr, and Vimeo online social networking services are fully integrated into iOS 7 and your iPad. The ability to share app-specific content with others from several different iPad applications is possible, plus you can use the official Twitter, Facebook, Flickr, or Vimeo apps to manage your respective online accounts.

> **NOTE** Twitter is a popular micro-blogging service that allows you to compose and send short (140-character) messages to your followers, plus read the Twitter feeds created by others. Facebook is a full-service online social networking service with more than one billion users worldwide. Flickr is an online-based photo sharing service, and Vimeo is a videosharing service (similar to YouTube).

The Twitter features built in to the iPad's operating system work with your existing Twitter account; however, you must download the free, official Twitter app to fully manage your account. You can also set up a free Twitter account if you don't already have one. Customize the settings as desired so you can send tweets from a variety of different iPad core apps, including Photos or Safari.

To set up your existing Twitter, Facebook, Flickr, or Vimeo accounts to work with your iPad, launch Settings. Scroll down on the left side of the screen until you see the service-specific options, and then tap on them, one at a time.

When prompted, enter your account username and password. You also need to install the official Twitter, Facebook, Flickr, or Vimeo apps by tapping on the Install button that's associated with each app.

From within Settings, you have the option to create new accounts for these services by tapping on the appropriate Create New Account buttons. Figure 1.22 shows the Twitter submenu screen within Settings.

> **NOTE** You need to enter your Twitter, Facebook, Flickr, or Vimeo account information once from within Settings to make each online social networking site integrate with the iPad's preinstalled apps. Then, after you install the official Twitter, Facebook, Flickr, and/or Vimeo app, you must enter your username and password information again, but this time in the actual app.

FIGURE 1.22

From Settings, set up your Twitter, Facebook, Flickr, and Vimeo accounts so other apps on your iPad can share content with these services.

MAKING APP-SPECIFIC ADJUSTMENTS

By launching Settings and scrolling downward on the main menu, it's possible to customize settings for some of the optional, third-party apps you have installed on your tablet.

To make adjustments that are specific to any of the apps listed, tap the app name (displayed in the left column of the Settings screen) and then adjust the app-specific settings on the right side of the screen. The customizations you can make are specific to each app.

For example, the Pages, Numbers, and Keynote apps are each listed within the Settings app after you install them.

USING THE iPAD'S DICTATION FEATURE

In addition to using Siri to issue commands and ask questions, iOS 7 continues to offer the Dictation feature, which offers an alternative to typing text using the virtual keyboard. Activate Dictation mode almost anytime the iPad's virtual keyboard is visible. Simply tap on the microphone key that's displayed between the .?123 and spacebar keys (see Figure 1.23).

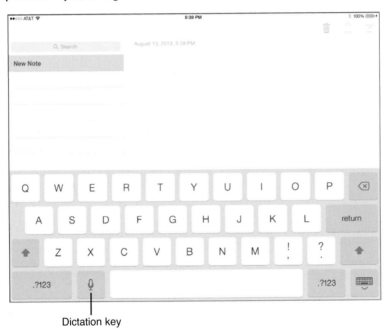

Dictation key

FIGURE 1.23

The Dictation feature enables you to speak directly to your tablet and have what you say translated into text. It's shown here within the Notes app.

Instead of manually typing information into the iPad when using a compatible app, tap on the Dictation key once, which causes a larger microphone icon to be displayed. At the same time, the iPad generates a quick tone. At this point, you can begin speaking into your iPad for up to 30 seconds in a normal voice.

In Dictation mode, anything you say is recorded by your tablet. Then, when you tap the Dictation key again on the virtual keyboard, your iPad translates whatever you said into text and inserts that text into the app you're using.

This feature works with many different apps on your iPad and can be a huge time-saver, as it is a viable alternative to touch-typing or manual data entry. As you're speaking to your iPad when the Dictation mode is active, speak as clearly as possible using a normal volume and speed.

As you're speaking, you can include punctuation into your text, by speaking that as well. For example, you can say, "comma," "period," "colon," "open quotes," "close quotes," "exclamation point," and so on. For example, as you're using the Pages or Notes app, you could say, "This is a test of the iPad's dictation mode period I really love this feature exclamation point." Your iPad translates this as, "This is a test of the iPad's dictation mode. I really love this feature!" and enters the text into your Pages or Notes document.

> **NOTE** Using Dictation requires Internet access. If your tablet is connected to the Web using a cellular data connection, this feature utilizes some of your monthly data allocation. However, the Dictation feature translates speech to text faster using a Wi-Fi connection.

Use Dictation mode to enter text into a text editor or word processor, compose tweets or Facebook page status updates, or insert text into virtually any compatible app without having to type. Keep in mind that the Dictation feature is different from Siri, which also allows you to utilize your voice in order to interact with your iPad. You learn more about Siri in Chapter 2, "Interacting with Siri: Your Voice-Controlled Assistant."

WORK WITH iOS 7'S MULTITASKING BAR

Your iPad is capable of running numerous apps simultaneously; however, you can only actively use one app at a time. To quickly switch between apps that are running, enter the multitasking bar. To do this, quickly press the Home button twice anytime you're using your tablet.

The newly designed multitasking bar (shown in Figure 1.24). displays a thumbnail of each app that's running on your tablet, as well as its respective app icon. Scroll left or right to view all apps that are currently running on your iPad.

To quickly switch between active apps, tap on the thumbnail for the app you want to use. To shut down an app, swipe your finger upwards, over the thumbnail for the app you want to close. It's also possible to swipe upwards with two fingers, over two different app thumbnails/icons to shut them both down at once.

> **NOTE** When you exit out of most apps by pressing the Home button or from the multitasking bar, the app will continue running in the background. To shut down the app, you must close it from within Multitasking mode or power down the iPad altogether.

FIGURE 1.24
The new multitasking bar that's built in to iOS 7 shows all apps that are currently running on your tablet.

NOW, LET'S PUT YOUR iPAD TO WORK

Now that you understand the basics of how to set up and interact with your iPad, let's start putting it to work by focusing on the job-related tasks for which you can use many of the tablet's preinstalled applications.

IN THIS CHAPTER

- How to use Siri
- Discover what Siri can be used to accomplish
- Speak so Siri understands you and complies with your requests
- Utilize Siri Eyes Free in your car

2

INTERACTING WITH SIRI:
YOUR VOICE-CONTROLLED ASSISTANT

For decades, science-fiction TV shows and movies like *Star Trek* have depicted mobile computers that respond to the human voice. Just as the concept for the iPad itself could have been lifted from imaginative science-fiction stories, the same is true for Siri. Built in to iOS 7 and accessible from the iPad, Siri takes the voice dictation feature that's built in to the tablet a step further by enabling you to control the device, issue commands, make requests, and ask questions using your voice.

To activate Siri, simply press and hold down the Home button on the iPad for 2 to 3 seconds. Regardless of which app you're running, the screen is replaced with a message that says, "What can I help you with?" (shown in Figure 2.1). At the same time, you hear an audible tone. Now, ask a question, issue a verbal command, or make your request. Speak in a normal voice using everyday language.

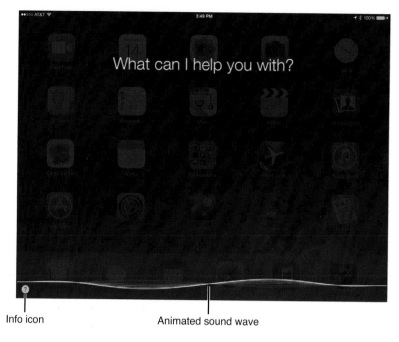

Info icon   Animated sound wave

FIGURE 2.1

When the animated sound wave appears on the tablet's screen and you hear the audible tone,
Siri is ready to accept your spoken command or request.

When you're finished with your command or request, stop speaking. However, if
you're in a very noisy area, it might be necessary to tap on the screen once, if Siri
can't discern your voice from the background noise.

> **TIP** After you activate Siri, hear the audible tone, and see the animated sound
> wave, you have several seconds to begin speaking. If you wait too long, Siri deacti-
> vates. To reactivate Siri, tap on the microphone icon once or press and hold down
> the Home button again.

In many instances, Siri offers an alternative to tapping onscreen icons or manually
entering data into your iPad. It also can be used to streamline the process of finding and using data that's stored on your tablet or retrieved from the Internet.

> **NOTE** Siri can create or access app-specific information or gather information
> directly from the Internet. For example, Siri can access information from Contacts,
> Calendar, Reminder, or Notes or control the Clock, Music, Messages, Safari, or
> Maps apps.

> **TIP** For Siri to function, your iPad must have access to the Internet using either a Wi-Fi or cellular data connection. Siri responds faster with a Wi-Fi connection.

> **CAUTION** When used with a cellular Internet connection, if you have a monthly data allocation from your wireless service provider, using Siri utilizes some of that allocation each time it's activated. Excessive use could lead to additional charges from your wireless data provider for extra data usage. The Siri feature, however, is free of charge to use, and there are no limitations if you use it with a Wi-Fi Internet connection.

CUSTOMIZING SIRI TO MEET YOUR NEEDS

From within Settings, it's now possible to customize Siri and give the feature a male or female voice. To do this, launch Settings, tap on the General option, and then tap the Siri submenu option. From the Siri menu screen within Settings (shown in Figure 2.2), turn on or off the Siri feature by tapping on the virtual switch near the top of the screen. Tap on the Voice Gender option to change Siri's voice.

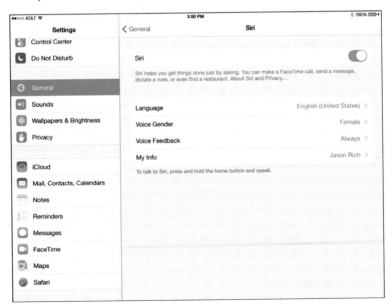

FIGURE 2.2
Use the Siri submenu within Settings to customize this feature.

In order for Siri to know who you are, where you live, where you work, and what your phone numbers and email addresses are, tap on the My Info option and then select your own entry within the Contacts database.

TIP   From within the Contacts app, be sure to create or edit your own entry to include as much detail about yourself as possible, since Siri refers to this information often.

SIRI CAN HANDLE A WIDE RANGE OF TASKS

Siri can be used for a wide range of tasks. After you learn the types of requests or commands Siri can handle, the next step is using the right commands or phrasing to generate the desired responses. Keep in mind that the technology Siri utilizes is constantly improving, so new functionality and improved accuracy are constantly being incorporated into this already powerful iPad feature.

In conjunction with iOS 7, Siri was given a handful of new capabilities. For example, you can now turn on or off iPad-related functions, like Airplane Mode, Wi-Fi, Do Not Disturb, or Bluetooth. Simply activate Siri and say, "Turn on Airplane Mode." or "Enable Wi-Fi." To adjust the iPad's screen brightness, issue the command, "Make the screen brighter" or "Make the screen dimmer."

You can also access specific submenus within Settings, by saying something like, "Open Mail settings."

Initiating a command with a specific word or phrase tells Siri which app to utilize. For example, when you begin a command with "Remind me to..." Siri creates a new item in the Reminders app. You can also begin a phrase by saying, "Search the Web for..." to instruct Siri to look up content from the Internet. If you say, "Create an appointment...," Siri creates a new event within the Calendar app.

CAUTION   Typically, not everything Siri does offers total hands-free operation. For example, when you compose a message or need to proofread something before it's sent, information is displayed on the iPad's screen. Also, some commands result in Siri displaying content on the screen in addition to or instead of Siri speaking the response. For example, if you ask, "What's today's weather?," an hour-by-hour forecast for the day is displayed at the same time Siri speaks the current temperature and forecast.

When your iPad is linked to your 2013 (or later) vehicle that has iOS In The Car integration built in, Siri Eyes Free is automatically used. Learn more about this function later in this chapter. However, if your car does not offer iOS In The Car integration, be careful how you utilize Siri while driving.

For additional advice on what types of commands, questions, or requests Siri can handle, activate Siri and then tap on the Info icon that's displayed in the lower-left corner of the screen (it's a circular icon with a question mark within it). Then, tap on an app or topic.

The following are just some of the tasks Siri can handle for you:

- Utilize information from the Contacts app. Ask, "What is [name]'s address?" or "What is [name]'s phone number?" You also can say something like, "Message Mom…," or "Show me [name]." This last request displays the contact's entry on the tablet's screen.

- Initiate a FaceTime call. Say, "Call [name]."

- Compose and add items to a list using the Reminders app. Say, "Remind me to…" followed by the item you want added. You can include specific information, such as a deadline. For example, you can say, "Remind me to pick up my dry cleaning tomorrow at 6 p.m."

- Compose and send an email message via the Mail app. Say, "Email [name] about [message subject.]" Follow the voice prompts to then compose and review the body of your email message.

- Launch an app. Say, "Open [app name]" or "Launch [app name]."

- Compose and send a message via iMessage (using the Messages app). Say, "Tell [name] [message]." For example, "Tell Jason Rich I am running 15 minutes late."

- Add an event to the Calendar app. Say, "Set up a meeting on Wednesday, November 14 at 10 a.m. to have lunch with Ryan at Morton's Steak House." This is shown in Figure 2.3. After you tap the Confirm button, a new event is created and added to the Calendar app.

> **TIP**   Siri can also verbally tell you about your upcoming meetings or overall schedule. Ask questions like, "What does my day look like?," "When is my next appointment?, "Where is my next appointment?", or "What time am I meeting with [name]?".

- Obtain the latest scores for your favorite sporting events or teams. Say, "Did the Boston Red Sox win their last game?" You also can ask something like, "When is the next [sports team]'s game?" or "Who won the last [sports team's] game?"

- Access detailed directions between locations using the Maps app. Say, "How do I get home from here?" or "How to I get to [name]'s house?" Siri can look up details from the Contacts app or find major locations (such as landmarks or airports) via the Internet. Thus, if you're in New York City, you could ask Siri, "How do I get to LaGuardia Airport?"

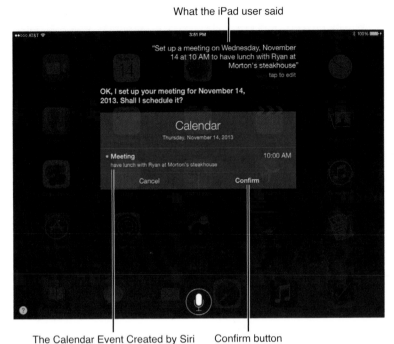

What the iPad user said

The Calendar Event Created by Siri   Confirm button

FIGURE 2.3

You can create new events in the Calendar app using Siri. Be sure to provide all the relevant details, such as the event name, time, date, and location.

- Compose and send a Tweet via Twitter to your followers. Say, "Tweet [message]."

- Compose and post status updates on Facebook. Say, "Post to Facebook, [message]." As shown in Figure 2.4, you could say, "Post to Facebook, I am going out for coffee to Starbucks. Would anyone care to join me question mark." Tap on the Post button to publish this status update on Facebook after Siri transcribes what you've said.

> **TIP**   As you're saying words to include within a Facebook update, tweet, note, email, or text message, for example, speak punctuation that should be included within the text, just as you do when using the Dictation feature (refer to Chapter 1).

Tap To Edit option

FIGURE 2.4
Begin composing a status update for Facebook using Siri by saying, "Post to Facebook…".
Tap the Confirm button to publish your Facebook status update online.

> **TIP** When reviewing your speech-to-text translated request, question, or command, in some cases a Tap To Edit option will be displayed allowing you to use the virtual keyboard to fine-tune your request. Refer to Figure 2.3 or 2.4 to see examples of this.

▣ Find a restaurant and/or make a reservation. Say, "Find a Chinese restaurant in [town or city]" or "Table for two at [restaurant name] in [insert city] for tonight at [time]." As shown in Figure 2.5, when you say, "Find a Chinese restaurant in Boston, Massachusetts," Siri displays a listing of related options. Each listing contains the restaurant's name, category, address, Yelp!'s star-based rating, Yelp's price range, and the distance you are from the restaurant's location. Tap on any listing (shown in Figure 2.6) to view more information about that restaurant.

> **TIP** Siri can work with the free (and optional) Yelp! or Open Table apps to help you find restaurants, access restaurant reviews or menus, and make reservations.

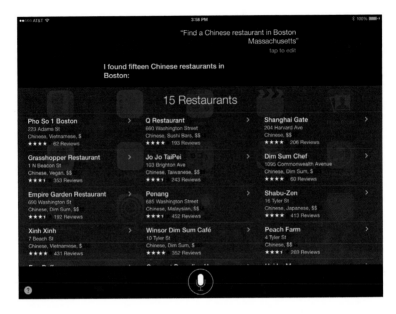

FIGURE 2.5

Use Siri to locate restaurants, learn about them using data from Yelp!, and even book a reservation using the free Open Table service.

FIGURE 2.6

Tap on a restaurant listing that Siri displays to view more information about that dining establishment, including its hours of operation, website address, and location on a map.

- Discover what movies are playing at local theaters. Say, "What movies are playing nearby?" or "What movies are playing at [theater name]?" You also can ask specific questions about any movie, such as "Who stars in [movie name]?" or "Who directed [movie name]?" To read the latest reviews for a movie, activate Siri and say, "Show me the movie reviews for [movie title]." Siri accesses the Rotten Tomatoes website and displays reviews that you can then read on the screen.

- Play music using the Music app. Choose individual songs, or choose a playlist that's stored on your iPad. Say, "Play [song title]," or "Play [artist name, album title, or playlist name]." As music is playing, you can also activate Siri and issue commands, such as Play, Pause, Skip, or Repeat.

- Check the weather. Say, "What is the weather today?" or "What is the weather forecast for tomorrow in New York City?" You can also ask to review the upcoming long-term forecast by saying, "What's the weather forecast for next week?" When you say, "What's the weather forecast for Los Angeles?" (shown in Figure 2.7), Siri displays a current and extended forecast.

FIGURE 2.7
Obtain an extended weather forecast for any city using Siri, just by asking for it.

- Obtain the latest stock quotes. Ask, "What is [company name]'s stock price?" or "What did [company name] close at today?"

- Set a wake-up call using the Clock app. Say, "Wake me up tomorrow at 7:15 a.m." or "Set an alarm for 8:00 p.m. tonight."

- Discover what time it is in other cities. Ask, "What time is it in London?"
- Set a timer. Say, "Set a timer for 15 minutes." You can then say, "Pause timer," "Show timer," "Resume timer," or "Stop timer."
- Find the location of your "friends" using the optional Find My Friends app. Say, "Where is Emily?" or "Who is near me?"
- Compose notes to yourself using the Notes app. Say, "Note that…" and dictate your note. You can then display your notes by saying something like, "Show me notes from [insert date]." When dictating a lot of text, you can speak for up to 30 seconds; however, you get better results by dictating one or two sentences at a time.
- Perform searches on the Web. Say, "Search the Web for…."
- Ask questions that require Siri to access the Internet to find an answer. Ask something like, "What is the state flower for Nebraska?" or "How many U.S. dollars is 50 Euros?"
- Perform mathematical calculations. Say, "What is two plus two?" or "What is 15 percent of $62.50?" As shown in Figure 2.8, Siri can be helpful if you need to quickly calculate a server's tip when dining out, for example.

FIGURE 2.8

Ask Siri, "What is 15 percent of $62.50?" and the answer is calculated and displayed promptly.

NOTE When you ask Siri a question, in some cases it automatically accesses the Internet and uses its artificial intelligence through a service called Wolfram|Alpha to figure out what you're asking and provide you with the most accurate response possible. For more information about how this works, visit www.wolframalpha.com/about.html.

CAUTION When using Siri to dictate text or compose content for an email, instant message, tweet, or Facebook posting, be sure to proofread the transcribed text carefully before sending it. Typos are common and could lead to you sending or posting something embarrassing.

SIRI RELIES ON CONTENT IN CERTAIN APPS

Not only does Siri require Internet access to function, but to handle certain types of requests, it needs access to data stored in various apps. As you begin using Siri, you must provide details about who you are and who you're related to. This allows Siri to know where you live; where you work; what your email address and phone number(s) are; as well as who your mother, father, brother, sister, and other relatives are.

SIRI TAPS INTO DATA STORED WITHIN THE CONTACTS APP

To fully customize Siri, create a detailed entry for yourself in the Contacts app. Be sure to include your home and work addresses and properly label all your phone numbers and email addresses. Also include details such as your birthday and Twitter and Facebook account information and use the Related People option.

The Related People option in the Contacts app enables you to link to a record in other contact entries that are somehow related, plus use labels, such as "Mother" or "Father," to describe the relationship.

First, create separate entries within Contacts for the people to whom you're related, such as your mother, father, brother, sister, spouse, assistant, and/or children. As you do this, be sure to properly use each field's label and differentiate between home and work phone numbers, addresses, and email addresses.

As you're creating or editing your own Contacts entry, tap on the Add Field option. Next, scroll down and tap on the Related People option. One at a time, link the entry for each related person by entering his name. Then, tap on the appropriate label to select how that person is related to you. Set up separate links in your own record for each relative.

> **TIP** As you create an entry in Contacts, if the person has a name that is difficult to spell or pronounce, consider using the Phonetic First Name and Phonetic Last Name fields in the entry. This enables you to also type and display the person's name as it sounds, as opposed to how it's actually spelled. Doing this also helps Siri understand what you're saying when referring to this person in the future. As you're creating or editing an entry in Contacts, tap on the Add Field option to find the Phonetic First Name and Phonetic Last Name fields.

Later, Siri uses this information. You can say, "Call Mom at home," and Siri knows who you're talking about and is able to access that record and obtain your mother's home phone number, assuming it's properly labeled and stored in the Contacts app. When you use the command "Call" with Siri on the iPad, whenever possible, a FaceTime video call connection is established.

> **TIP** Siri also needs to know where you are to be able to provide directions and local weather forecasts, find local restaurants, locate your friends (related to your location), and tell you what movies are playing nearby.
>
> To do this, launch Settings, tap on Privacy, tap on Location Services, and then turn on the virtual switch for Location Services. Next, scroll down and make sure the virtual on/off switch associated with Siri is also turned on. This enables Siri to access and use your exact location as needed to fulfill your requests.

SIRI ALSO USES DATA FROM CALENDAR AND OTHER APPS

Depending on your command or request, Siri uses information that's stored in other apps as well. For example, you can say, "Show me appointments related to Jane Doe," and Siri searches your Calendar database for any appointments containing "Jane Doe." You could also say, "Search emails for John Doe," to view any incoming or outgoing emails related to John Doe.

Likewise, if you tell Siri to play Madonna, it launches the Music app and begins playing songs by Madonna, assuming you already have Madonna songs stored in your tablet.

Siri can find major locations and landmarks. If you're in New York City, for example, you can ask Siri, "How do I get to the Empire State Building?" or "Where is Lincoln Center?" You can also ask for information relating to a local airport.

> **TIP** By default, Siri determines where you are and finds the geographically closest thing that you ask for. If you want to find something in another area, city, state, or country, you have to ask for it specifically. For example, if you ask, "Where is a gas station?," Siri automatically shows you the gas stations closest to your current location. However, if you ask, "Where is an Apple Store in Los Angeles?" Siri shows the listings for all Apple Stores in that city.

> **NOTE** The difference between Siri and Dictation mode is that Siri enables you to issue commands or requests to which your iPad responds. The Dictation mode simply records what you say, transcribes the words into text, and then inserts that text into the app you're using.

USING SIRI EYES FREE WHILE DRIVING

When you use Siri, information that's requested is often displayed on the iOS device's screen. Siri Eyes Free, however, offers much of the same functionality as Siri but turns off the iPad's screen altogether. Thus, it offers only verbal responses to a user's requests, commands, and questions.

> **TIP** Using Siri Eyes Free while driving only works with iPad Wi-Fi + Cellular models that have a cellular data connection to the Internet readily available. This feature does not work while the tablet is in Airplane Mode, for example.

Siri Eyes Free offers the perfect solution to drivers who must pay attention to the road, yet who want to access content from their Internet-connected iOS mobile device to look up information, access email or text messages, or obtain turn-by-turn driving directions to a specific location (using the Maps app).

When an iPad is paired with a compatible car via Bluetooth, drivers can press the Siri or voice recognition button that's built in to their steering wheel or their car's in-dash infotainment system. This activates Siri Eyes Free on the iPad (or iPhone). There is never a need for a driver to search around for her iOS mobile device or even momentarily divert her eyes to the tablet or smartphone's screen.

Thanks to Siri Eyes Free, all compatible cars now have access to GPS navigation via the Maps app; can utilize Internet connectivity; and be used for a growing selection of voice-activated tasks, such as accessing weather forecasts, finding nearby gas stations, looking up or adding appointments to the Calendar app, obtaining sports scores, locating nearby restaurants (and making dining reservations), and playing music that's stored on the iOS mobile device.

Again, all responses from Siri Eyes Free are spoken, not displayed on a screen, allowing the driver's attention to continuously remain on the road for safety.

Siri Eyes Free does not handle features that would ordinarily require Siri to display content on the screen. For example, if you ask for a weather forecast, Siri Eyes Free says the current temperature but does not display an extended forecast on the screen. Likewise, Siri Eyes Free reads aloud an incoming email or text message and allows a response to be verbally created, but the message does not appear on users' screens as they're driving.

All conversations between the driver and Siri are conducted using the speaker(s) and microphone built in to the vehicle itself—not through the iPad. Thus, privacy between Siri and the driver isn't possible, as all in-vehicle passengers can hear the interactions. The benefit of this is that music or audiobooks stored on the tablet, for example, can be played wirelessly through the vehicle's speaker system for all to enjoy.

Siri Eyes Free is currently available in all 2013 (or later) GM vehicles (including Chevrolets, Buicks, Cadillacs, and GMC trucks). Within their 2014 or 2015 model year vehicles, Audi, BMW, Ferrari, Honda, Jaguar, Land Rover, Mercedes-Benz, and Toyota will also be compatible with Siri Eyes Free and other iOS In The Car functionality. Each vehicle manufacturer is implementing Siri Eyes Free and iOS In The Car integration with their vehicles' in-dash infotainment systems differently.

> **NOTE**   The 2013 and 2014 Cadillac XTS sedans (www.cadillac.com/xts) come equipped with an iPad that's bundled with several proprietary apps for controlling the CUE in-dash infotainment system, OnStar, and certain vehicle functions. These Cadillacs were among the first vehicles to offer Siri Eyes Free and iOS In The Car integration.

The ultimate goal of Siri Eyes Free is to allow a driver to press a single button located on her steering wheel, activate her iPad or iPhone remotely, and then take advantage of the device's cellular Internet connection to transform her iOS mobile device and the car she's driving in into a hands-free and eyes-free virtual assistant.

To accomplish this task, even experienced iPad users who have mastered how to utilize Siri may experience a slight learning curve because communicating with an iPad using only one's voice while driving and not having access to the tablet's screen is an entirely new experience.

If you ask Siri to read an incoming text message, and the message asks you to meet a friend for lunch tomorrow at 2 p.m., activate Siri and verbally check the Calendar app to determine your availability. You can then verbally reply to that text message—all within a short period of time—using only your voice and without ever touching or looking at your iPad.

Other tasks that you can utilize via Siri, such as finding a restaurant and then making a reservation, or accessing movie listings and finding the closet theater that's playing a certain movie, are handled slightly differently using Siri Eyes Free.

For example, if you ask a question such as "What is the state flag of Massachusetts?", Siri displays the flag on the iPad's screen, but Siri Eyes Free informs you that the requested task is not possible while you're driving.

Any time you leave your vehicle, Siri Eyes Free automatically deactivates and gives you full access to all of Siri's regular features.

IN THIS CHAPTER

- Setting up an iPad to work with your existing email accounts
- Using the Mail app to compose, send, and manage emails
- Communicating with instant messages via the Messages app

3

STAYING IN TOUCH USING EMAIL AND INSTANT MESSAGES

As long as your iPad has access to the Internet via a Wi-Fi or cellular (3G/4G LTE) connection, it has the capability to securely access virtually any type of email account. In fact, using the tablet's preinstalled Mail app, you can manage multiple email accounts simultaneously without having to open and close accounts to switch between them.

Meanwhile, if you want to use real-time instant messages to communicate with coworkers, your employer, customers, clients, friends, or family, this too is possible using the Messages app in conjunction with Apple's iMessage service.

For business professionals on the go, the Mail and Messages apps can become indispensible communication tools, plus help make down time more productive.

USING THE MAIL APP TO MANAGE YOUR EMAIL ACCOUNTS ON YOUR iPAD

The newly revamped Mail app that comes preinstalled with iOS 7 offers a more streamlined interface for reading, composing, sending, and managing one or more email accounts from your tablet. If you're already familiar with the Mail app from iOS 6, all of the same features are intact, but the user interface of the app is new, and some of the command icons and menu options look different and are in a different location within the app.

SETTING UP YOUR iPAD TO WORK WITH EXISTING EMAIL ACCOUNTS

The email account setup process described here works with virtually all email accounts. If you have an email account through your employer that doesn't initially work using the setup procedure outlined in this chapter, contact your company's IT department or Apple's technical support for assistance.

NOTE For certain types of email accounts, such as Gmail or Yahoo! Mail, instead of using the Mail app, you can download a third-party app that works specifically with that email service. The drawback is that these apps only work with one email account, while the Mail app allows you to manage multiple email accounts of any type at once.

NOTE The process for setting up an existing email account to use with your iPad and the Mail app only needs to be done once per account.

Follow these steps to set up your iPad to work with your existing email account(s):

1. From the Home screen, launch Settings.

2. Tap on the Mail, Contacts, Calendars option on the left side of the screen.

3. When the Mail, Contacts, Calendars submenu is displayed (see Figure 3.1), tap the Add Account option that's displayed near the top of the screen, below the Accounts heading. If you've already set up iCloud on your iPad when you initially set up the tablet, your free iCloud-related email account is already listed under the Accounts heading, just above the Add Account option.

FIGURE 3.1

Tap on the Mail, Contacts, Calendars option within Settings, and then tap on the Add Account option to set up a preexisting email account to work with the Mail app.

4. From the Add Account screen, select the type of email account you have: iCloud, Microsoft Exchange, Google Gmail, Yahoo!, AOL Mail, Outlook.com, or Other (see Figure 3.2). If you have a POP3- or IMAP-compatible email account, tap the Other option and follow the onscreen prompts.

   If you have an existing Yahoo! Mail account, for example, tap the Yahoo! option. When the Yahoo! submenu appears (shown in Figure 3.3), use the iPad's virtual keyboard to enter your full name, existing Yahoo! email address, account password, and a description for the account (such as My Yahoo! Account).

5. Tap the Next button that's located in the upper-right corner of the window. Your iPad connects to the email account's server and confirms the account details you entered.

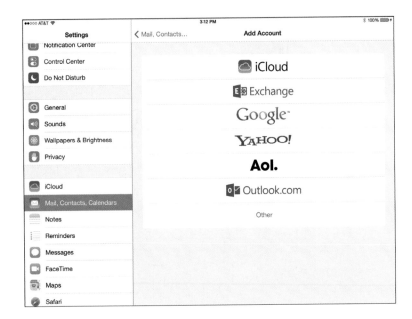

FIGURE 3.2
Select the type of email account you are setting up by tapping the appropriate icon.

FIGURE 3.3
Using the iPad's virtual keyboard, enter the details pertaining to your existing email account.

6. After the account has been verified, a new window with multiple options, such as Mail, Contacts, Calendars, and Notes, is displayed. The options listed vary based on the type of email account you're setting up. These options relate to what account-related data syncs with your iPad.

7. Tap the Save option that's located near the upper-right corner of this window. Details about the email account you just set up are added to your iPad and accessible from the Mail app.

8. If you have another existing email account to set up, from the Mail, Contacts, Calendars screen within Settings, tap the Add Account option and repeat the preceding steps.

TIP If you're trying to set up a POP3, IMAP, or Microsoft Exchange account, you are prompted for additional information, such as your incoming mail server hostname, incoming mail server port number, outgoing mail server, and outgoing server authentication type. If you do not have this information, contact your Internet service provider or the company that provides your email account. If you already have this email account configured on a different computer or device, you can often obtain the information you need from that account setup.

Depending on the type of email account you're setting up, the information you are prompted for varies slightly.

TIP When you purchase an iPad, it comes with free technical support from AppleCare+ for 90 days. This includes the ability to make an in-person appointment with an Apple Genius at any Apple Store to get help setting up your email accounts on your tablet. To schedule a free appointment, visit www.apple.com/retail/geniusbar. Or call Apple's toll-free technical support phone number and have someone talk you through the email setup process. Call (800) APL-CARE.

CUSTOMIZING YOUR EMAIL ACCOUNT SETTINGS

Once you have set up your email account(s), you can turn to a variety of customizable options pertaining to the Mail app available from the Mail, Contacts, Calendars submenu in Settings (refer to Figure 3.1). Tap each of the options that are displayed under the Mail heading, one at a time, to personalize the settings based on your preferences and needs.

FETCHING NEW DATA

Set up your iPad to automatically access the Internet and retrieve new email messages by tapping the Fetch New Data option and adjusting its settings. You also can turn on the Push option, listed at the top of the Fetch New Data screen (see Figure 3.4). This enables the iPad to automatically retrieve new emails from the server on an ongoing basis.

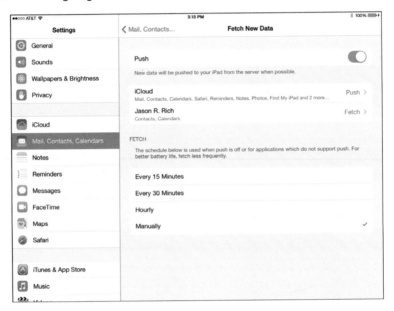

FIGURE 3.4

Turn on the Push option to enable your email provider to automatically send emails to your iPad, without the tablet needing to retrieve them.

> **TIP**   The Fetch New Data option is listed between the Accounts and Mail headings on the Mail, Contacts, Calendars submenu screen. Tap on it, and then for each separate email account, determine how often the Mail app should automatically check for new incoming emails (using the Fetch option). Alternatively, it's possible to turn on the Push option for all accounts (or for specific accounts) and have the Mail app continuously check for new incoming emails. The Push option utilizes more of your monthly cellular data allocation if your tablet is utilizing a 3G or 4G (LTE) Internet connection, plus the additional Internet connectivity drains your tablet's battery faster.
>
> To conserve cellular data usage and conserve the tablet's battery, turn off the Push option and set up the Fetch option for each account, and then select the Manual

option. This allows you to manually refresh your Inbox only when you access the Mail app and at your discretion. To do this, launch Settings; tap on the Mail, Contacts, Calendars option; and then tap on the Fetch New Data option. From the Fetch New Data menu, tap on each email account listing separately and select the Fetch or Manual option.

Keep in mind, not all email accounts support the Push option. Some only work with the Fetch option.

If you turn off the Push option, it's possible to set the Fetch option to check for new emails every 15 minutes, every 30 minutes, hourly, or manually.

CUSTOMIZING MAIL OPTIONS

Under the Mail heading of the Mail, Contacts, Calendars menu (within Settings) are a handful of additional customizable features pertaining to how your iPad handles your email accounts. These options include the following:

- **Preview:** As you look at your Inbox using the Mail app, determine how much of each email message's body text is visible from the Inbox summary screen, in addition to the From, Date/Time, and Subject lines. Options include between zero and five lines of the message.

- **Show To/Cc Label:** To save space on your screen as you're reading emails, you can turn off the To and CC label within each email message by tapping the virtual switch associated with this option.

- **Flag Style:** Choose between using an orange flag graphic icon (Shape) or a colored dot (Color) to showcase email messages that you manually flag as important within the Mail app.

- **Ask Before Deleting:** This option serves as a safety net to ensure you don't accidently delete an important email message. When this feature is turned on, you are asked to confirm your message deletion request before an email message is actually deleted. Keep in mind that for most email accounts, by default, you cannot delete email messages stored on your email account's server. When you delete a message, it is only deleted from your iPad. Your iCloud-related email account works differently. When you delete a message on your tablet, it does get deleted from your account altogether. Check with your email account provider to determine how it handles messages deleted from your iPad.

- **Load Remote Images:** When an email message has a photo or graphic embedded with it, this option determines whether that photo or graphic is automatically downloaded and displayed with the email message. You can opt to have your iPad refrain from automatically loading graphics with email messages. This reduces the amount of data transferred to your tablet, and it can help to protect against spammers who use image tracking to verify valid email addresses. You always have the option to tap an icon in the email message to download the graphic content of that message, including photos.

■ **Organize By Thread:** This feature enables you to review messages grouped by subject if a single message turns into a back-and-forth email conversation, where multiple parties keep hitting Reply to respond to messages with the same topic. When turned on, this makes keeping track of email conversations much easier, especially if you're managing several email accounts on your iPad. If turned off, messages in your Inbox are displayed in reverse chronological order as they're received and are not grouped together by subject or sender.

■ **Always Bcc Myself:** To ensure you keep a copy of every outgoing email you send, turn on this feature. A copy of every outgoing email is sent to your Inbox if this feature is turned on. When you send emails from your iPad, this feature ensures those messages also appear within the Sent folder of the mail app you use on your primary computer.

■ **Increase Quote Level:** This feature can be turned On (the default selection) or Off. When turned On, any time you forward or reply to an email message, the original message will be displayed but be indented, which makes it easier to visually separate the original message content from your reply.

■ **Signature:** For every outgoing email that you compose, you can automatically add an email signature that's displayed at the bottom of your email messages. The default signature is "Sent from my iPad." By tapping this option, it's possible to compose customized signatures for each email account. A signature might include your name, mailing address, email address, phone number(s), website address, Twitter username, and/or or your company's marketing slogan.

■ **Default Account:** If you're managing multiple email accounts, when you reply to an email message, by default it will be sent from the email account to which the original email was sent. However, if you're composing an email from scratch, this feature enables you to choose a default email account from which the new email will be sent. As you're composing the email, you can always change the From account by tapping on the From field, and then select one of your other email accounts.

After you make whatever adjustments you want to the Mail app-related options, exit Settings by pressing the Home button on your iPad to return to the Home screen. You're now ready to begin using the Mail app to access and manage your email account(s).

MANAGING YOUR EMAIL ACCOUNTS WITH THE MAIL APP

The Mail app that is preinstalled on your iPad is loaded with features to make managing one or more email accounts a straightforward process.

NOTE If you need to manage multiple email accounts with your iPad, it's important to understand that although the Mail app enables you to view email messages in all of your accounts simultaneously (when the All Inboxes option is selected), the app actually keeps messages from your different accounts separate.

As you view your incoming email messages, by default, the app groups emails together by message thread, enabling you to follow an email-based conversation that extends through multiple messages and replies. When turned on, this feature displays emails within the same thread in reverse chronological order, with the newest message first.

After you've initially set up your existing email accounts to work with the Mail app, use this app to manage your email accounts from anywhere. Launch the Mail app from the Home screen.

To alert you of incoming messages, without having the Mail app running, have the iPad display a badge on the Mail app icon that's displayed on the Home screen as new emails arrive. By default, this feature is turned on. To modify this, launch Settings, tap on the Notification Center option, and then under the Include heading tap on the Mail option. Next, tap on each email account listing and turn on the virtual switch that's associated with Badge App Icon for each (shown in Figure 3.5).

NOTE A badge is a small number that appears in the upper-right corner of the Mail app's icon on the Home screen. In this case, it indicates how many new emails your iPad has received.

At the same time you set up the Badge App Icon feature, set up the Notification Center to list incoming emails. Then, when the Notification Center window displays a new incoming message alert (shown in Figure 3.6), tap the message listing in order to automatically open the Mail app and display that new message. From the Notification Center window, tap on the All tab to view new Mail message notifications.

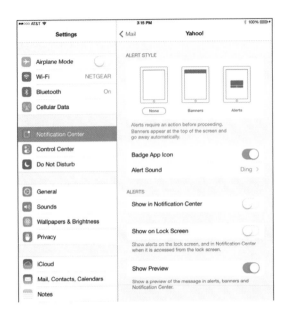

FIGURE 3.5

Within Settings, turn on the Badge App Icon option for each of your email accounts (shown here for a Yahoo! account), plus have new incoming emails listed within the Notification Center.

FIGURE 3.6

This is what the Notification Center window looks like when incoming email message alerts are displayed. Tap on the All tab near the top-center of the screen.

After you launch the Mail app, you can access the Inbox folder for one or more of your existing email accounts, compose new emails, or manage your email accounts. Just like the Inbox folder on your main computer's email software, the Inbox folder of the Mail app (see Figure 3.7) displays your incoming emails.

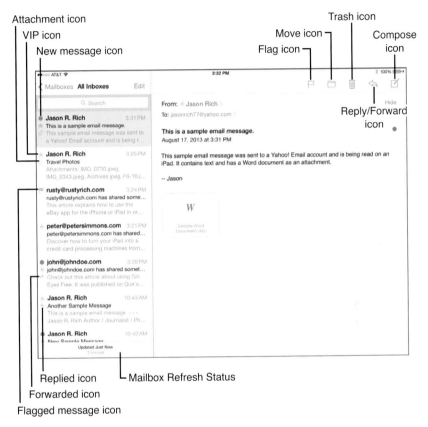

FIGURE 3.7

The Mail app's inbox screen. In this example, just one email account is set up to work with the app.

WORKING WITH THE INBOX

On the left side of the Mail app's screen is a list of the individual emails in your Inbox folder.

> **TIP** A blue dot associated with an email listing within your Inbox (refer to Figure 3.7) indicates that a message is new and unread. An orange flag icon (or multicolored dot) indicates the message is urgent. A curved, left-pointing

arrow icon indicates you have already sent a reply to that message. A curved, right-pointing arrow indicates you have forwarded the message to one or more recipients. A star icon means the sender of the incoming email message is on your VIP List, while a paperclip icon shows that there's an attachment associated with the email.

Based on the customizations that you made from within Settings, the Sender, Subject, Date/Time, and up to five lines of the message's body text are displayed for each incoming message.

The email message that's highlighted in blue on the left side of the screen is the one that's currently being displayed in its entirety on the right side of the screen.

TIP   To refresh your Inbox and manually check for new incoming emails, swipe your finger downward within the Inbox listing on the left side of the Mail app's screen. The Updated message displayed at the bottom of the Inbox folder listing is accompanied by the Just Now message or the date and time of the last time your Inbox was refreshed.

NOTE   If you're managing multiple email accounts from your iPad, you can view the Inbox folder for any single email account or choose to view a comprehensive listing of all inboxes by selecting the All Inboxes option. It's also possible to select just your VIP inbox folder by tapping on the VIP option from the Mailboxes selection menu, as explained later in this chapter.

At the top of the Inbox message listing are two buttons labeled Mailboxes (or the name of the email account whose Inbox folder you're viewing) and Edit. Between these two icons is the Inbox heading.

Just below the Inbox heading is a Search field. Tap this Search field to enter a search phrase and quickly find a particular email message. You can search the content of the Mail app using any keyword, a sender's name, or email subject, for example.

TIP   The Search field within the Mail app only allows you to search for content within the app. To search your entire iPad for specific content, access the Spotlight Search feature from the Home screen.

ORGANIZING MAILBOX ACTIONS WITH THE MAILBOXES OPTION

When looking at your Inbox, the Mailboxes button is displayed near the upper-left corner of the screen. If you're managing just one email account with the Mail app, when you tap on this button, you can immediately access your Drafts folder, Sent Message folder, Trash folder, Bulk Mail folder, or other folders associated with your email account.

However, if you're managing multiple email accounts, when you tap the Mailboxes button, the Mailboxes selection menu is displayed. This includes a listing for each email account's Inbox folder, as well as each email account, displayed on the left side of the screen. You also see a listing for your VIP inbox and flagged messages inbox (if you've previously flagged one or more messages).

At the top of this listing, tap on All Inboxes to view a listing of all of your incoming emails, from all your accounts, on a single screen. These messages are displayed together but are actually kept separate by the Mail app.

> **TIP** When you're managing multiple accounts, you can tap the Mailboxes option to switch between individual email account inboxes. Under the Accounts heading, you can also access the Inbox, Drafts, Sent, Trash, Bulk Mail, or other folders for each account separately.

Depending on the email account, you might be able to add new folders for storing and organizing email messages on your iPad. As you're looking at the current list of folders associated with one email account, tap the Edit button that's displayed at the top of the screen next to the Mailboxes heading. At the bottom of the screen, near the lower-right corner of the left mailbox folder column, you may see a new option labeled New Mailbox (shown in Figure 3.8).

Tap the New Mailbox button to manually enter the name of a new folder, and decide under which email account (Mailbox Location) the folder should be displayed. When you create a new folder on your iPad for an email account, that folder (and its contents) syncs with the other computers and/or mobile devices you access this email account from.

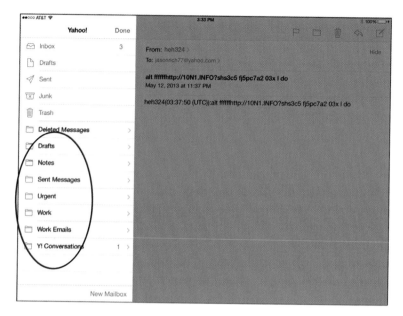

FIGURE 3.8

For most types of email accounts, you can create an unlimited number of mailbox folders (each with a custom name) for organizing email messages.

SELECTING MESSAGES FOR MANAGING WITH THE EDIT OPTION

Located on top of the Inbox folder message listing (to the right of the Inbox heading) is an Edit button. When you tap this button, you can quickly select multiple messages from your Inbox to delete or move to another folder (see Figure 3.9).

After you tap the Edit button, an empty circle displays to the left of each email message summary. To move or delete one or more messages from this Inbox listing, tap the message listing. A blue-and-white check mark fills the empty circle when you do this, and the Mark, Move, and Trash options are displayed near the bottom-left corner of the screen.

NOTE Also, after you tap the Edit button, a Mark All option now appears in the lower-left corner of the screen. This allows you to select all of the messages in the displayed Inbox and either Flag them all at once or mark all of them as read.

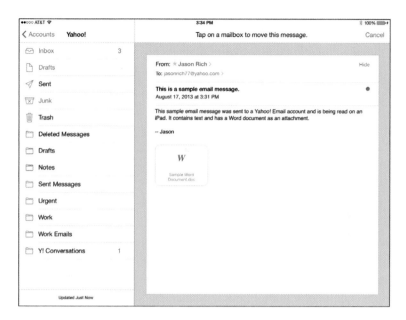

FIGURE 3.9

After tapping the Edit button, you can quickly delete or move multiple email messages currently stored in your Inbox.

After you've selected one or more messages, tap the Trash option to quickly delete the messages from your Inbox (which sends them to the Trash folder). Tap the Move option, and then select the folder to which you want to move the selected email messages. Tap on the Mark option to flag the message(s) as important, mark the message(s) as read/unread, or move the messages to your email account's Junk (spam) folder. A pop-up menu offering these three options appears.

DELETING INDIVIDUAL INCOMING MESSAGES

As you're looking at the listing of messages in an Inbox folder, it's possible to delete individual messages, one at a time, in several ways. Swipe your finger from right to left over a message listing on the left side of the screen. Keep in mind, in iOS 6 (and earlier versions of the iOS), this action required a left-to-right swipe, so the finger motion is now reversed. A red-and-white Trash option and a gray-and-white More option display on the right side of that email message listing. Tap the Trash option to delete the message. Tap on the More option to access a pop-up menu that offers the following options: Reply, Forward, Flag/Unflag, Mark As Read/ Unread, Move To Junk, and Move Message.... These options allow you to manage just the selected email.

TIP Another way to delete a single message from your Inbox (or any folder) is to tap the message listing that's displayed on the left side of the screen, which highlights the message in blue. At the same time, the entire message is displayed on the right side of the screen. Tap the Trash icon displayed near the upper-right corner of the screen to delete the message.

VIEWING YOUR EMAIL

When a single email message is highlighted on the left side of the Inbox screen (when the iPad is in landscape mode), that message is displayed, in its entirety, on the right side of the screen. At the top of the message, you see the From, To, Cc, Bcc, Subject, and Date/Time lines. When held in portrait mode, only the selected email message is displayed. To view the Inbox mailboxes, swipe your finger from left to right, starting at the left edge of the screen.

TIP As you then look at your Inbox listing, messages that have been flagged are accompanied by an orange flag icon or colored dot. From the Mailboxes listing on the left side of the screen, if you tap on the Flagged Inbox, only flagged messages from your various email accounts are displayed.

Displayed near the top-right corner of the mail screen are five command icons that allow you to manage the email message you're currently viewing. From left to right, here's a rundown of what these icons are used for:

- **Flag:** Tap on this flag-shaped icon to access a menu that allows you to Flag/Unflag the message, mark the message as Read/Unread, or move the message to the email account's Junk (spam) folder.
- **Move:** When you tap on this folder-shaped icon, a listing of all folders associated with the email account is displayed along the left margin of the screen. Tap on the folder to which you want to move the selected message.
- **Trash:** Delete the message you're currently viewing and erase it from your iPad (but not necessarily from the online-based email server).
- **Reply:** Tap on this curved, left-pointing arrow icon to access a menu that allows you to Reply to, Forward, or Print the email message you're viewing.
- **Compose:** Tap on the compose icon to create a new email from scratch. A blank New Message window appears. The message you were currently viewing remains intact.

ACCESSING INCOMING EMAIL ATTACHMENTS

The Mail app enables you to access certain types of attachment files that accompany an incoming email message. Some of the file formats that are viewable and can be accessed include photos (in the .JPEG, .GIF, .PNG, and .TIFF formats); audio files (in the .MP3, .AAC, .WAV, and .AIFF formats), PDF files; and Pages, Keynote, Numbers, Microsoft Word, Microsoft Excel, and Microsoft PowerPoint files.

> **NOTE** Depending on which optional apps you have installed on your tablet, additional email attachment file formats become accessible when you place your finger on the attachment file's icon and hold it there for 1 to 3 seconds.

If an incoming email message contains an attachment that is not compatible or accessible from your iPad, you see that an attachment is present but you aren't able to open or access it. In this case, you must access this content from your primary computer.

To open a compatible attached file within an incoming email message, tap and hold down the attachment icon for 1 to 3 seconds. If the attachment is compatible with an app that's installed on your iPad, you are given the option to transfer the file to that app and directly open the file using that app. Or, you can open a compatible attachment in the Mail app's own viewer.

TRANSFERRING MESSAGES TO OTHER FOLDERS

As you're viewing an email message on the right side of the screen, you can move it from your Inbox to another folder in one of two ways. First, you can tap the Edit button, or you can tap the file folder–shaped icon that's displayed in the upper-right corner of the screen. When you tap this icon, the various folders available for that email account are displayed on the left side of the screen. Tap the folder to which you want to move the message. The folders available vary for different types of email accounts.

FORWARDING, REPLYING TO, AND PRINTING EMAILS

From within the Mail app, you can reply to the message, forward any incoming message to someone else, or print the email by tapping the curved, left-pointing arrow icon that's displayed in the upper-right corner of the main Inbox screen (next to the Trash icon). A menu is then displayed in the upper-right corner of the screen (see Figure 3.10).

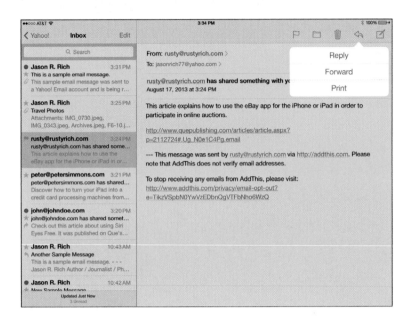

FIGURE 3.10
As you're reading any email message, tap the curved left-pointing arrow icon to reply, forward, or print that message.

To reply to the message you're reading, tap the Reply button. An email message template appears on the screen. See the "Composing Messages" section later in this chapter for details on how to write and send an email message from the Mail app.

To forward the email you're reading to another recipient, tap the Forward button. If an attachment is associated with this email, you are asked whether you want to include the attachments from the original email. You see two options, labeled Include and Don't Include. Choose the appropriate response.

Start the message forwarding process by filling in the To field. You can also modify the Subject field (or leave the message's original Subject) and then add to the body of the email message with your own text. The newly added text displays above the forwarded message's content.

> **NOTE** To forward an email to multiple recipients, enter each person's email address in the To field of the outgoing message, but separate each address with a comma. You also can tap the plus icon (+) that appears to the right of the To field to add more recipients. This also works when composing a new message to several recipients.

NOTE If you're sending an email to a contact that's stored in your Contact app's database, instead of manually typing the personal's email address, you can begin typing the person's name. The Mail app offers suggestions based on the information stored in the Contacts app.

When you're ready to forward the message to one or more recipients, tap the Send option that appears in the upper-right corner of the email message window. Or tap the Cancel button (located in the upper-left corner of the message window) to abort the message forwarding process.

If you have an AirPrint-compatible printer set up to work with your iPad (see Chapter 11, "Wireless Printing and Scanning via Your iPad"), you can print incoming or outgoing emails directly from your tablet using the Print command.

CREATING A VIP LIST IN THE MAIL APP

Although you can flag individual emails as being important, if you often receive emails from specific senders, such as important clients or your boss, that are extremely important to you, it's possible to designate those people as VIPs within the Mail app. Then, any messages you receive from those senders are displayed with a blue star in your Inbox folder, plus you can view the separate VIP Inbox to quickly view only incoming emails from people on your VIP lists that have been received in all of your email accounts.

To do this, as you're reading an incoming email from someone you want to add to your VIP list, tap on the From field of the message. Details about the sender are displayed in a pop-up window (shown in Figure 3.11). Tap on the Add To VIP option to add this person to your VIP list. A blue star appears next to their name in the From field.

TIP To remove someone from your VIP list, view an incoming email from that individual and tap on the From field. When the Sender pop-up window is displayed, tap on the Remove From VIP button.

As you're viewing the main Mailboxes listing on the left side of the Mail app's screen, tap on the VIP listing (shown in Figure 3.12), to view all the incoming emails from people on your VIP list in a centralized listing for easy reference. As you're looking at your All Inboxes listing or the Inbox for an individual email account, messages received from people on your VIP list have a blue star displayed to the left of them rather than a blue dot.

Add To VIP option

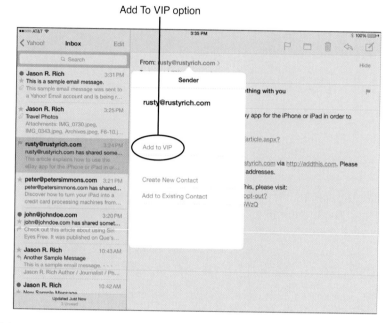

FIGURE 3.11

Add people who are important to you to your VIP list so you can easily identify incoming emails from them.

VIP Mailbox folder

FIGURE 3.12

Tap on the VIP listing under Inbox to display only incoming emails from people on your VIP list. This is a comprehensive listing from all your email accounts that the Mail app is managing.

COMPOSING EMAIL MESSAGES

From within the Mail app, you can easily compose an email from scratch and send it to one or more recipients. To compose a new email, tap the Compose icon that's displayed near the upper-right corner of the main Inbox screen. The Compose icon looks like a square with a pencil on it.

When you tap the Compose icon, a blank New Message window (shown in Figure 3.13) displays. Using the virtual keyboard, fill in the To, Cc, Bcc, and Subject fields. At the very least, you must fill in the To field with a valid email address for at least one recipient. The other fields are optional.

FIGURE 3.13

After tapping the Compose icon, you can create an email from scratch and send it from your iPad.

You can send the same email to multiple recipients by either adding multiple email addresses to the To field or adding additional email addresses to the Cc or Bcc fields.

> **TIP** If you're managing just one email address from your iPad, the From field automatically fills with your email address and is not displayed. However, if you're managing multiple email addresses from the tablet, tap the From field to select the email address from which you want to send the message.

Tap the Subject field and use the virtual keyboard to enter the subject for your message. As you do this, the Subject displays in the title bar of the Compose window, replacing the New Message heading.

To begin creating the main body of the outgoing email message, tap in the main body area of the message template and use the virtual keyboard (or the external keyboard you're using with your iPad) to compose your message.

Instead of manually typing an email message, you can use the Dictate feature. Refer to Chapter 1, "Activating and Personalizing Your Tablet," for information about using this feature.

The signature you set up within Settings is displayed automatically at the bottom of the newly composed message. You can return to Settings to turn off the Signature feature, or you can modify or delete the signature that appears directly within the compose message window.

When your email is fully written and ready to be sent, tap the Send option that's found near the upper-right corner of the Compose window. In a few seconds, the message is sent from your iPad, assuming the tablet is connected to the Internet. A copy of the message goes to your Sent or Outbox folder.

SAVING UNSENT DRAFTS OF AN EMAIL MESSAGE

If you want to save a draft of an email without sending it, tap the Cancel button that appears in the upper-left corner of the compose message window. The Delete Draft and Save Draft buttons display. Tap Save Draft to save it in your Drafts folder until you either send it or delete it.

SENDING AN EMAIL WITH AN ATTACHMENT

To send an email message that contains an attachment, such as a Pages document, those attachments must be sent from within a specific app (such as Pages), not from the Mail app. However, from within the Mail app, you can attach photos or video clips that are stored in your iPad.

> **NOTE** It's also possible to send photos via email directly from the Photos app. To do this, select up to five images from within Photos, tap on the Share icon, and then select the Mail option.

To add a photo or video clip attachment, press and hold your finger on the screen where you want the image to be inserted for about 2 seconds. A command bar appears. Tap on the Insert Photo or Video option that's displayed (shown in Figure 3.14).

Insert Photo or Video tab

FIGURE 3.14

Tap on the Insert Photo or Video tab to select and insert an image or video clip into your outgoing email.

When the Photos window appears, tap on the album that contains the image or video clip you want to include in the email, and then tap on the thumbnail for the actual image. From the Choose Photo window, tap on the Use button to select the image and embed it into the outgoing email. The image is now displayed in the outgoing email message you're composing (shown in Figure 3.15). Pay attention to the file size to ensure the message is not larger than what your email account provider (or the recipient's email account provider) allows. If it is, you need to decrease the photo's image size.

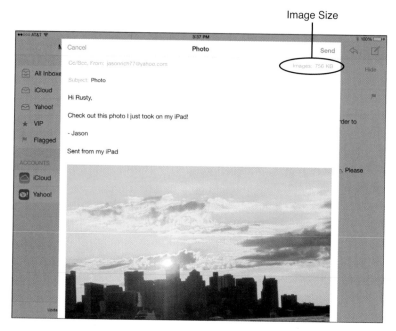

Image Size

FIGURE 3.15

You can embed one or more images (or video clips) into an outgoing email message from within the Mail app.

> **TIP** Anytime you add a photo as an attachment to an outgoing email in the Mail app, the app keeps the photo at its current file size. To change the image file size, look to the right of the From field for a message that says Images, and tap on it.
>
> An Image Size tab bar (shown in Figure 3.16) is displayed that includes four buttons, Small, Medium, Large, and Actual Size. Tap on the image file size you want. Remember that most email accounts do not allow extremely large files to be sent or received, so if you're sending multiple high-resolution images in a single email, you may need to decrease the image sizes. Doing this also speeds up the sending and receiving process significantly, especially if you're using a 3G or 4G cellular data connection.

Keep in mind that you can send a Pages, Word, or PDF document from the Pages app, or a Numbers or Excel (spreadsheet) file from the Numbers app. It's also possible to send photos or video clips from the Photos app.

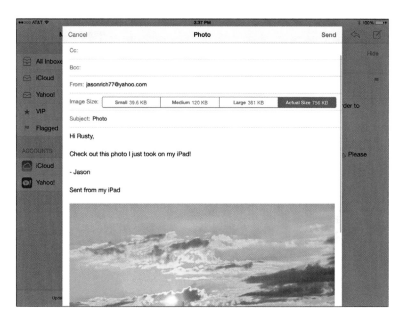

FIGURE 3.16

You can change the file size of images being embedded into your outgoing emails when using the Mail app.

Other apps also enable you to attach app-specific files to outgoing emails that are composed and sent from within that app. To do this, tap the Share icon that's displayed within the app and choose the Email option.

ADDITIONAL MAIL APP FEATURES

The Mail app offers much of the same functionality as the email program you use on your primary computer or on the Web. In addition to utilizing a built-in spell checker, for example, Mail is compatible with the Select, Copy, Cut, and Paste features built in to the iOS operating system. This enables you to move text and email message content between messages or into other apps with ease.

Plus, the Mail app automatically links with the Contacts app to pull email addresses from your Contacts database. So instead of entering someone's email address into the To field of a message you're composing, you can begin typing the recipient's name, and the app automatically pulls email addresses from your Contacts database and gives you a list of potential recipients.

USING THE WEB OR OTHER APPS TO ACCESS EMAIL

In addition to using the Mail app to access your email, for some types of email accounts, you can also use the Safari web browser to access your email account directly from the server.

When you visit the App Store, you can also find third-party iPad apps that can replace the Mail app and help you better manage one or more email accounts. To find these apps, launch the App Store app, and enter the keyword "email" into the Search field.

ACCESSING YOUR iCLOUD-RELATED EMAIL ACCOUNT FROM iCLOUD.COM

All content related to your iCloud-related email account automatically syncs with iCloud. To manage your iCloud-related email account from any or computer that's connected to the Internet, point your web browser to www.icloud.com, sign in using your Apple ID and password (or iCloud log-in information), and then click on the Mail app icon. This launches the online version of the Mail app, which is automatically populated with your iCloud-related email account content.

COMMUNICATING VIA INSTANT MESSAGES VIA THE MESSAGES APP

Using short, text-based messages and a special "language" composed of abbreviated terminology, such as "LOL" (meaning "laugh out loud") or "BRB" (meaning "be right back"), people have begun to rely on text messaging and instant messaging as a convenient way to communicate. On your iPad, this type of communication is possible using the Messages app.

The Messages app works with Apple's own iMessage service, which allows Mac, iPhone, and iPad users to communicate for free and on an unlimited basis with one another via the Internet. SMS text messaging, however, is typically done using a smartphone and a cellular data network. You can find other text/instant messaging apps that are compatible with other services available from the App Store.

> **NOTE** If the person you're communicating with via the Messages app has an entry in your Contacts app database and that entry contains his photo, it is displayed within the Messages app. Otherwise, the person's initials are displayed by default where the photo would otherwise be seen. If you receive a message from someone who is not in your Contacts database, a generic head silhouette appears.

> **TIP** It's possible to use Siri in order to dictate and send text messages using your voice. To do this, activate Siri and say something like, "Send text message to Rusty Rich." When Siri says, "What would you like it to say?," speak your message, and then confirm it. When prompted, tell Siri to send the text message you dictated. This feature works best if details about the person to which you're sending a text message are already stored in your Contacts database.
>
> Siri can also be used to read your newly received text messages without having to look at or touch the tablet's screen.

QUICK START: APPLE'S iMESSAGE SERVICE

The Messages app taps into your iPad's other functions and allows for the easy sharing of photos, videos, locations, and contacts; plus, it works seamlessly with Notification Center.

> **TIP** When the iMessage service is used with the Messages app, it enables you to send the same text message to multiple recipients. It uses a feature referred to as *group messaging* that enables everyone in that group to participate in the same text-message–based conversation.

iMessage enables you to participate in text-based but real-time conversations. You can see when someone is typing a message to you, and then you can view and respond to the message a fraction of a second after it is sent.

SETTING UP A FREE iMESSAGE ACCOUNT

The first time you launch the Messages app to use it with the iMessage service, you're instructed to set up a free account using your existing Apple ID. Or, instead of using your Apple ID, tap on the Create New Account option to create an account that's linked to another existing email address.

> **NOTE** iPhone users can associate their cellphone number with their iMessage account to send and receive text messages using this service. However, an Apple ID or existing email address can be used as well if you're an iPhone and iPad user.

> TIP If you've upgraded your iPad to iOS 7, when you first launch Messages, you might discover the app automatically uses your existing Apple ID to establish your free iMessage account. You can modify this by selecting the Messages option from the Settings app and then tapping Send & Receive if you want to create or use a different existing Apple ID account for use with these services.

Just as when you're using FaceTime, the unique Apple ID, email address, or iPhone phone number you use to set up your iMessage account is how people find you and are able to communicate with you via instant messages. So if you want someone to be able to send you messages via iMessage, that person needs to know the iPhone phone number, Apple ID, or email address you used to set up the account. Likewise, to send someone a message via iMessage, you need to know the iPhone phone number, Apple ID, or email address the recipient used to set up her iMessage account.

If you attempt to send a message to someone's email address that is not registered with iMessage as an active account, the message is sent as a traditional email and appears in the recipient's email inbox.

PROS AND CONS OF USING iMESSAGE

The biggest benefits to using iMessage over other text-messaging services are that it's free and you can send/receive an unlimited number of messages. And because iMessage utilizes the Messages app, the app itself nicely integrates with other features, functions, and apps on your iPhone or iPad.

Using the Camera app, for example, you can easily snap a photo or shoot a video clip using your iOS mobile device and then use Messages to send that image or video clip to one or more friends via iMessage. Or if you're enjoying a cup of coffee at a local cafe, you can quickly share your exact location with a handful of friends and use iMessage to send out an invite for other people to join you.

If you're away from your iPad when an incoming message arrives, don't worry. The Notification Center app can continuously monitor the Messages app and inform you of any missed messages in the Notification Center window.

Another convenient feature of iMessage is that you can begin a message-based conversation using your iPhone, for example, and then at any time switch to using your iPad or Mac and continue that conversation using the iMessage service.

All messages that are sent and received are saved and categorized by the person you communicated with. Until you manually delete the conversation, you always have a record of what was said, accompanied by the time and date messages were sent/received.

STRATEGIES FOR USING THE MESSAGES APP

The main Messages app screen is divided into two main sections (shown in Figure 3.17). On the left is a listing of previous text-based conversations you've participated in.

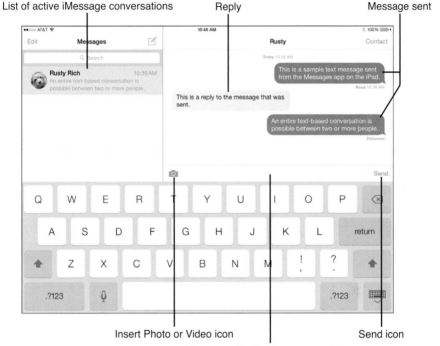

List of active iMessage conversations   Reply   Message sent

Insert Photo or Video icon   Send icon

Type outgoing instant message here

FIGURE 3.17

The main Messages screen on the iPad.

When Messages is running, the right side of the screen is the active conversation window. From here, you can initiate a new conversation or respond to incoming messages, one at a time.

> **NOTE** When you need to type messages, the iPad's virtual keyboard appears. To give you more onscreen real estate to reread a long conversation, tap on the Hide Keyboard key that always appears near the lower-right corner of the virtual keyboard.

CREATING AND SENDING A TEXT MESSAGE

The first time you launch Messages on the iPad, the New Message screen is visible, with the cursor flashing on the To field and the virtual keyboard displayed. If you have contact information stored in the Contacts app, as soon as you start typing in the To field, Messages attempts to match up existing contacts with the name, cell-phone number, or email address you're currently typing. When the intended recipient's name appears (because it's already stored in Contacts), tap on it.

To enter a recipient's name, cellphone number, Apple ID, or email address from scratch, simply type it into the To field using the iPhone or iPad's virtual keyboard.

> **TIP** After you've sent and received text messages using the Messages app, to initiate a new text-message conversation with someone, tap on the New Message icon that appears to the right of the Messages heading in the left column.

To quickly search your Contacts database to find one or more recipients for your messages, you can also tap on the plus sign icon in the To field as you're composing a new message. A scrollable list of all contacts stored in Contacts displays, along with a Search field you can use to search your contacts database from within the Messages app.

After filling in the To field with one or more recipients, tap on the optional Subject field to create a subject for your text message, and then tap on the blank field located to the left of the Send icon to begin typing your text message. If you're only sending text within your message, enter the text and then tap on the Send option. Or to attach a photo or video clip to your outgoing text message, tap on the camera icon that's displayed to the left of the field where you're typing the text message.

> **TIP** When you tap on the camera icon as you're composing a text message, two command options are displayed: Take Photo or Video and Choose Existing. Tap on the Take Photo or Video option to launch the Camera app from within Messages, and quickly snap a photo or shoot a video clip using your iPad's built-in camera.
>
> If you already have the photo or video clip stored on your tablet that you want to share, tap on the Choose Existing option to launch the Photos app from within Messages, and then tap on the thumbnail for the photo or video clip you want to attach to the message.

When the photo or video clip has been attached to the outgoing text message, and you've typed any text that you want to accompany it, tap on the Send key to send the message.

It's also possible to send a photo via iMessage from within the Photos app. To do this, select the image you want to share, tap the Share icon, and then select Message. Fill in the To field and then tap on the Send option.

PARTICIPATING IN A TEXT-MESSAGE CONVERSATION

As soon as you tap Send to initiate a new text-message conversation and send an initial message, the New Message window transforms into a conversation window, with the recipient's name displayed at the top center. Displayed on the right side of the conversation window are the messages you've sent. The responses from the person you're conversing with are left-justified and displayed in a different color on the screen with text bubbles.

As the text-message–based conversation continues and eventually scrolls off the screen, use your finger to swipe upward or downward to view what's already been said.

TIP Whenever there's a pause between the sending of a message and the receipt of a response, the Messages app automatically inserts the date and time in the center of the conversation window so that you can later easily track the time period during which each conversation took place. This is particularly helpful if there are long gaps in the conversation.

To access command icons for deleting individual text messages, deleting entire text-message conversations, or forwarding a single message (or complete conversation) to someone else, while viewing an instant message conversation, hold your finger for 2 seconds or so on any individual message and then tap on the More option. You can then select messages to delete, and tap on the Delete All option (to delete the entire conversation). Once selected, tap on the Trash icon to delete the selected content or tap on the Forward icon to share it with others.

TIP From the Messages conversation window, tap on the Contact button in the upper-right corner to view the complete Contacts database entry for the person you're conversing with.

To delete entire conversations, swipe your finger from left to right along the Messages listing for the conversation you want to delete. When the red-and-white Delete icon appears, tap on it to delete that entire conversation (as opposed to individual text messages within a conversation). You can also quickly delete multiple conversations with specific people. To do this, tap on the Edit button at the top-left of the Messages listing and then tap the red-and-white negative sign icon that's displayed next to the listings.

RESPONDING TO AN INCOMING TEXT MESSAGE

Depending on how you set up the Messages app from within Settings, you can be notified of an incoming message in a number of ways. For example, notification of a new message can be set to appear in the Notification Center. Or if the Messages app is already running, a new message alert sounds and a new message listing appears under the Messages heading on the left side of the iPad screen.

> **TIP**   When a new message arrives, a blue dot appears to the left of the new message's listing indicating a new, unread message.

To read the incoming text message and enter into the conversation window and respond, tap on the incoming message listing. If you're looking at the listing in the Notification Center window, for example, and you tap on it, the Messages app launches and the appropriate conversation window automatically opens.

After reading the incoming text message, use the virtual keyboard to type your response in the blank message field, and then tap the Send icon to send your response.

RELAUNCHING OR REVIEWING PAST CONVERSATIONS

From the left side of the screen when the Messages app is running, you can view a listing of all saved text-message conversations. The Messages app automatically saves all text messages until you manually delete them.

The Messages listing contains all the conversations you've participated in to date, displayed in reverse chronological order. Each listing displays the person's name, the date and time of the last message sent or received, and a summary of the last message sent or received.

Tap on any of the listings to relaunch that conversation in the Conversation window. You can either reread the entire conversation or continue the conversation by responding to the last message that was sent or by sending a new message to that person.

TIP   By tapping on one conversation listing at a time, you can quickly switch between conversations and participate in multiple conversations at once.

TIP   To exit a conversation, tap on one of the other listings under the Messages heading on the left side of the screen. However, to exit the Messages app altogether, press the Home button.

TIP   By default, Notification Center will alert you of new incoming text messages in the Notification Center window. You can change this option from within Settings. You can also set it up so that your iPad displays a banner or an alert on the screen, shows a Badge App Icon, and/or displays a message on the Lock Screen when a new incoming text message arrives.

To adjust these option, launch Settings from the Home Screen; tap on the Notification Center option; and then adjust the Notification Center, Show, Alert Style, Badge App Icon, Show Preview, Repeat Alert, and View in Lock Screen options that are displayed under the Messages heading.

CUSTOMIZING THE MESSAGES APP

From Settings, you can customize several options related to the Messages app. To do this, launch Settings from the Home screen and then tap on the Messages option.

From the Messages submenu, turn on or off the iMessage service altogether, plus make adjustments that are relevant to sending and receiving text messages from your tablet.

For example, by adjusting the virtual switch associated with the Send Read Receipts option to the on position, the people who send you messages to will be notified immediately when their messages to you have been read.

CAUTION   Beware of the iPad's auto-correction feature when using the Mail and Messages apps. When turned on, your iOS device automatically "fixes" misspelled or incorrectly typed words. However, this auto-correction feature is not always accurate, especially if you're using abbreviations in your email or instant messages, and this could result in an embarrassing situation.

To control the Auto-Correction feature, launch the Settings app and select the General option. Scroll down to the Keyboard option, and tap on it. Tap on the virtual on/off switch associated with the Auto-Correction feature to enable or disable it.

Before sending any email or instant message from your iPad, be sure to proofread it carefully to avoid an embarrassing and potentially unprofessional situation or miscommunication.

TIP   When using the Messages app, you can take advantage of keyboard short-cuts and special keyboard layouts to increase your text entry speed and accuracy, plus give you a greater selection of special characters, symbols, and emoticons. To create keyboard shortcuts, launch Settings, tap on the General option, and then tap on the Keyboard option. To create a new Keyboard Shortcut that can be used from any app, including Messages, tap on the Add New Shortcut... button.

To activate a special keyboard layout, such as the Spanish or French keyboard, launch Settings, tap on the General option, and then tap on the Keyboard option. From the Keyboard submenu, tap on the Keyboards option. Then, from the Keyboards submenu, tap on the Add New Keyboard... option and select the appropriate option by tapping on it. Now, when the virtual keyboard is displayed, a globe-shaped icon appears between the 123 key and the Dictation key (the microphone). Tap on this new key to reveal the alternative keyboard layout(s).

IN THIS CHAPTER

■ Managing your schedule using the
  Calendar app
■ Taking advantage of the Clock app

4

USING THE CALENDAR AND CLOCK APPS TO ORGANIZE YOUR PERSONAL AND PROFESSIONAL LIFE

As you know, iOS 7 offers a plethora of useful apps that come preinstalled with the operating system, many of which can become indispensible tools in your personal and professional life.

The Calendar app, for example, not only enables you to create and manage your schedule, it's possible to create separate calendars (for your work, personal life, travel schedule, kids' schedule, and so on), and view them on a single screen. Calendar is also fully compatible with iCloud, so your scheduling data syncs with your other computers and iOS mobile devices automatically and is accessible anytime directly from the iCloud website.

Meanwhile, in addition to serving as a reliable alarm clock, the Clock app features world clock functionality (showing the specific countries you're interested in), plus it can serve as a stopwatch or timer.

TIP   When traveling on business and staying at hotels, instead of relying on notoriously unreliable hotel wake-up calls, you can set your iPad to wake you up at a predetermined time using the alert tone (or even a song) of your choosing. Just be sure that your tablet is fully charged or plugged in and is not powered down.

CALENDAR APP BASICS

With its multiple viewing options for keeping track of the scheduling information, Calendar is a highly customizable scheduling tool that enables you to easily sync your scheduling data with your primary computer's scheduling software (such as Microsoft Outlook on a PC or the Mac version of Calendar), as well as with your iPhone or smartphone. Like many other apps, Calendar works seamlessly with Notification Center and Apple's iCloud service.

NOTE   When using the Calendar app, appointments, meetings, and other items you enter are referred to as *events*.

TIP   The iCloud website offers an online-based version of the Calendar app that is accessible from any computer or mobile device that's connected to the Internet. Visit www.icloud.com, log in using your Apple ID and password (or your iCloud account information), and then click on the Calendar app icon within the browser window. As long as you have the Calendar app set up to sync Calendar data with iCloud, all of your up-to-date schedule information is automatically loaded into the online edition of the Calendar app.

Using Calendar, it's easy to share some or all of your schedule information with colleagues and maintain several separate, color-coded calendars of your own to keep personal and work-related responsibilities and projects listed separately while still being able to view them on the same screen.

TIP   The Calendar app is designed to work seamlessly with Apple's iCloud service, Microsoft Exchange, as well as other software and online-based calendar/scheduling programs (including Google Calendar, Facebook, and Yahoo! Calendar). This file compatibility enables you to easily synchronize your scheduling data between your iPad and other devices and/or online-based scheduling apps. If you opt to sync Calendar app-specific data with iCloud, however, do not also attempt to sync this data with another online-based service, or you wind up with duplicate entries.

CONTROLLING THE VIEW

When you launch the Calendar app, choose which viewing perspective you'd like to use to display your schedule data in. Your options, selectable by tapping the tabs displayed near the top-center of the screen, include the following:

DAY VIEW

In one-hour increments, this view (shown in Figure 4.1) displays a day's worth of events on the left side of the screen, based on the time each event is scheduled for. When you tap on a specific event listing (on the left side of the screen), all of the details pertaining to that individual event are then displayed on the right side of the screen and become editable.

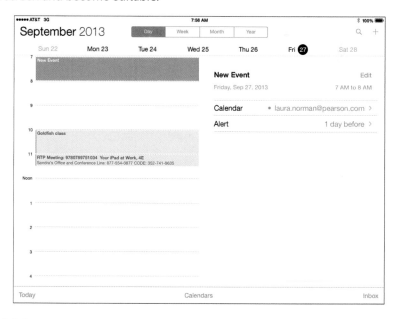

FIGURE 4.1

The Calendar app's Day view.

> **TIP** When utilizing the Day view, you can swipe up and down on the left side of the screen to scroll through your day, hour by hour. Near the top of the screen, you can scroll horizontally along the days of the week to advance or go back a week at a time. Tap on a specific day to view its schedule of events/appointments. Access the current day by tapping on the Today button.

WEEK VIEW

This view uses a grid format (shown in Figure 4.2) to display the days of the week along the top of the screen and time intervals along the left side. With it, you have an overview of all events scheduled in a particular week (Sunday through Saturday).

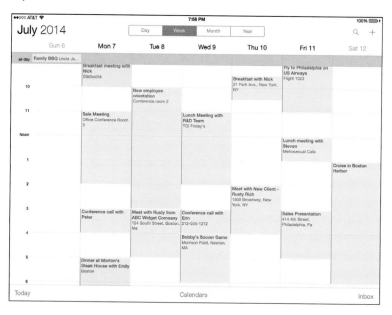

FIGURE 4.2

The Calendar app's Week view.

> **TIP** When utilizing the Week view, it's possible to swipe upward or downward to view more of each day or swipe a finger horizontally to advance or go back one week at a time.

MONTH VIEW

The month-at-a-time view (shown in Figure 4.3) enables you to see a month's worth of events at a time. You can tap any single day to immediately switch to the Day view in order to review a detailed summary of events slated for that day.

> **TIP** When accessing the Month view, swipe your finger upward to manually advance to a future month or swipe downward to go back and view previous months.

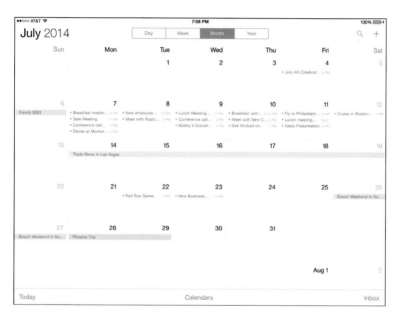

FIGURE 4.3

The Calendar app's Month view.

YEAR VIEW

This view (shown in Figure 4.4) enables you to look at 12 mini calendars. From the Year view, swipe your finger upward to manually advance to a future year (an additional 12-month group of mini calendars) or swipe downward to go back and view previous years.

Regardless of which view you select, view the current day's schedule by tapping the Today option located in the lower-left corner of the screen. On the calendar itself, the current date is always highlighted in red.

Search icon   Event icon

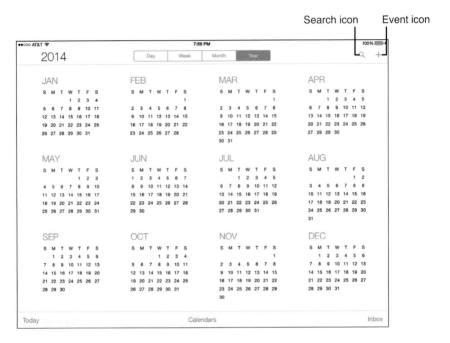

FIGURE 4.4

The Calendar app's Year view.

NOTE The Calendar app works with the iPad held in either landscape or portrait mode, so which you choose is a matter of personal preference. Regardless of which direction you hold your tablet, the onscreen information pertaining to your schedule is the same.

COMMAND OPTIONS AVAILABLE FROM ALL CALENDAR VIEWS

Regardless of which calendar view you're using, the Search icon and the Add Event icon (refer to Figure 4.4, for example) are continuously displayed near the top-right corner of the screen.

Tap the Search icon (which looks like a magnifying glass) to search the contents of your Calendar app's database for a specific event. You can enter a time, date, person's name, location, or any keyword associated with the appointment you're looking for. Keep in mind, as you create a new event, all data you enter pertaining to that event becomes searchable, so to quickly find events later (using this search feature, iOS 7's Spotlight Search feature, or Siri), add as much detail as possible, including who it involves, where it takes place, and when the event takes place.

If you're managing multiple calendars using the Calendar app, you have the option to view events from all calendars on a single screen in a color-coded format or display each calendar one at a time. To determine what calendar data is visible, tap on the Calendars option that's displayed at the bottom-center of the screen.

One of the features that makes the Calendar app useful in a work environment is the ability for groups of people to share their calendars (or event-specific information) via the Internet. When you're invited to participate in a new event by someone else, you receive an alert within the app. You can then opt to attend, decline, or do nothing with the electronic invitation. To manage all incoming event invitations from others, tap on the Inbox option in the lower-right corner of the screen.

> **NOTE** Once you confirm an incoming event invitation, it will be automatically added to your own calendar.

CREATING A NEW APPOINTMENT

No matter which calendar view you're using, to create a new event, tap the Add Event icon (the plus sign icon) that's displayed in the top-right corner of the screen. This displays an Add Event window (shown in Figure 4.5).

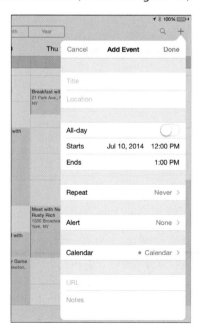

FIGURE 4.5

From the Add Event window, it's possible to add a new appointment to the Calendar app and associate an audible alarm with that event.

The first field in the Add Event window is labeled Title. Enter a heading for the event, such as "Lunch with Bob," "Sales Meeting," or "Conference call with Natalie."

Next, if there's a location associated with the meeting or appointment, tap the Location field and enter the address or location of the appointment. Entering information into the Location field is optional. You can be as detailed as you want when entering information into this field.

To set the time and date for the new appointment to begin and end, use the Starts and Ends fields. These fields expand to allow you to set dates and times for the event using scrolling dials, as shown in Figure 4.6.

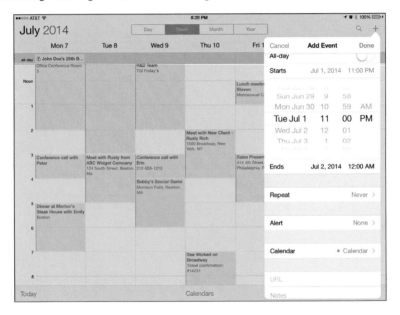

FIGURE 4.6

From the Start and End fields, select the start and end times and the dates for each new event you manually enter into the Calendar app.

TIP If the new event will last the entire day, tap on the virtual switch that's associated with the All-Day option to turn it on. Then, you no longer need to utilize the Starts and Ends options for the event.

After you enter the start time and end time for the appointment, scroll down to add additional details to the event listing.

TIP If the appointment you're entering repeats every day, every week, every two weeks, every month, or every year, tap Repeat and choose the appropriate option. The default for this option is Never, meaning it is a nonrepeating, one-time only event.

TIP When using almost any app, when you enter a day, such as "Monday" or "Wednesday"; a time; or a specific date, this information becomes an active link. By tapping on the link, a New Event window is displayed that allows you to quickly create a new event within the Calendar app. This also applies to text within incoming emails or text messages.

ASSOCIATING ONE OR TWO ALERTS WITH EACH EVENT

To set an audible alarm for the appointment, tap the Alert option displayed in the Add Event window. The Event Alert window temporarily replaces the Add Event window. In the Event Alert window, tap to specify when you want the audible alarm to sound in order to remind you of the appointment.

Your options are None (which is the default), At Time of Event, 5 Minutes Before, 15 Minutes Before, 30 Minutes Before, One Hour Before, Two Hours Before, One Day Before, Two Days Before, or One Week Before.

When you add an alert, a Second Alert option displays within the Add Event window. If you want to add a secondary alarm to this event, tap the Second Alert option, and when the Event Alert window reappears, tap when you want the second alarm to sound.

ADDITIONAL WAYS TO CUSTOMIZE EACH EVENT LISTING

When you return to the Add Event window, if you're maintaining several separate calendars using the Calendar app, it's possible to choose which calendar you want to list the event by tapping on the Calendar option and then selecting the appropriate calendar.

TIP Once events are scheduled within the Calendar app, the time within the day can be displayed as Free or Busy. As you're creating an event, tap on the Show As option to switch between these two settings. The default is Busy for a scheduled event.

Continue to scroll down in the Add Event window to access optional URL and Notes fields. You can enter a website address (URL) that corresponds to the event. Likewise, tap on the Notes field and manually type notes pertaining to the appointment (or paste data from other apps into this field). You can use the Dictation feature as another way to input notes or other Calendar data.

CAUTION It is absolutely essential that you tap the red Done option that's displayed near the top-right corner of the Add Event window in order to save the new event information; otherwise, the information you entered is not saved to your calendar.

TIP The Calendar app works with several other iPad apps, including Contacts and Notification Center. For example, in Contacts, you can enter someone's birthday in their entry, and that information can automatically be displayed by the Calendar app.

To display birthday listings within Calendar, tap the Calendars button, which is displayed at the bottom-center of the screen, and then tap the Birthdays option to add a check mark to that selection. All recurring birthdays stored in your Contacts app appear in Calendar.

The alternative to manually entering appointment information into the Calendar app is to enter your scheduling information within a scheduling program on your primary computer, such as Microsoft Outlook (PC), the Mac version of Calendar (Mac), or Microsoft Entourage (Mac), and then sync this data with your iPad using the iTunes sync process, iTunes Wireless Sync process, or via iCloud. You can also sync scheduling data with your iPhone, as well as several different online or network-based scheduling applications.

USING SIRI TO ENTER AND VIEW CALENDAR DATA

Instead of manually typing new events into the Calendar app, it's possible to dictate the information using Siri. To create a new event, activate Siri by pressing and holding down the Home button for 2 to 3 seconds, and then say something like the following:

- "Set up a meeting at 10 a.m. with Emily at her office."
- "Meet with Ryan at noon at Starbucks."
- "New appointment with John Doe on Thursday, July 18, at 2 p.m. at his office."

TIP When using Siri, if you give only a time for the meeting, Siri assumes you're referring to the present day and schedules the meeting accordingly. However, you can also refer to a date in the future by saying something like, "next Wednesday at 2 p.m.," or you can provide a detailed date and time (such as July 7, 2013 at 4:14 p.m.).

After events are entered into the Calendar app, it's possible to use Siri to cancel (delete) or reschedule them. For example, you can say, "Cancel my meeting at 3 p.m. today," "Reschedule my appointment with Natalie to next Wednesday at 11 a.m.," or "Move my 4 p.m. meeting to 4:30 p.m."

It's also possible to use Siri to review your schedule. For example, you can ask Siri, "What does the rest of my day look like?", "When is my next appointment?", or "When am I meeting with Ryan?" You can also issue Siri a command, such as "Show me my schedule for today" or "Show me my appointments for this week."

TIP By utilizing the Location field within the Add Event window as you're creating a new event, you can later reference this information by asking Siri a question like, "Where is my next appointment?" or "How do I get to my next appointment?"

VIEWING INDIVIDUAL EVENT DETAILS

From the Day, Week, or Month view within the Calendar app, tap any individual event to view all of the details related to that item. When you tap a single event in the Week or Month view, a new window opens. If you're in the Day view, the event's details are displayed on the right side of the screen.

In the upper-right corner of the event window is an Edit button. Tap it to modify any aspect of the event listing, such as the title, location, start time, end time, alert, or notes.

To delete an event entry entirely, tap the Edit button followed by the red-and-white Delete Event button that's displayed near the bottom of the Edit window.

TIP When you're done making changes to an event entry, don't forget to tap on the Done option that's displayed near the upper-right corner of the window to save your updated event information.

SUBSCRIBING TO CALENDARS

From within Calendar, it is possible to subscribe to read-only Google, Yahoo!, or calendars saved in the .ics format. To subscribe to a calendar, which enables you to view events created on other devices or services, but not edit or create new events within those calendars, follow these steps:

1. From the iPad's Home screen, launch Settings.

2. Tap on the Mail, Contacts, Calendars option.

3. Under the Accounts heading on the right side of the Settings screen, tap the Add Account option.

4. From the bottom of the list of account types, tap the Other option.

5. When the Other menu appears on the right side of the display, tap the Add Subscribed Calendar option.

6. In the Subscription window that appears, enter the address for the calendar you want to subscribe to in the field labeled Server. Enter this information using the following format: *myserver.com/cal.ics*.

7. Tap the Next icon that's located in the upper-right corner of the screen to validate the subscription, and then tap the Save button. Your tablet must be connected to the Internet to do this.

If you use the Calendar app on a Mac, for example, you can publish (and share) a Calendar via a web server and make it available to be subscribed to on your iPad. This is a useful feature if you want to share Calendar-related data, such as a conference schedule, with other people and make events displayable on their respective devices (within the Calendar app) but not give those people the ability to edit or modify listed events.

From the Calendar app on your Mac, select the calendar you want to publish from the listing on the left side of the screen (on your Mac). After it's highlighted, click on the Edit pull-down menu and then click on the Share Calendar… option. When prompted, create a name for the calendar and one at a time, enter the name or email addresses for the people you want to share the calendar with (or tap on the Public option).

The Apple website also publishes dozens of read-only calendars that you can subscribe to on your iPad. These read-only calendars list major holidays, game schedules for your favorite sports teams, moon phases, new song releases on iTunes, new DVD releases, and more. For a listing of these calendars, visit www.apple.com/downloads/macosx/calendars.

TIP If your primary work schedule is handled on a computer or network that is compatible with the industry-standard CalDAV format, you can easily sync this data with the Calendar app on your iPad. To subscribe to a CalDAV calendar, launch Settings on your iPad, and then choose the Mail, Contacts, Calendars option. Tap the Add Account option, and then choose Other from the bottom of the list.

When the Other screen appears, select the Add CalDAV Account option. A CalDAV window displays, and you are prompted to enter the server address (*cal.example.com*), your username, password, and a description for the calendar. This is information you can obtain from your company's network system administrator or IT department.

After entering all the requested information in the CalDAV window on your iPad, tap the Next button to verify the account. Tap the Save button when this process is completed. The events included in the calendar you just subscribed to now appear in their own color-coded calendar when you launch the Calendar app on your iPad.

FINDING AN EVENT

In addition to viewing the Day, Week, or Month view in Calendar to find individual events, use the Search option. Tap the Search icon in the top-right corner of the screen (to the left of the Add Event icon), and then use the virtual keyboard to enter any keyword or phrase associated with the event you're looking for.

Or, from the iPad's Home screen, place your finger near the center of the screen and swipe downward in order to access the tablet's main Spotlight Search feature.

In the Search field that appears, enter a keyword, search phrase, or date associated with an event. When a list of relevant items is displayed, tap the event you want to view.

TIP You can also use Siri to help you find a appointment. Activate Siri and say something like, "When am I meeting with [name]?" or "When is my next meeting?"

INVITING PEOPLE TO MEETINGS OR EVENTS

The Calendar app is compatible with Microsoft Exchange as well as the Calendar app running on any other Mac, iPhone, or iPad. Thus, if you have the appropriate feature turned on and your company uses a CalDAV-supported scheduling app on its network, you can invite other people on that network to your events and respond to other people's event invites.

To respond to an event invitation, your iPad must have access to the Internet. When you receive an invitation, a notice is placed in the Calendar app's Inbox. Tap the Inbox option to view options enabling you to see who the invitation is from and who is attending the event. You can also set your iPad to alert you of the meeting and add comments of your own that pertain to the meeting invite.

As the invitee, you can then accept or decline the invitation or tap the Maybe option. The person who invited you to the event automatically receives your response.

CUSTOMIZING THE CALENDAR APP

There are many ways to customize the Calendar app beyond choosing between the Day, Week, Month, or Year view. For example, from within the Calendar app you can set audible alerts to remind you of upcoming events. To customize the audio alert you hear, launch Settings and select the Sounds option from the left side of the screen. Next, tap the Calendar Alerts option displayed on the right side of the screen and choose a sound or music clip to use as the audible alert.

> **TIP** If you have the ability to receive meeting or event invites from others, from Settings, tap the Mail, Contacts, Calendars option. Then scroll down to the Calendars heading and make sure the Shared Calendar Alerts option is turned on. This enables you to be notified when you receive a new group invitation for a Shared Calendar Event. Turn on the New Invitation Alerts option to be alerted when an individual invites you to a single event.

Also from Settings, listed under the Calendars heading on the right side of the display, it's possible to determine how far back in your schedule you want to sync appointment data between your iPad and iCloud (or another scheduling app). Tap on the Sync option to do this. Your options include Events 2 Weeks Back, Events 1 Month Back, Events 3 Months Back, Events 6 Months Back, or All Events.

When the Time Zone Support option is turned on and you've selected the major city that you're in or near, all alarms are activated based on that city's time zone. However, when you travel, turn off this option. With Time Zone Support turned off, the iPad determines the current date and time based on the location and time zone you're in (when it's connected to the Internet) and adjusts all your alarms to go off at the appropriate time for that time zone.

To access the Time Zone Support feature, launch Settings and select the Mail, Contacts, Calendars option. On the right side of the screen, scroll down to the options listed under Calendars, and then tap the Time Zone Support option. When the Time Zone Support screen appears, you see a virtual on/off switch. When it's turned on, below the switch is a Time Zone option. Tap it and then choose your home city (or a city within the time zone you're in).

Meanwhile, the Default Alert Times option (shown in Figure 4.7) enables the Calendar app to automatically generate alerts. These auto alerts can be scheduled for the day of the event (at 9 a.m.), one day before the event (at 9 a.m.), two days before the event (at 9 a.m.), or one week before the event. You can adjust the settings differently for Birthdays, Events, and All-Day Events.

FIGURE 4.7

To customize the Calendar app from within Settings, select the Mail, Contacts, Calendars option on the left side of the screen and then scroll down to the Calendars heading.

If you have birthdays displayed in the Calendar app (using data from the Contacts app), this feature reminds you of upcoming birthdays with ample time to send a card or gift.

> **TIP**   Managing multiple calendars simultaneously is common, such as main-
> taining separate calendars for personal and work-related events. From the Mail,
> Contacts, Calendars screen within Settings, tap on the Default Calendar option
> to choose which calendar is used as the default when new events are added. As
> you're entering the event, however, you can always change the calendar.

SYNCING SCHEDULING DATA WITH YOUR PRIMARY COMPUTER OR SMARTPHONE

Depending on whether you want to sync your Calendar app with a standalone PC or Mac or wirelessly access scheduling data on a network, the process for setting up the connection and syncing scheduling data is slightly different.

SYNCING CALENDAR DATA WITH A PC OR MAC USING iTUNES SYNC

The process for syncing data between the Calendar app and your primary computer using the iTunes sync process involves connecting the two devices using the white USB cable that came with your iPad. You also need the free iTunes software to be running on your primary computer. Customize the Sync Calendars option within iTunes on your computer, which is found under the Info tab when your iPad is connected to your PC or Mac and iTunes is running.

Using the Wireless iTunes Sync process, you can sync your iPad with your Mac or PC that's running the iTunes Software, as long as the two devices are connected to the same wireless network. This feature does not work over the Internet, so you need to be within close proximity to your primary computer to perform the data sync.

SYNCING CALENDAR DATA WIRELESSLY USING iCLOUD

It's also possible (and recommended) to sync your Calendar data with other iOS mobile devices, as well as your computer(s), using Apple's iCloud online service. After you have created an iCloud account, set up your iPad for automatic Calendar app syncing.

To do this, launch Settings and select the iCloud option displayed on the left side of the screen. On the right side of the screen, when the iCloud submenu appears, make sure the Calendars option is turned on.

You also must turn on Calendar syncing via iCloud on your computer(s), iPhone, and/or other iOS mobile devices that are linked to the same iCloud account. Once you do this, the online version of the Calendar app is available to you as well by visiting www.icloud.com.

SYNCING CALENDAR DATA WIRELESSLY WITH SCHEDULING SOFTWARE ON A MICROSOFT EXCHANGE–COMPATIBLE NETWORK

To set up the Calendar app to sync data with Microsoft Exchange–compatible scheduling software used in a corporate environment, launch Settings on your tablet and choose the Mail, Contacts, Calendars option.

Tap the Add Account option, and then select Microsoft Exchange from the menu displayed on the right side of the screen. Enter your account information when prompted. This information is typically supplied by your company's system administrator or IT department.

As you're setting up the Microsoft Exchange connection with your iPad, be sure to add a check mark next to the Calendar option so you can sync this data.

TIP Many company networks and virtual private networks (VPNs) utilize scheduling software that is CalDAV-compatible. To synchronize your scheduling information between your tablet and a CalDAV-compatible calendar/scheduling software package on a corporate network, contact your company's IT department or system administrator to obtain the necessary account settings and passwords to make this connection.

On your iPad, set up this connection from the Settings app. If your company's system administrator or IT department is not able to help you sync your tablet with the company's network, make an appointment with an Apple Genius at any Apple Store or call AppleCare's toll-free phone number (800-APL-CARE) and have a technical support person walk you through the setup process.

SYNCING CALENDAR DATA WIRELESSLY WITH GOOGLE CALENDAR, YAHOO! CALENDAR, AOL, OR OUTLOOK.COM

If you maintain your scheduling information using an online-based scheduling application, such as Google Calendar or Yahoo! Calendar, you can use your iPad to wirelessly sync scheduling data.

To set this up, launch Settings on your iPad; select the Mail, Contacts, Calendars option; and then tap the Add Account option.

Choose the Google, Yahoo!, AOL, or Outlook.com option based on where you maintain an online-based calendar. When prompted, enter your name, the existing email address and password used for that service, and a brief description for the account.

Finally, tap the services you want to link with your iPad, such as Calendars, Contacts, and so on. The available options vary based on the service you use. To sync your calendar data between the online service and the Calendar app, be sure to turn on the virtual switch associated with the Calendars option.

> TIP Thanks to Facebook integration with iOS 7, it's possible to set it up so your Calendar app syncs event-related details with your online Facebook Events calendar. To do this, launch Settings, tap on the Facebook option, and then turn on the virtual switch associated with the Calendar app that's listed under the "Allow These Apps To Use Your Account" heading.

> CAUTION If you opt to sync your data between your iPad and an online service (such as Google, Yahoo!, AOL, Outlook.com, or Microsoft Exchange), be sure to turn off iCloud syncing for the Calendar app. Otherwise, you may wind up with duplicate entries.

USING THE CLOCK APP

The Clock app that comes preinstalled with iOS 7 is designed to serve as a world clock (enabling you to view the current time in numerous cities simultaneously), an alarm clock, a stopwatch, and a countdown timer. When you launch this app, you'll see four command icons displayed along the bottom of the screen that enable you to choose which function you want to utilize.

WHAT TIME IS IT IN TOKYO, LONDON, AND DALLAS?

When you tap on the World Clock option, displayed along the top of the screen are six clock faces, each of which can represent a different city (shown in Figure 4.8). When you swipe your finger from right to left along the clock faces, six additional clocks are revealed.

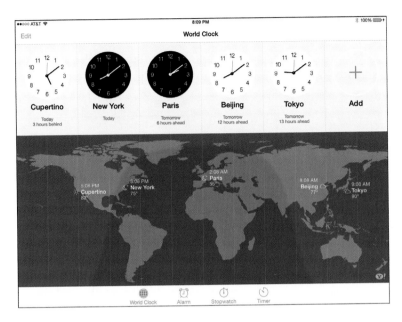

FIGURE 4.8
View the current time in up to a dozen cities around the globe.

Tap on the Add clock icon to create a new clock associated with any major city on the planet. Or once a clock is associated with a city, tap on the Edit option that's displayed near the upper-left corner of the screen to change the city each clock face is associated with. When you do this, the Choose a City window appears. In the search field, enter the name of any major city in the world or scroll down the detailed list that's displayed and tap on your selection.

Once a clock face is associated with a city, it displays the current time in that city. Plus, the city is displayed (along with the current time and temperature) on the world map found in the lower section of the screen (see Figure 4.9).

As you're looking at the World Clock display, tap on any clock face for a specific city to view a full-screen version of that clock.

USING YOUR iPAD AS A RELIABLE ALARM CLOCK

Unlike the wake-up call services offered by most hotels, which are notoriously unreliable, you can use your iPad as an alarm clock. You can set an alarm to sound anytime you wish and have the tablet play the audio alert of your choosing or a song that's stored in the Music app.

To use this feature, launch the Clock app and tap on the Alarm icon at the bottom of the screen. To set a new alarm, tap on the plus sign icon that's displayed at the upper-right corner of the screen. The Add Alarm window is displayed. Once an Alarm is created, you always have the option to edit it (shown in Figure 4.9).

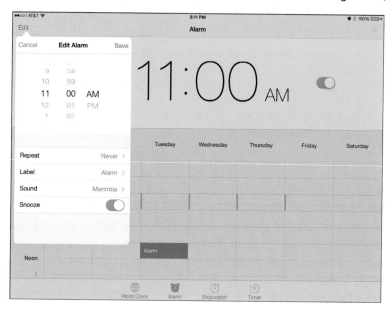

FIGURE 4.9

You can set as many separate alarms for the alarm clock as you want and then turn each of them on or off separately.

From the Add Alarm window, you can choose whether the alarm will repeat and, if so, when. Tap on the Sound option to choose an alarm sound (or a song that's stored on your tablet) for each separate alarm. As a preview of the alarm is playing, use the Volume Up or Volume Down button to adjust its volume.

> **TIP** Just like a traditional alarm clock, you can set the Alarm within the Clock app to offer a snooze option. From the Add Alarm window, turn on the virtual switch associated with the Snooze option to activate this feature.

You can also custom create the label associated with each alarm. The default option is Alarm, but you can change it to anything you'd like, such as Wake Up, Meeting, or Take Medication. Finally, use the dials to choose the time you want each alarm set for. The Alarm feature enables you to set as many separate alarms as you'd like, but each must be set one at a time.

A listing for each alarm that's programmed into the Clock app is displayed on the Alarm screen. To edit any of the alarms, tap on the Edit button that's displayed near the upper-left corner of the screen. You can then turn on or off individual alarms by tapping on their listing and then turning on or off the virtual switch that's associated with each.

USING THE STOPWATCH AND TIMER FEATURES

The Stopwatch feature of the Clock app enables you to time events and monitor how long they take down to a fraction of a second. You can pause the stopwatch at any time, restart or reset the timer, or use the stopwatch's lap feature. The Stopwatch feature starts at 00:00.0 and counts upward.

The Timer feature of the Clock app enables you to set a timer for a specific period. Then, after you start the timer (by tapping on the Start button), the timer counts down and sounds an alarm when it reaches zero. You can pause or resume the timer at any time by tapping on the Pause or Resume button.

You can use the Stopwatch or Timer feature for a wide range of tasks, such as tracking the length of phone calls or meetings.

TIP　Siri also works very well with the alarm clock and timer features of the Clock app. You can tell Siri to set an alarm by saying, "Set an alarm for 7:30 a.m. tomorrow" or "Set a wake-up call for 7 a.m. tomorrow." You can also set a timer by telling Siri to "Set a timer for 15 minutes," for example. You can also say something like, "Wake me up in four hours."

If you need to know what time it is in a specific country or city, just ask Siri by saying, "What time is it in London?" You can also ask for the current time or date where you are by asking, "What's today's date?" or "What time is it?"

5

WORKING WITH THE CONTACTS APP

The art of networking is all about meeting new people; staying in contact with them; making referrals and connections for others; and tapping the knowledge, experience, or expertise of the people you know to help you achieve your own career or work-related goals.

If you become good at networking, regardless of which field or industry you work in, over time you establish a contact list comprised of hundreds, or even thousands, of individuals and companies.

In addition to the contacts you establish and maintain within your network, your contacts database might also include people you work with, customers, clients, family members, people from your community you interact with (doctors, hair stylists, barbers, dry cleaners, and so on), and friends.

The easiest way to keep your contacts database organized is to utilize some type of contact management application on your primary computer or online. On a Mac, you might use

the popular Contacts app (which is included with OS X Mountain Lion and OS X Mavericks) or Microsoft Entourage. On a PC, Microsoft Outlook is a popular tool. There are also many web-, network-, and online (cloud)-based contact management applications available that are used by professionals and businesses of all sizes.

CUSTOMIZING THE CONTACTS APP

Chances are that the contacts database upon which you rely at your office can be synced with your tablet and made available to you using the Contacts app on your iPad. As you're about to discover, Contacts is a customizable contact management database tool that works with several other apps which also came preinstalled on your iPad, including Mail, Calendar, Safari, FaceTime, and Maps. It also integrates with the Facebook and Twitter apps, as well as Siri, plus is fully compatible with iCloud.

> TIP   Once you create and start managing a Contacts database using the Contacts app on your iPad, Mac, or iPhone, thanks to iCloud, it can remain synced with all of your other computers and mobile devices. Plus, you can access the online version of the Contacts app using any computer by visiting www.icloud.com and have complete and secure access to all of your Contacts data.

Of course, Contacts can be used as a standalone app on your iPad, enabling you to enter new contact entries as you meet new people and need to keep track of details about them.

The information you maintain in your Contacts database is highly customizable, which means you can keep track of only the information you want or need. For example, within each contact entry, you can store a lot of information about a person, including the following:

- First and last name
- Name prefix (Mr., Mrs., Dr., and so on)
- Name suffix (Jr., Sr., Ph.D., Esq., and so on)
- Job title
- Company
- Multiple phone numbers (work, home, cell, and so on)
- Multiple email addresses
- Multiple mailing addresses (work, home, and so on)

- Multiple web page addresses
- Facebook, Twitter, Skype, AOL Instant Message, or other online social networking site usernames

You can also customize your contacts database to include additional information, such as each contact's photo, the person's nickname, their spouse and/or assistant's names, the contact's birthday, as well as detailed notes pertaining to the contact.

Using the Contacts app, your entire contacts database is instantly searchable using data from any field in the database, so even if you have a database containing thousands of entries, you can always find the person or company you're looking for in a matter of seconds. Plus, other apps can pull information from your Contacts database automatically to make communication with those people more efficient.

ALLOWING THE CONTACTS APP TO WORK SEAMLESSLY WITH OTHER APPS

After your contacts database has been populated with entries, other apps can utilize that information in a handful of ways. Here are some examples:

- When you compose a new email message in Mail, in the To field you can begin typing someone's full name or email address. If that person's contact information (including their email address) is already stored in Contacts, the relevant email address automatically displays in the email's To field.
- If you're planning a trip to visit a contact, you can pull up someone's address from your Contacts database in order to obtain driving directions to the person's home or work location using the Maps app.
- If you include each person's birthday in your Contacts database, that information can automatically be displayed by the Calendar app to remind you in advance to send a card or gift.
- As you're creating each contact entry, you can include a photo of that person by either activating the Camera app from within the Contacts app to snap a photo or using a photo that's already stored in the Photos app and linking it with a contact. It's also possible for the Contacts app to display someone's Facebook profile picture automatically, plus update their entry whenever a Facebook friend's profile information is updated.
- From within FaceTime, you can create a Favorites list of people you often engage in video calls with. You can compile this list from entries in your Contacts database but access it from within FaceTime.

■ From within the Messages app, it's possible to access your Contacts database when filling out the To field as you compose new messages to be sent via iMessage. As soon as you tap the To field, an All Contacts window appears, enabling you to select contacts from your Contacts database (or you can manually enter the recipient's info).

■ Using Siri, you can refer to people in your Contacts database by name (or their Related Name label), and Siri enables you to verbally compose emails to them, send them instant messages, determine their location (using the optional Find My Friends app), display their Contacts entry, or look up details about that person. For example, you could say, "Where does John Doe live?", "When is John Doe's birthday?", or "What is John Doe's work phone number?", and Siri accesses that information from your Contacts database for you.

TIP   If you activate Siri and say, "How do I get to John Doe's office from here?", assuming you have an entry for John Doe in your Contacts database, Siri accesses this information and then displays detailed, turn-by-turn directions to John Doe's office from your current location using the Maps app.

■ From any app with a Share icon or button, you can access information from your Contacts database to send other people app-specific content via email, messages, and so on.

GETTING STARTED USING THE CONTACTS APP

When you first launch this app, its contents are empty. However, you can create and build your contacts database in two ways. The first way is to sync the Contacts app with your primary contact management application on your computer; network; or online (cloud-based) service, such as iCloud. You can also manually enter contact information directly into the app.

You can enter new contact information or edit entries on either your tablet or within your primary contact management application and keep all the information synchronized regardless of where the entry was created or modified. The easiest way to do this is with iCloud, if you want to sync data with your primary computer, iPhone, and/or other iOS mobile devices that are linked to your iCloud account.

From the iPad's Home screen, tap the Contacts app to launch it. At the top-left side of the screen is the All Contacts heading, and below it is a Search field. After you have populated your contacts database, the entries are all listed alphabetically on the left side of the screen below the Search field (shown in Figure 5.1).

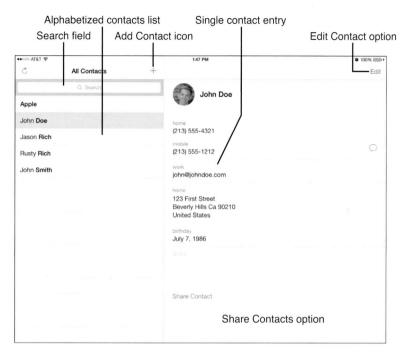

FIGURE 5.1

This is the main Contacts screen. The Contacts database in this example contains just a few entries. Tap the plus sign icon (displayed to the right of the All Contacts heading) to create a new entry.

> **TIP** Quickly find a particular entry by entering any keyword associated with an entry, such as a first or last name, city, state, job title, or company name, into the Contacts app's Search field. You can also use the Spotlight Search feature of your iPad, which is accessible from the Home screen, by swiping your finger downward, starting near the center of the screen.

To see the complete listing for a particular entry, tap its listing on the left side of the screen. That entry's complete contents are then displayed on the right side of the screen.

CREATING NEW CONTACT ENTRIES

To create a new contact entry, tap the Add Entry icon (which looks like a plus sign) that's displayed near the top-center of the Contacts screen (refer to Figure 5.1). When you do this, the right side of the Contacts screen is replaced by the New Contact form.

Within the New Contact form are a handful of empty fields related to a single contact entry, starting with the First Name field. By default, the fields available in this app include First Name, Last Name, Company, Photo, Add Phone, Add Email, Ringtone, Text Tone, Add URL (Website), Add Address, Add Birthday, Add Date, Add Related Name, Add Social Profile, Add Instant Message, Notes, and Add Field (see Figure 5.2).

FIGURE 5.2

From the New Contact form, you can enter details about a new contact and create a new entry within the Contacts app.

Some of these fields, like Add Phone, include a green-and-white plus-sign icon to the left of them. These fields enable you to enter multiple listings, one at a time. Thus, in the Add Phone field, for example, you could include someone's home, work, fax, and mobile phone numbers within the entry. Likewise, you can include multiple email addresses, as well as home and work addresses for an individual.

TIP   When entering data into some fields, such as Add Phone, Add Email, or Add Address, you can customize the field name by tapping on the blue label associated with the field. For example, if you tap on the Phone label, you can choose between Home, Work, iPhone, Mobile, Main, Home Fax, or Work Fax (shown in Figure 5.3). It's important to differentiate phone numbers, addresses, and other types of content by accurately labeling all relevant fields.

For many of the fields that allow you to change the field label, it's possible to create a custom label. For example, when you tap on the Home label that's associated with an Email Address, tap on the Add Custom Label, if you want to create your own label instead of using Home, Work, iCloud, or Other.

FIGURE 5.3
For any field that has a blue label, tap that label (not the empty field) to change the label. A Label window then displays. Tap on your new label selection.

Begin by filling in one field at a time. To jump to the next field, tap it. For example, after filling in the First Name field, tap the Last Name field to fill it in, and then move on to the Company field, if applicable, by tapping it. For each type of field, the iPad's virtual keyboard modifies itself accordingly, giving you access to specialized keys.

NOTE As you're creating each contact entry, fill in any fields you want, leaving the others blank. You can always go back and edit a contact entry to include additional information later.

TIP When you enter a contact's phone numbers, it's important to differentiate between a mobile phone number and an iPhone phone number. If you know someone has an iPhone, use the iPhone label because the FaceTime and Messages apps use what's in this field to identify someone's FaceTime or Messages user ID (which, if they're an iPhone user, is usually their iPhone's phone number).

At the bottom of the New Contact window is the Add Field option. Tap this to reveal a menu containing additional fields you can add to each contact entry, such as Prefix, Phonetic First Name, Middle Name, Phonetic Middle Name, Phonetic Last Name, Suffix, Nickname, Job Title, and Department.

TIP When entering a phone number, simply enter the 10 digits of that number for U.S. phone numbers. There is no need to include parentheses around the area code or a dash between the exchange and main number. This formatting is done for you by the app. The Contacts app can also accommodate international phone numbers, along with related country codes and/or dialing prefixes.

NOTE Use the Add Related Name field to include the names of your contact's mother, father, parent, brother, sister, child, friend, spouse, partner, assistant, manager, or other. You can even add your own labels within this Related Name field.

ADDING A PHOTO TO A CONTACT ENTRY

To the immediate left of the First Name field is a circle that says Add Photo. When you tap this field, a submenu with two options, Take Photo and Choose Photo, is displayed. If you tap Take Photo, the iPad's Camera app launches from within the Contacts app so that you can snap a photo to be linked to the contact entry you're creating.

If you tap on the Choose Photo option, a pop-up window that lists the Albums stored within the Photos app is displayed. Tap on an Album to view thumbnails for all images within it. Choose any digital image that's currently stored on your tablet.

When you tap the photo, a Move and Scale window displays on the Contacts screen, enabling you to reposition and/or zoom the image with your finger, as shown in Figure 5.4.

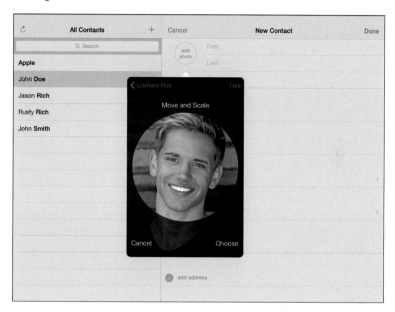

FIGURE 5.4

Select a photo stored on the iPad and link it to someone's contact entry. After choosing the photo, you can move and scale the image to make it fit within the window's virtual frame.

After cropping or adjusting the photo selected, tap the Use option in the upper-right corner of the Move and Scale window to link the photo with that contact's entry.

> **TIP** When you set up Facebook integration with your iPad (from within Settings), you can import the profile photos and Facebook usernames of your online "friends," and use them as the photo in your Contacts database. To do this, first create your Contacts app entries as you normally would. Then, launch Settings, tap on the Facebook option, enter your Facebook account information, and tap on the Update All Contacts button that's displayed near the bottom of the screen. As long as your iPad has Internet access, it compares your online friends to entries in your Contacts database, and downloads each friend's Facebook username for the Facebook field, as well as their photo. Then, in the future, as each online friend changes his profile picture on Facebook, it is automatically updated in your Contacts database.

To automatically add a Twitter field for the people in your Contacts database whom you follow on Twitter, tap on the Twitter option on the left side of the Settings menu. Enter your Twitter account information. Next, tap on the Update Contacts button. The appropriate information is downloaded and incorporated into your Contacts database when your iPad discovers matches between entries in your Contacts database and the people you follow on Twitter.

Periodically, you should re-launch Settings, access the Facebook or Twitter submenus, and tap the Update Contacts button again for each service. Over time, the people in your Contacts database may establish new Facebook or Twitter accounts, or as you add new contact entries, the Facebook or Twitter information will need to be downloaded.

Keep in mind, if you create an entry for someone, and then sync your contacts database with Facebook or Twitter, if that person uses a different name than what's in your Contacts database, a second Contacts entry for that person is created. It's then possible to link the two related entries. For example, within your Contacts database, if you have an entry for Jason Rich, but his Facebook account lists him as Jason R. Rich, two entries are created upon syncing your Contacts Database with your Facebook friends database. Learn how to link contact entries later in this chapter.

If you also use an iPhone or use FaceTime on your iPad, from the Ringtone option in the New Contact form you can select the ringtone you hear each time the contact calls you. Your iPad has more than two dozen preinstalled ringtones (Marimba is the default); however, from the iTunes Store, you can purchase and download thousands of additional ringtones, many of which are clips from popular songs. You can also set up a separate ringtone or sound and associate it with the Messages app for when you receive instant messages from that person.

NOTE Each time you add a new mailing address to a contact's New Contact form, the Address field expands to include Street, City, State, ZIP, and Country fields (as shown in Figure 5.5).

In the Notes field, it's possible to enter as much information pertaining to that contact as you want. Or, you can paste content from another app into this field using the iOS 7's Select, Copy, and Paste commands, along with the multitasking capabilities of your iPad to quickly switch between apps. Press the Home button twice to access the multitasking bar and quickly switch between apps.

FIGURE 5.5

Using the virtual keyboard, you can add multiple addresses, one at a time, for each contact in your Contacts database. This enables you to include a home address and a work address, for example.

After you have filled in all the fields for a particular entry, tap the Done option, which is displayed near the upper-right corner of the New Contact form. Your new entry gets saved and added to your Contacts database. Then, if you have Contacts set up to sync with iCloud, that new entry automatically syncs with your iCloud account as long as your iPad is connected to the Internet.

EDITING OR DELETING AN ENTRY

As you're looking at the main Contacts screen, it's possible to edit an entry by selecting it from the left side of the screen. Tap its listing to view the complete entry on the right side of the screen. Then, tap the Edit option that's displayed in the top-right corner of the screen to edit the selected entry.

When the contact's editable entry form appears, tap any field to modify it using the iPad's virtual keyboard. You can delete a field by tapping the red-and-white minus icon.

You can also add new fields to an entry by tapping any of the green-and-white plus icons and then choosing the type of field you want to add.

> **TIP**   When you're done editing a contact entry, be sure to tap the Done option to save your revisions. If you have the iCloud sync function activated, your revisions are automatically reflected on your computer(s) and other iOS mobile devices that are linked to the same iCloud account, within seconds.

You can also delete an entire entry from your Contacts database. As you're editing a contact entry, scroll down to the bottom of it and tap the red Delete Contact option. If you have your Contacts database set up to use the iCloud sync feature, the entry is also immediately deleted from all of the computers and devices that are linked to your iCloud account. Keep in mind, there is no "undo" option for this feature.

> **TIP**   When you're viewing a contact entry, tapping a listed email address causes the iPad's Mail app to launch, which enables you to compose an email message to that recipient. The To field of the outgoing email is filled in with the email address you tapped in Contacts.
>
> Likewise, in any Contacts entry, tap a website URL that's listed, and the iPad launches the Safari web browser with the appropriate web page automatically loaded.
>
> This technique also works with the Twitter field if you have the Twitter app installed. Or, if you tap a street address, Contacts automatically launches the Maps app, which displays that address. From that point you can tap the Directions icon displayed near the upper-left corner of the screen to obtain directions to that contact's location.

To link contact entries together within your database, when you're in edit mode for an entry, scroll down to the very bottom of the entry form and tap on the Link Contacts… option. From the All Contacts window that appears, select the contact entries you want to link with the entry you're creating or editing.

One reason why you might want to link Contacts entries together is if two related entries are created for the same contact when you sync your Contacts database with Facebook or Twitter, for example.

SHARING CONTACT ENTRIES

From the main Contacts screen, tap a contact listing on the left side of the screen that you want to share details about. When the contact's entry is displayed on the right side of the screen, scroll to the bottom of the entry until you see the Share Contact option displayed (refer to Figure 5.1) and tap it.

Next, choose to email or message the contact entry you've selected to another person. If you choose Mail, an outgoing email message form displays on your iPad's screen. Fill in the To field with the person or people with whom you want to share the contact info. The default subject of the email is Contact; however, you can tap this field and modify it using the virtual keyboard. If you select Message, enter the recipient in the To field of the message composition window that is displayed. When you choose either of these options, you can add multiple recipients to the To field.

The contact entry you selected (stored in .vcf format, which is an industry standard format used by many contact management applications) is already embedded in the message. When you've filled in all the necessary fields in the outgoing email form and added additional text to the body of the message (or have filled in the To field in the Messages window), tap the Send option to send the selected contact entry to the intended recipient(s). After doing this, you are returned to the Contacts app.

When the recipient clicks on the email's attachment (the contact entry you sent), he can automatically import that data into his contact management application as a new entry.

If someone sends you an email with a contact's entry attached, it is displayed in the body of the email as an attachment. After tapping the email's attachment icon, tap the Create New Contact or Add to Existing Contact option to incorporate this information into your own Contacts database.

> **TIP** If someone hands you a printed business card, consider using the optional Business Card Reader HD business card scanner app ($6.99) to snap a digital photo of the card using your tablet's camera, and then have the app automatically convert the contents of the card into a new entry for your Contacts database.

SYNCING CONTACT DATA WITH OTHER CONTACT MANAGEMENT SOFTWARE

If you maintain your primary contacts database using the Contacts app on your Mac, you can sync the Contacts app on your iPad via the iTunes Sync process, or you can sync the contacts wirelessly using iCloud (which is a more convenient and fully automated method).

You can also synchronize your contacts database on your iPad with Microsoft Outlook (or Outlook.com), Microsoft Entourage (on a Mac), any Microsoft Exchange–compatible contact management software that is running on your company's network, or a variety of other online (cloud)-based contact management tools. To synchronize contacts data wirelessly, you must first do some initial setup (just once) using Settings on your tablet.

SYNCING CONTACTS DATA FROM YOUR iPAD WITH iCLOUD

After setting up a free iCloud account, launch Settings on your iPad. On the left side of the screen, tap the iCloud option to access the iCloud submenu. Enter your Apple ID and password to turn on the main iCloud functionality. Next, scroll down within the iCloud submenu and make sure the virtual switch associated with the Contacts option (shown in Figure 5.6) is turned on.

Contacts option

FIGURE 5.6
For the iCloud sync feature to work with Contacts, it must be turned on from within the Settings app.

TIP   To customize certain features and functions of the Contacts app, launch Settings and select the Mail, Contacts, Calendars option. Scroll down on this submenu to the Contacts heading, where you can change the Sort Order, Display Order, Short Name, and My Info options.

Turning on the iCloud Sync option for Contacts enables your iPad to automatically sync your Contacts data with your iCloud account (as long as your tablet is connected to the Web). Also make sure you turn on iCloud functionality—as well as the Contacts sync feature—for your primary computer, iPhone, and other iOS devices that are linked to the same iCloud account.

SYNCING WITH MICROSOFT EXCHANGE–COMPATIBLE APPLICATIONS

To set up your Contacts database to sync with a Microsoft Exchange account, from the iPad's Home screen, launch Settings and then choose the Mail, Contacts, Calendars option. Tap the Add Account option displayed under the Accounts heading on the right side of the screen.

Choose to set up a Microsoft Exchange account. When prompted, enter your email address, domain, username, password, and an account description. This is information that should be supplied by your network administrator or IT department. Next, turn on the Contacts option and save your new settings.

Contacts is compatible with any contact management software that uses the industry-standard CardDAV and LDAP formats. Thus, if you have a Microsoft Exchange account and activate the contacts sync feature, you can wirelessly keep your primary contacts database perfectly synchronized with your Contacts database as long as your iPad has access to the Web.

SYNCING WITH CARDDAV- OR LDAP-COMPATIBLE APPLICATIONS

To set up the wireless sync process between a CardDAV-compatible application and Contacts, launch Settings on your iPad and select the Mail, Contacts, Calendars option. Under the Add Account heading, tap the Other option. Next, choose either the Add LDAP account or Add CardDAV account option, depending on the application you are syncing with.

You are prompted for a server address, username, password, and account description. Obtain this information from your network administrator or company's IT department.

HOW DOES SYNCING YOUR CONTACTS INFO HELP YOU?

After the iPad is set up to sync your Contacts app with another contact management application, whenever you make a change, deletion, or addition to your contacts database (either from your iPad, your primary computer, or your smartphone that's also synced with the database), those modifications are automatically reflected on all the devices from which you access your contacts database.

If you have questions about how to configure your iPad to sync correctly with your primary contact management application, make an appointment with an Apple Genius at any Apple Store, or call AppleCare's toll-free phone number at (800) APL-CARE and have a technical support specialist talk you through the setup and initial data sync process.

NOTE In addition to or instead of using the Contacts app to manage your contacts, the App Store has a selection of optional third-party apps that offer slightly different, or sometimes enhanced, functionality when compared to Contacts. When visiting the App Store, enter the search phrase "Contact Management," "CRM" (Contact/Customer Relationship Manager), or "Contacts" into the Search field. There you can also find utility apps, such as Remove Duplicate Contacts ($0.99), which can help you streamline your contacts database and avoid duplicates.

TIP Instead of just maintaining a contacts database using the Contacts app on your iPad, consider using the optional VIPorbit for iPad app ($4.99, www.viporbit.com) to transform your tablet into a feature-packed customer relationship manager. This enables you to maintain a contacts database and combine it with scheduling and note-taking elements, thus allowing you to track and manage many aspects of professional relationships while on-the-go, using a single app.

A CRM app, like VIPorbit, is ideal for mobile executives, salespeople, telemarketers, or anyone who maintains ongoing relationships with customers or clients and needs to keep detailed and constantly updated records about their interactions. You'll find the VIPorbit app in the App Store. A Mac version of VIPorbit ($29.99) was recently launched as well and is available from the Mac App Store. Both versions can easily and seamlessly sync data with each other via the Internet.

IN THIS CHAPTER

- Create and manage to-do lists
- Compose, view, print, and share text-based notes using the Notes app
- Syncing app-specific data with iCloud and other mobile devices

6

MANAGING INFORMATION USING THE REMINDERS AND NOTES APPS

On the surface, Reminders is a straightforward to-do list manager. However, after you start using this easy-to-use app, you may find it offers a plethora of useful features.

Reminders works seamlessly with Notification Center and iCloud and easily syncs with the Reminders app on your Mac (that's running OS X Mountain Lion or OS X Mavericks) or iPhone, as well as with Outlook on your primary computer (a Mac or PC). Plus, you can create as many separate to-do lists as you need to properly manage your personal and professional life or various projects you're responsible for.

> **TIP** Using iCloud, Reminders can automatically sync with your primary computer, iPhone, or other iOS devices. Be sure to turn on the iCloud functionality for Reminders from within the iCloud submenu of the Settings app to initiate real-time, automatic syncing.

Once this is done, from any computer or mobile device that's connected to the Internet, it's possible to access the online version of Reminders by pointing the web browser to www.iCloud.com. Log in with your Apple ID and password (or iCloud username and password), and then click on the Reminders app icon. The online version of the app is populated with the most recent version(s) of your to-do list(s) and app-related settings.

To make it easier for you to juggle tasks and keep track of deadlines and ongoing responsibilities, you can give every item on your to-do list a unique alarm, which can be associated with specific times, dates, or both.

When you launch Reminders for the first time, on the left side of the screen you see the control center for this app. On the right side of the screen (shown in Figure 6.1) is a simulated sheet of blank paper.

To begin creating a single to-do list, tap the top empty line on the right side of the Reminders screen. Using the virtual keyboard, enter the first item to be added to your list, and then tap the Return key on the keyboard.

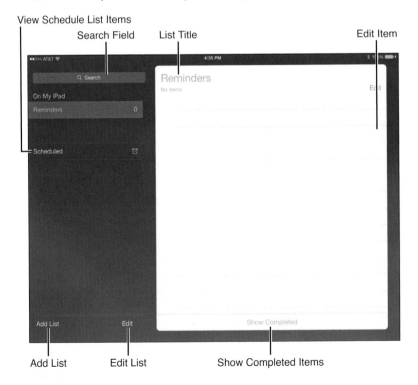

FIGURE 6.1

This is what the Reminders screen looks like when you launch the app for the first time.

When you tap the Return key, an empty circle displays in the margin, to the left of the item you just entered (as shown in Figure 6.2). You can later mark the completion of this task by tapping on this circle to fill it in. Then, at the bottom of the list, tap on the Show Completed option to display only items you've completed.

Tap on the circle when an item is completed.   Item Info icon

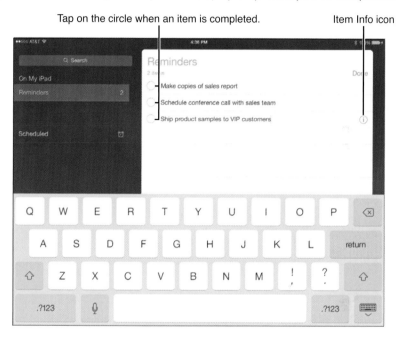

FIGURE 6.2
As soon as you create an item within a to-do list, an empty circle displays to the left of it.

> **TIP** It's possible to use Siri to enter new to-do list items with verbal commands. To do this, activate Siri and begin your command by saying, "Remind me to…" or "Add [item] to my [list name]."
>
> As you're speaking, you can include a date and time for your reminder, which allows Siri to associate an alarm with that to-do list item. For example, you could say, "Remind me to pick up my dry cleaning tomorrow at 2 p.m."

As you're entering the to-do list item (or anytime after), tap on it to edit the entry. An Info icon (a circular icon with an "i" within it) appears to the right of the listing. Tap on this Info icon to access the Details window, and then customize the individual to-do item on the list. For example, you can change the item's title or set an alarm by tapping on the Remind Me On A Day option. You can also set a Priority for the item, change the list it's associated with, or add unlimited text-based notes to the item—all from the Details window (shown in Figure 6.3).

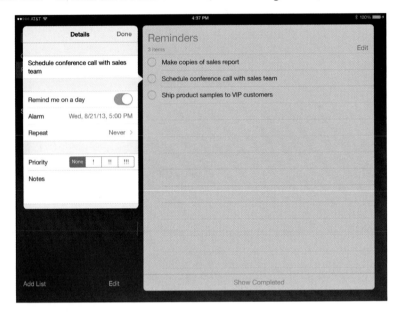

FIGURE 6.3

From the Details window, it's possible to customize each list item, add an alert, or set a priority for it.

When you set a Priority, this does not impact the order in which items on your list are later displayed. It simply displays a Priority icon (up to three exclamation points) to the immediate left of an item listing. As you set a priority, your options include None, Low Priority (!), Medium Priority (!!), or High Priority (!!!).

After a to-do item on a list has been created, to delete it from the list altogether, swipe your finger from right to left across the listing. The Delete and More buttons appear. Tap the red-and-white Delete button to erase the item from the list. Tap on the More button to quickly access the Details menu that's associated with the item.

> **NOTE** Alarms can be associated with each item in each of your to-do lists. You also have the option of creating a to-do list item without associating any type of alert or alarm with it.
>
> When any alarm goes off that's related to a to-do list item, a notification automatically displays as part of your iPad's Notification Center, assuming you have this feature turned on.

To ensure Reminders works with the Notification Center, launch Settings and tap the Notification Center option. When the Notification Center submenu appears on the right side of the screen, tap the Reminders option. From the Reminders submenu, make sure the Show In Notification Center option is turned on. You can then modify the Include option and/or set up banners or alerts related to the Reminders app that appear when an alarm is generated by the app.

TIP To alter the order that items within a specific list are displayed, as you're viewing the list, tap on the Edit option that's displayed near the top-right corner of the screen. Then, place your finger on the Move icon (which looks like three horizontal lines) that's associated with the item listing you want to move up or down the list and drag it upward or downward. To delete the item, tap on the negative sign icon. When you're done rearranging the list, tap on the Done option, which is displayed near the top-right corner of the screen.

MANAGING MULTIPLE TO-DO LISTS SIMULTANEOUSLY

To create a new list from scratch, tap on the Add List option that's displayed near the bottom-left corner of the Reminders app screen. If you have Reminders set up to sync with iCloud and with another online service, such as Yahoo! or Outlook.com, a Select Account pop-up menu appears with your available options. Choose where you want to save the new list.

When the New List heading appears near the top-center of the screen, type in the New List's title and select a color for it. Tap the Done option to save this information and then begin populating the list with individual items, one at a time.

As you're working with a specific to-do list, tap on the Edit option that's displayed at the top-right corner of the screen in order to edit the list's title and change the color associated with the list. Tap on the title to edit it, or tap on the Color option to change the list's default color. Tap the Done option (displayed at the top-right corner of the screen) to save your changes.

Also while in Edit mode for a list, it's possible to delete the list altogether by tapping the Delete List button at the bottom of the list.

You can also delete a list by tapping the Edit button at the bottom right of the left column of the Reminders screen and then tapping the red minus-sign icon to the left of the list name you wish you delete. To change the order of your lists, place your finger on the icon that looks like three horizontal lines and drag it upward or downward. To exit Edit mode, tap the Done button.

> **CAUTION** If you delete an entire list or an item from a list, that change immediately syncs with iCloud. There is no "undo" feature when you delete or edit a list or item.

In addition to managing general lists using the Reminders app, from the left side of the screen, you can create a date-specific "smart list" based on the time/date alerts you've set up for specific items. When you tap on the Scheduled option, a comprehensive listing of all items with an alarm scheduled for the current day, as well as future dates, will be displayed in chronological order. This information can also be displayed when you tap on the Today tab within Notification Center.

> **TIP** To quickly find items within any of your to-do lists, tap the Search field that's displayed near the upper-left portion of the screen and then use the virtual keyboard to enter any text that is associated with what you're looking for. From the Home screen, you also have the option to use the Spotlight Search feature in order to find Reminder-related information.

The Reminders app can be used to manage many different types of information in your personal and professional life.

> **NOTE** If you use the Reminders app on your iPhone, each list item can be associated with a date/time-based alarm or a location-based alarm. However, the iPad edition of the app does not currently support location-based alarms.

SETTING UP REMINDERS TO WORK WITH iCLOUD AND OTHER ONLINE SERVICES

To set up the Reminders app to work with iCloud, launch Settings and tap on the iCloud option to access the iCloud submenu. Then, turn on the virtual switch that's associated with the Reminders app. This only needs to be done once on your iPad, but it also needs to be done on each Mac and iPhone you use the Reminders app with.

Once you set up Reminders to sync with iCloud, you can access the iCloud.com website (www.iCloud.com) and utilize the online-based edition of Reminders (shown in Figure 6.4). This app is compatible with the iPad edition of Reminders and is automatically populated with your app-specific data.

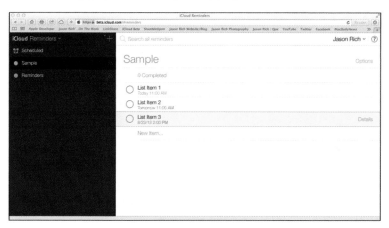

FIGURE 6.4

This is the online version of the Reminders app, accessible from www.iCloud.com. It is fully compatible with the iPad edition of the app.

Keep in mind, if you're using the online app from someone else's computer (or from a public computer within the business center of a hotel or an Internet café, for example), be sure to log off of your iCloud account when you're done using the online version of the Reminders app. To do this, click on your username that's displayed near the top-right corner of the browser window and then click on the Sign Out menu option. This also applies when using the iCloud.com version of Contacts, Calendar, Notes, Pages, Numbers, or Keynote.

To set up the Reminders app to work with Outlook; Outlook.com; Yahoo!; or another online-based service, such as one that's compatible with Microsoft Exchange, launch Settings and tap on the Mail, Contacts, Calendars option. Next, tap on the Add Account option (found under the Accounts heading).

Choose the type of preexisting account you want to add. If the type of account isn't listed within the Add Account menu, tap the Other option. When prompted, enter your account-specific username, password, and/or other information that's requested. Once the account has been verified, be sure to turn on the virtual switch that's associated with the Reminders option (which is shown within Figure 6.5, related to a Yahoo! account).

FIGURE 6.5
After setting up an online account within Settings, be sure to turn on the Reminders app sync feature for that online account. Shown here is the Settings submenu for customizing a Yahoo! account.

USING YOUR TABLET AS A NOTE-TAKING DEVICE WITH THE NOTES APP

While the Reminders app allows you to create, edit, view, and maintain detailed to-do lists that can be synced between your iOS mobile devices and Mac(s), the Notes app serves as a basic text editor that allows you to create, edit, view, and manage notes.

> NOTE The Notes app offers very basic formatting functionality, but if you need the features and functions of a full-featured word processor, you should use the optional Pages app or another word processing app on your iPad. Notes is designed more for basic note-taking, not word processing. There are also far more powerful note-taking apps available from the App Store that also allow you to write or even draw using a stylus, instead of typing.
>
> Some third-party note-taking apps worth looking into include Evernote, Notepad+, Notes Plus, Microsoft OneNote, and Penultimate. Learn more about some of these apps in Chapter 15, "Discovering 'Must-Have' Business Apps."

Just like Reminders, the Notes app comes preinstalled with iOS 7. In addition, a similar Notes app comes preinstalled on the iPhone, as well as Macs running OS X Mountain Lion or OS X Mavericks. Plus, an online edition of the Notes app is available on iCloud.com. So, if you set up this app to work with iCloud, all of your notes remain synced on all of your computers and/or iOS mobile devices that are linked to the same iCloud account.

On the iPad, the Notes app screen is divided into two sections (shown in Figure 6.6). On the left is a comprehensive listing of individual notes stored within the app, and on the right, a selected note can be viewed and edited.

FIGURE 6.6
The iPad displays all aspects of the Notes app on a single screen.

To create a new note, tap on the Compose icon that's displayed near the top-right corner of the screen. On the virtual note page, begin typing your note using the virtual keyboard, activate the Dictation function, or utilize an external keyboard.

> **NOTE** By default, the first line of text you enter into a new note becomes that note's title, which is displayed in the Notes listing on the left side of the screen.

When you're done typing, dictating, or editing a note, tap on the Compose button to add another note, tap on a note in the listing to switch to that note, or exit the Notes app. Your note is automatically saved.

The left side of the main Notes screen allows you to see the title for each note that's stored within the app. From this listing, to delete a note, swipe your finger from right to left across the note's title. Confirm your decision by tapping on the Delete button. To open and view a note, tap on its listing.

Tap on the trash can icon to delete the note you're currently viewing.

Tap on the Share icon to send the note to one or more recipients via email or the Message app. You can also print or copy a note by tapping on the appropriate option displayed within the Share menu. When you use the copy command the note's content gets saved within your iPad's virtual clipboard (so you can then paste the contents of the note into another app).

> **TIP** The Notes app works with the Select, Select All, Copy, Cut, and Paste features of iOS 7. Thus, you can select and copy text from one note and then paste it into another note or into another app altogether.

As you're creating or viewing a note, press and hold your finger on any word to make the Copy, Select All, and/or Paste menu options appear. Once you select a word, you'll also see a Define and Replace option displayed (shown in Figure 6.7).

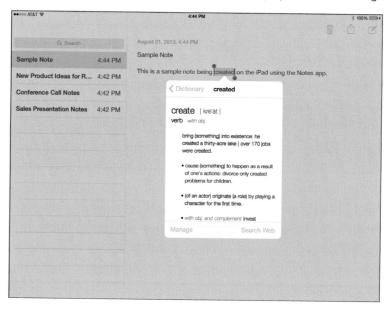

FIGURE 6.7

As you're typing text into the Notes app, hold your finger on a word and tap on the Define option to view a definition (and the correct spelling) of that word.

It's also possible to tap on Define to look up the definition of the selected work. A pop-up window displaying the definition is displayed. When you use this feature for the first time, you're prompted to download the Dictionary tool. This process takes just 5–10 seconds and only needs to be done once.

> **TIP** Syncing notes with iCloud works exactly the same as syncing Contacts, Calendar,s or Reminders app-specific data; however, once iCloud is set up on your iOS device, you still need to turn on the iCloud syncing function that's specific to the Notes app from the iCloud Control Panel within Settings.

Once you set up the Notes app to sync app-specific data with iCloud, access the iCloud.com website (www.icloud.com) at anytime using any computer or Internet-enabled device; log in to your account using your Apple ID and password (or iCloud username and password); and then click on the Notes app icon to use the online-based Notes app, which is populated with all of your Notes data from your iPhone, iPad, and/or Mac(s).

The Notes app's functionality is relatively basic and straightforward. However, this app comes in particularly handy for jotting down ideas or memos without having to worry about formatting text (as you would when using a word-processing app). To help keep you organized, the time and date you create each note is automatically saved in conjunction with the note itself.

> **TIP** To quickly find content within a specific note, tap on the Search field that's displayed near the top-left corner of the Notes app screen. Enter a keyword, date, or search phrase to quickly find similar content stored within the Notes app. To search your entire iPad for that content, however, you need to use the Spotlight Search feature from the Home screen.

ORGANIZING YOUR NOTES

The Notes app allows you to set up separate folders, within which you can store multiple notes. To do this, tap on the Folders button that's displayed at the top-left corner of the screen to create or manage folders, which are then listed on the left side of the screen.

CERTAIN CONTENT WITHIN NOTES IS INTERACTIVE

Anytime you include an address, for example, within a note, tap on its link to launch the Maps app and view that address on a detailed map. Or when a website URL is included within a note, tap on it to launch Safari and visit that website.

Likewise, if you enter a day of the week, time, or date within a note, that information automatically becomes an active link. Then, when you tap on that link, you have the option to quickly create a new event within the Calendar app related to that link, without first having to launch the Calendar app. So, within a note, if the text says, "On Monday, July 7th, 2014…," once you save that note, the Monday, July 7th, 2014, text is highlighted and underlined. Tap on it and a pop-up menu with the following options are displayed: Create Event, Show In Calendar, and Copy. Tap on Create Event to create a new event within the Calendar app. Tap Show In Calendar to simply view the Day View within the Calendar app for that date, or tap Copy to copy the date information into your iPad's virtual clipboard and paste it elsewhere.

Meanwhile, if there are sentences or phrases that you use often within your notes, set up keyboard shortcuts for them to reduce the amount of typing that's necessary. To do this, launch Settings, tap on General, select the Keyboard option, and then tap on Shortcuts.

For example, if you constantly incorporate the phrase, "For more information, please visit my website at www.JasonRich.com." into notes, documents, emails, or instant messages, it's possible to create a keyboard shortcut for that phrase, using the shortcut "FMI" (For More Information). Then, when you type FMI into almost any app, including Notes, the full phrase that "FMI" is associated with is incorporated into the app. This can be used as a time-saving tool, plus help reduce typos.

IN THIS CHAPTER

- Discover what's new with the iOS 7 edition of the Safari web browser
- Take advantage of iCloud Keychains, Reading List, and iCloud Bookmarks
- Manage online social networking accounts

7

SURFING THE WEB USING SAFARI

The Safari web browser on your iPad (shown in Figure 7.1) offers the same basic functionality as the web browser for your desktop or notebook computer, but it's designed to maximize the iPad's touchscreen and screen size, as well as offer iCloud integration. As you're about to discover, the iOS 7 edition of Safari has a new look plus a handful of useful new features that make surfing the Web using your tablet more efficient.

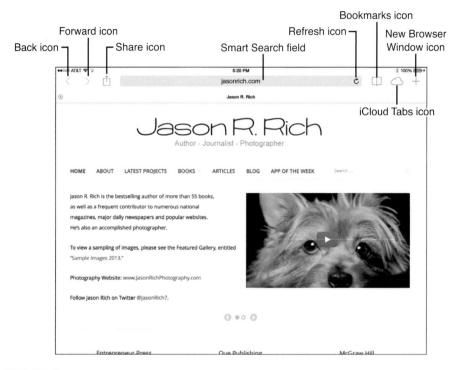

FIGURE 7.1

The main screen of the Safari web browser on the iPad.

TIP   Your iPad enables you to visit virtually any website and navigate around the World Wide Web with ease using now-familiar finger motions on the tablet's touch screen.

As you visit web pages using Safari, you can utilize hyperlinks or activate command icons with a tap, scroll up or down on a web page with a finger swipe, perform a reverse pinch or double-tap to zoom in on specific areas of a web page, or flick your finger to scroll left or right.

NOTE   In addition to having a new look, Safari on the iPad now features a single Smart Search field and tabbed browser windows. The Reading List feature is easier to use, and it allows you to read everything on your Reading List at once or read each article separately. One of the most useful new Safari features is iCloud Keychain, which is also covered in this chapter.

YOU'RE READY TO BEGIN SURFING

To access the Web using your iPad, make sure it's connected to the Internet, and then tap the Safari app icon that's displayed on the Home Screen. The main Safari web browser screen appears.

USING SAFARI'S NEW TOOLBAR ICONS

Displayed along the top of the Safari app screen is the Toolbar (refer to Figure 7.1), which includes a handful of command icons you can use to navigate around the Web. Although the icons look different than what you're used to when surfing the Web using the browser installed on your primary computer, their features and functions are similar.

> **TIP** As you surf the Web using Safari, you can hold your tablet in portrait or landscape mode. Landscape mode makes the portion of the websites you're viewing appear larger on the screen, but portrait mode enables you to see more of the web page vertically.

The Back and Forward Icons

Displayed near the upper-left corner of the Safari screen are the Back and Forward arrow-shaped icons used for jumping to a previous web page you've visited, while staying within the same browser window.

The Share Icon

Tap on this icon to access the expanded Share Menu, which offers a handful of features.

The Smart Search Field

Instead of having a separate Address Bar and Search Field, the iOS 7 version of Safari has a single Smart Search Field. Within it, you can either type what you're looking for and perform a search using the browser's default search engine (Google, Yahoo!, or Bing), or you can enter a website URL to access a specific website.

The Bookmarks Icon

The Bookmarks icon that resembles an open book enables you to access your Reading List, History, Bookmarks Folder(s), and Favorites Bar content. Later in this chapter, you learn how to sync your bookmarks between Safari on your iPad with the bookmarks stored on your primary computer's web browser software using iCloud.

> **TIP** To edit the Bookmarks menu, first tap on the Bookmarks icon and then tap on the Edit option that's displayed near the lower-right corner of the menu. Once in Edit mode, it's possible to move items up or down within the menu listing, delete saved bookmarks, and/or create new folders (by tapping on the New Folder option) within which you can group bookmarks.

To switch between Bookmarks and Reading List content, tap on either the Bookmarks or Reading List tab that's dislayed near the top-center of the Bookmarks window. Then, tap on the listing you want to open within your browser.

The Shared Links ("@") tab allows you to view and access website links shared by your online friends who are active on select online social networks, including Twitter.

The iCloud Tabs Icon

The cloud-shaped icon is used to access iCloud Tabs, as explained later in this chapter.

Tabbed Browser Icon

Use this feature, which is explained later in the chapter, to quickly switch between open browser windows.

CUSTOMIZING SAFARI'S SETTINGS

To customize your web surfing experience, launch Settings and then tap on the Safari option. When the Safari submenu appears (as shown in Figure 7.2), you have a handful of customizable options, as follows:

- **Search Engine**—The new Smart Search field is used to enter specific website URLs (addresses), as well as to find what you're looking for on the Web via a search engine, such as Google, Yahoo!, or Bing. This option enables you to select your default (favorite) Internet search engine. So if you select Google as your default, whenever you perform a search using Safari's Search field, the browser automatically accesses Google to obtain your search results.

FIGURE 7.2

Customize your web surfing experience when using Safari from within Settings on your iOS device.

> **TIP** Regardless of which Internet search engine (Google, Yahoo!, or Bing) you select to be your default from within Settings, you can always add the other two (or any other search engine) to your Bookmarks folder or Favorites Bar, so that you can access the other search engines directly by pointing Safari to www.Google.com, www.Yahoo.com, www.Bing.com, and so on.

■ **Passwords & AutoFill**—One of the more tedious aspects of surfing the Web is constantly having to fill in certain types of data fields, such as your name, address, phone number, email address, and website-related passwords.

This feature, when turned on, remembers your responses and automatically inserts the data into the appropriate fields. It also pulls information from your own contacts entry in the Contacts app. To customize this option and link your personal contact entry to Safari, tap on the AutoFill option, turn on the Use Contact Info option, and then tap on My Info to select your own contact entry in Contacts. You can also set whether Safari remembers Names and

Passwords for specific websites you visit, as well as your credit card information that you use to make online purchases.

- **Favorites**—This feature serves as a shortcut for accessing websites you frequently visit. As you begin typing a website address or website name into the Search field, Safari accesses your Bookmarks folder(s), Favorites Bar content, and History, and then automatically suggests related website URLs.

- **Open New Tabs in Background**—When turned on, this feature enables you to open up new web pages in separate tabs when you tap on an active link within a website. If turned on, you remain on the web page you're currently viewing, but a new tabbed browser window opens that displays the content from the link you've tapped on. Then, when you're ready, tap on the other tab(s) to view the additional websites.

- **Block Pop-Ups**—When turned on, this feature prevents a website you're visiting from creating and displaying extra windows or opening a bunch of unwanted browser pages. The default for this option is turned on. You will probably enjoy your web surfing experience more if you leave it that way.

- **Do Not Track**—By default, when you surf the Web using Safari, the web browser remembers all of the websites you visit and creates a detailed History list that you can access in order to quickly revisit websites. By turning on the Do Not Track feature, Safari does not store details about the websites you visit or maintain a History folder.

- **Block Cookies**—Many websites use cookies to remember who you are and your personalized preferences when you're visiting that site. This is actually data that gets saved on your iPad, but that's accessible by the websites you revisit. When this option is turned on and set to Never, Safari does not accept cookies from websites you visit. Thus, you need to reenter site-specific preferences and information each time you visit that site. Your other two options are Always (meaning that Safari accepts all cookies) and From Third Parties and Advertisers (which is the option selected by most iPad users).

- **Smart Search Field**—Tap on this Settings option to reveal a submenu that allows you to turn on or off the Search Engine Suggestions feature altogether. The second option is Preload Top Hit. This determines what suggestions Safari makes as you use the Search field to find information on the Web.

- **Fraudulent Website Warning**—This feature helps prevent you from visiting impostor websites designed to look like real ones, which have been created for the purpose of committing fraud or identity theft. It's not foolproof, but keeping this feature turned on gives you an added level of protection, especially if you use your iOS device for online banking and other financial transactions.

- **Clear History**—Using this feature, you can delete the contents of Safari's History folder that stores details about all the websites you have visited.

> **TIP** Safari automatically keeps a detailed listing of every website you visit. When you tap the Clear History button, this listing is reset and deleted.

- **Clear Cookies and Data**—Use this command to delete all cookies related to websites you've visited that Safari has stored on your iOS device.
- **Use Cellular Data**—This option allows your tablet to use the cellular data service (instead of only a Wi-Fi Internet connection) to download Reading List information to your device (from your iCloud account) so that it can be read offline. While this feature is convenient, it also utilizes some of your monthly cellular data allocation, which is why there's an on/off option associated with it. This feature applies onlly to iPad Wi-F1+ Cellular models.
- **Advanced**—From this submenu, you can view details about website-specific data that Safari has collected (and if you choose, manually delete this information). You can also turn on or off the JavaScript feature.

> **TIP** As you make changes within Settings relating to Safari, they are automatically saved and those changes take effect the next time you launch the Safari app.

WHERE'S THE FLASH?

The one main drawback to surfing the Web using Safari on your iPad is the web browser's inability to display Adobe Flash–based graphics and animations. This limitation is not due to lack of technological capability of your tablet, however. It's the result of ongoing disagreements between Apple and Adobe with regard to offering Flash compatibility through the iOS operating system.

Unfortunately, websites that rely heavily on Flash are not accessible using Safari. If you want limited Flash compatibility on your iPad, try using a third-party web browser app, such as Photon Flash Web Browser for iPad ($4.99). It's available from the App Store and offers compatibility with many (but not all) Flash-based content on the Web.

HOW TO USE TABBED BROWSING WITH SAFARI

Safari's new Toolbar contains the various command icons used to navigate the Web. These icons are located along the top of the screen. Immediately below the Toolbar, if you have the option turned on, your personalized Favorites Bar is displayed. Below the Favorites Bar, the Tabs bar becomes visible if you have more than one web page open at any given time.

When you tap on a link in a web page that causes a new web page to automatically open, a new tab in Safari is created and displayed (shown in Figure 7.3).

Favorites Bar   Tabbed Browser bar with open tabs   Toolbar

FIGURE 7.3

Instead of separate windows, Safari on the iPad uses onscreen tabs that enable you to instantly switch between open web pages.

> **TIP** On the iPad, in addition to showing open browser windows as tabs, you can display the Favorites Bar, which can be fully customized. From the Safari menu within Settings, determine whether or not the Favorites Bar is displayed.

As you're viewing a web page, you can simultaneously open another web page by tapping on the New Browser Window icon (which looks like a plus sign). It's displayed near the top-right corner of the Safari screen. When you do this, a new tab is created and you can visit a new web page without closing the previous page.

Along the Tab bar, you can have multiple web pages accessible at once. Simply by tapping on a tab, you can instantly switch between web pages.

To close a tab, tap on the small "x" that appears on the left side of that tab.

TAKING ADVANTAGE OF THE NEW iCLOUD TABS FEATURE

You already know that iCloud can be set up to sync app-specific data between your iPhone, iPad, Mac(s), and PC(s) that are linked to the same iCloud (Apple ID) account. In addition to syncing your Bookmarks, Favorites Bar, and Reading List information, the iOS 7 version of Safari also syncs, in real-time, your open Safari browser windows.

Thus, if you're surfing the Web on your Mac and have one or more browser windows open, you can pick up your iPad, tap on the iCloud Tabs option (the icon on the Toolbar that looks like a cloud), and then open that same browser window(s) on your tablet (or vice versa), without having to reenter the web page's URL.

When you tap on the iCloud Tabs option, a separate window opens that lists open browser windows on each of your computers and/or devices. Tap on a listing to open that browser window on the iPad.

> **CAUTION** With this feature turned on, as you're surfing the Web on your iPad, someone can literally follow along and see what web pages you're visiting in real time online by tapping on the iCloud Tabs option while using Safari on your primary computer if they are logged in to your user account on that computer.

REMOVING SCREEN CLUTTER WITH SAFARI READER

The Safari Reader feature enables you to select a compatible website page; strip out graphic icons, ads, and other unwanted elements that cause onscreen clutter; and then read just the text (and view related photos) from that web page on your iOS device's screen.

The Safari Reader icon works only with compatible websites, including those published by major daily newspapers and other news organizations. If the feature is available while you're viewing a web page, a newly designed Reader icon (as shown in Figure 7.4) is displayed to the left of that web page's URL in Safari's Smart Search field.

170   YOUR iPAD AT WORK

WHAT'S NEW The Reader button within the iOS 7 version of Safari now looks like a series of horizontal lines that appears on the edge of the Smart Search field. It no longer actually says "Reader."

Reader icon

FIGURE 7.4

When you see a Reader icon appear in the Smart Search field within Safari, you can open that content in the Reader window and view it clutter free.

When you see the Reader icon displayed, tap on it. An uncluttered window that contains just the article or text from that web page, along with related photos, is displayed. Use your finger to scroll up or down.

To exit the Reader window and return to the main web page, tap anywhere in the margins of the screen, outside the Reader window.

CREATING AND MANAGING READING LISTS

As you're surfing the Web, you may come across specific web pages, articles, or other information that you want to refer to later. From within Safari, you can create a bookmark for that website URL and have it displayed in your Bookmarks folder or on your Favorites Bar, or you can add it to your Reading List, which is another way to store web page links and content that's of interest to you.

NOTE The iOS 7 version of Safari allows the Reading List feature to download entire web pages for offline viewing, as opposed to simply storing website addresses that you are able to refer to later. While this feature downloads text and photos associated with a web page, it does not download animated graphics, video, or audio content associated with that page.

To add a website to your personalized Reading List for later review, tap on the Share icon that's displayed on the left side of the Toolbar and then tap on the Add to Reading List button.

Figure 7.5 shows an example of a Reading List, which you can access by first tapping on the Bookmarks icon and then tapping on the Reading List tab (which looks like eyeglasses).

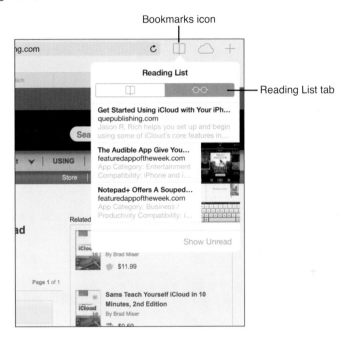

FIGURE 7.5

Creating a Reading List is another way to store links related to specific content on the Web that you want to easily be able to find again and access later.

When you want to refer to items stored in your Reading List, tap on the Bookmarks icon and then tap on the Reading List tab. A listing of your saved web pages or articles previously saved to your Reading List is displayed.

> **TIP**   Like your Bookmarks folder and Favorites Bar, the items stored in your Reading List can automatically be synced with iCloud.

NEW OPTIONS FOR SHARING WEB CONTENT IN SAFARI

There are often times when you're surfing the Web and come across something funny, informative, educational, or just plain bizarre that you want to share with other people, add to your Bookmarks folder, or print. The iOS 7 version of Safari makes sharing web links extremely easy, plus it now gives you a handful of new options.

Anytime you're visiting a web page that you want to share with others, tap on the Share icon to reveal a newly expanded Share menu (as shown in Figure 7.6). The Share icon can be found to the immediate left of the Smart Search field.

Share Icon   Share Menu

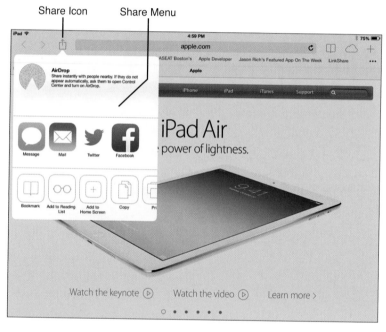

FIGURE 7.6
Safari's Share menu offers a handful of ways to store and share web page content.

Depending on which features you have set up and activated on your tablet, the following options can be available from the Share menu:

- **Message**—Send details about the web page you're currently viewing to one or more other people via instant message using the Message app (without having to leave Safari). Tap on Message, fill in the To field, and then tap the Send button. The website title and URL are automatically embedded within the instant message.

▪ **Mail**—To share a website URL with others via email, as you're looking at the web page or website you want to share, tap on the Share icon and select the Mail option from the Share menu. In Safari, an outgoing email window will appear.

Simply fill in the To field with the recipient's email address and tap the Send icon. The website URL automatically is embedded within the body of the email, with the website's heading used as the email's subject. Before sending the email, you can add text to the body of the email message and/or change the Subject.

▪ **Twitter**—If you have an active Twitter account that's set up for use with iOS 7, tap on the Twitter option from the Share menu to create an outgoing tweet that automatically has the website URL attached.

When the Tweet window appears, enter your tweet message (up to 140 characters, minus the length of the website URL). Tap the Send icon when the tweet message is composed and ready to share with your Twitter followers.

> TIP If you're managing multiple Twitter accounts from your iOS device, within the outgoing tweet window, tap on the From field and then select from which of your Twitter accounts you want to send the tweet you're composing.

▪ **Facebook**—Thanks to Facebook integration within iOS 7, when you tap on the Facebook option, you can update your Facebook Status and include details about the web page you're currently viewing in Safari.

▪ **Bookmark**—Tap on this option to add a bookmark to your personal Bookmarks folder or Favorites Bar that's stored in Safari. You can later access your bookmarks and/or Favorites by tapping on the Bookmark icon.

When you opt to save a bookmark, an Add Bookmark window appears (as shown in Figure 7.7). Here, you can enter a title for the bookmark and decide whether you want to save it as part of your Bookmarks folder or as part of your Favorites Bar. It's also possible to create separate Bookmark subfolders within your Bookmarks folder in order to organize your saved Bookmarks.

▪ **Add to Reading List**—Instead of adding a web page URL to your Bookmarks folder or Favorites Bar, it's possible to save it in your Reading List for later reference. (It will be downloaded to your iPad for later viewing, so you can access it even if no Internet connection is later available.) To access your Reading List, tap on the Bookmarks icon, and then tap on the Reading List tab.

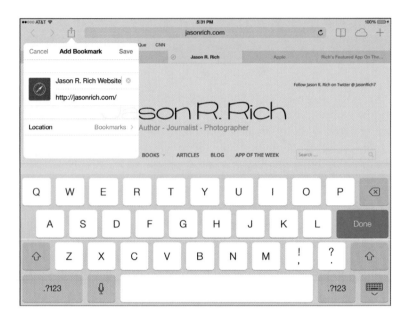

FIGURE 7.7

You can save a website URL as a bookmark in your Bookmarks menu or to be displayed as part of Safari's Favorites Bar.

■ **Add to Home Screen**—In addition to saving a website URL in the form of a bookmark or within your Reading List, another option is to save it as a Home screen icon. This feature is explained shortly.

■ **Copy**—Use this command to copy the web page URL you're looking at to the virtual clipboard that's built in to iOS 7. You can then paste that information into another app.

■ **Print**—It's possible to wirelessly print a website to any AirPrint-compatible printer that's set up to work with your iOS device. To print a web page, tap on the Print command. From the Printer Options screen, select the printer you want to use, and then choose the number of copies you want printed. Tap the Print option at the bottom of the Print Options window to send the web page document to your printer.

CREATING, MANAGING, AND SYNCING SAFARI BOOKMARKS

Thanks to the fact that Safari is fully integrated with iCloud, if you have an active iCloud account, your tablet can automatically sync your Bookmarks, Favorites Bar content, and related Safari data with your other iOS mobile devices, as well as the compatible web browsers on your primary computer(s).

To activate this iCloud sync feature, launch the Settings app and then tap on the iCloud option. When the iCloud submenu appears, make sure your iCloud account is listed at the top of the screen, and then make sure the virtual on/off switch associated with the Safari option is turned on.

Your Bookmarks list, Favorites Bar, open browser windows (tabs), and Safari Reading List will now automatically be continuously synced with your iCloud account. Thus, when you add a new bookmark while surfing the Web on your iPad, within seconds that same bookmark appears in your Bookmarks folder on your iPhone and Safari on your Mac.

SYNCING USERNAMES AND PASSWORDS USING iCLOUD KEYCHAIN

Another new feature within the iOS 7 version of Safari which also utilizes iCloud is called iCloud Keychain. Once this feature is turned on (on each of your iOS mobile devices and Macs), anytime you enter a username and password for a website you visit, that information is stored by Safari and synced with iCloud.

Then, anytime you revisit that website on any of your iCloud-linked devices or computers, your username and password for that website are remembered and you're automatically logged in.

> NOTE   iCloud Keychain also remembers credit card information you use when making online purchases from a website. All usernames, passwords, and credit card details are stored using 256-bit AES encryption to maintain security.

To turn on and use the iCloud Keychain feature, launch Settings and tap on the Safari option. Next, tap on the Passwords & AutoFill option. Turn on the virtual switch that's associated with the Names and Passwords option.

For security, this feature does not automatically work with certain online banking-related websites, for example. If you want iCloud Keychain to remember these usernames and passwords as well, turn on the virtual switch that's associated with the Always Allow option.

If you also want iCloud Keychain to remember your credit card information to make online shopping easier, also turn on the virtual switch that's associated with the Credit Cards option.

If you opt to have iCloud Keychain remember your credit card details, also from this Passwords & AutoFill menu screen within Settings, manually enter your credit card details by tapping on the Saved Credit Cards option. This only needs to be done once.

iCloud Keychain-related information will automatically sync with your computers and other iOS mobile devices that are linked to your iCloud account. So, if you visit a website and create a username and password to access it, the next time you visit that website, even if it's from one of your other computers or iOS mobile devices, Safari will automatically insert the appropriate log-in information, so you will not have to remember your username and password and enter this information manually.

LAUNCHING YOUR FAVORITE WEBSITES FAST WITH HOME SCREEN ICONS

If you regularly visit certain websites, you can create individual bookmarks for them. However, to access those sites, you still need to launch Safari, tap on the Bookmarks icon (or Favorites Bar), and then tap on a specific listing to access the related site.

A time-saving alternative is to create a Home screen icon for each of your favorite websites (as shown in Figure 7.8).

To create a Home screen icon, surf to one of your favorite websites using Safari. After it loads, tap on the Share icon, and tap on the Add to Home Screen button from the Share menu.

A new Add to Home window appears. It displays a thumbnail image of the website you're visiting and enables you to enter the title for the website (which is displayed below the icon on your device's Home screen). Keep the title you choose short. When you've created the title (or if you decide to keep the default title that Safari creates), tap on the Add option that's displayed in the upper-right corner of the window.

cnn.com icon

Jason R. Rich icon

FIGURE 7.8
Create Home screen icons for your favorite websites so that you can launch them directly from your iOS device's Home screen with a single tap.

> **NOTE** When you use the Add to Home Screen feature in Safari, if you're creating a shortcut for a website designed to be compatible with an iPad, a special website-related icon (as opposed to a thumbnail) is displayed. The CNN logo icon is an example of this. Otherwise, a thumbnail of the home page is displayed. Refer to Figure 7.9 to see examples of these two types of Home screen icons.

Displayed on the Home screen is what looks like a new app icon; however, it's really a link to your favorite website. Tap on this icon to automatically launch Safari from the Home screen and load the web page the shortcut is associated with.

After a Home screen icon is created for a web page, it can be treated like any other app icon. You can move it around on the Home screen, add the icon to a folder, or delete the icon from the Home screen.

ACCESSING SOCIAL NETWORKS ON YOUR iPAD

Whether you use Facebook, Twitter, Google+, YouTube, LinkedIn, Tumblr, Vine, or Instagram to promote your business, a product, or service to help position yourself as an expert in your field; to meet new people; or simply to stay in touch with your friends and family, you can fully utilize these online social networking sites using specialized apps available from the App Store.

The capability to share information using online social networking from virtually anywhere using your iPad brings a new level of interactivity to these services.

WORKING WITH FACEBOOK

In addition to offering Facebook integration in iOS 7 and some of the core apps, the official Facebook for iPad app is available for free from the App Store. It offers almost all the functionality of Facebook on your tablet's screen, including the capability to access your Wall, update your Status, send/receive messages, manage your photo albums, upload and share photos shot using your iPad, and chat in real time with your Facebook Friends.

NOTE   The official Facebook Pages app (which is separate from the Facebook app for managing an individual account) can be used to easily manage the Facebook page for a business, organization, public figure, or charitable organization, for example. To learn more about publishing a free Facebook page for your business, visit www.Facebook.com from any web browser, scroll down to the bottom of the page, and click on the Create Page option.

TIP   To download the Facebook app and configure Facebook integration with your iPad, launch Settings and then select the Facebook option from the menu. Then, on the Facebook submenu, tap on the Install icon to install the official Facebook app on your iPad. Add your existing Facebook account information in Settings, and then again when you launch the actual Facebook app for the first time.

When you tap on the Update All Contacts button on the Facebook screen in Settings, your iPad syncs your Contacts database with your active friends list on Facebook automatically.

TWEETING FROM YOUR iPAD

There is a free official Twitter app, designed specifically for the iPad, as well as dozens of third-party apps that work with Twitter. Twitter functionality has also been fully integrated into iOS 7, so you can tweet from a variety of different apps. However, to be able to manage your existing Twitter accounts, you should install the official Twitter app onto your tablet.

To initially set up Twitter on your iPad, launch Settings and tap the Twitter option in the menu. On the Twitter submenu, you have the option to install the official Twitter app by tapping the Install icon.

After installation, launch the Twitter app. You can then sign in using one or multiple Twitter accounts or create a new account (which is also something you can do from the Twitter screen in Settings, by tapping the Create New Account option).

You can use the official Twitter app to create and send tweets, access your Twitter timeline, and see what the people you're following are tweeting about. In addition, various other core apps—including Photos, Safari, Camera, Contacts, and Maps—are fully integrated with Twitter and allow you to send tweets with an app-related attachment.

> **TIP** For Twitter integration to work with the core apps built in to your iPad (as opposed to just the official Twitter app), you must sign in to your Twitter account from within Settings just once.

TAPPING INTO LINKEDIN TO NETWORK WITH BUSINESS PROFESSIONALS

More than 250 million business professionals, working in thousands of different fields and industries, are active participants on the LinkedIn online social networking service (www.linkedin.com).

To access LinkedIn from your iPad, download the free LinkedIn for iPad app available from the App Store. This is a useful online tool for professional networking, job searching, recruiting, exchanging information with peers working in your industry, and/or for seeking out answers to business- or career-related questions.

Using the LinkedIn app, it's possible to quickly search for other members based on their name, job, employer, or a group/affiliation, for example. You can also manage and update your own profile, view and save recommended job listings, read industry news, research companies, monitor online social interest groups, manage endorsements, and build your online reputation, as well as handle other commonly used tasks.

MANAGING YOUR GOOGLE+ ACCOUNT FROM YOUR iPAD

Also available from the App Store is the free Google+ app, which enables you to manage most aspects of your Google+ account directly from your tablet. From this app, you can join a Hangout, post a photo, see what your online friends are up to, see the What's Hot stream, and view the Nearby stream, for example.

SHARING YOUR PHOTOS WITH INSTAGRAM

Whereas Twitter enables you to send text-based messages to your followers (that can include an attached website link or photo), Instagram is designed specifically for sharing digital photos shot using your mobile device.

TIP If you know you're shooting a photo on your iPad to share via Instagram, use the Square shooting mode within the Camera app or use the camera functionality built in to the Instagram app.

Using this app, you can take pictures on your iPad, edit and crop them, add special effects (filters), and then publish them on the Instagram service. Photos can be accompanied by a text-based caption and/or hash tags. The free Instagram app also enables you to view the public photo feed from the Instagram service, plus view the photo feeds of the people you're following.

NOTE The official Instagram app is currently an iPhone-specific app that works flawlessly on the iPad, but it does not use the iPad's larger screen size unless you use the 2x feature.

MANAGING YOUR YOUTUBE CHANNEL FROM YOUR TABLET

In late-August 2013, the official YouTube app for the iPad was redesigned, giving users the ability to manage their YouTube Channel directly from their tablet, as well as view their favorite YouTube Channels and videos. Virtually all of the YouTube functionality that's available from the www.YouTube.com website (when accessed from your computer) is now offered from within the free iPad app.

MOBILE BLOGGING AND WEBSITE MANAGEMENT IS EASY FROM YOUR iPAD

More and more businesses and entrepreneurs are using blogs to communicate with their (potential) customers and clients in an informal way. If you want to maintain your blog while on-the-go, specialized apps are available that are designed for use with the most popular blogging services, including WordPress, Blogger.com, and Tumblr.

The WordPress app, for example, offers all of the functionality you need to compose, format, and publish new blog entries as well as manage WordPress websites, moderate comments, and track your blog/website's traffic stats. When used in conjunction with the Camera and Photos apps, bloggers and website managers can easily shoot and edit photos or videos on their tablets, and then publish that content, along with related text, directly to a blog or website.

In addition, a handful of audio recording apps are available for the iPad that make it easy to record studio-quality audio that can be used for podcasts. Specialized apps can then be used to edit and publish the audio podcast directly from the tablet. To produce even better quality audio, consider connecting an external microphone to the iPad.

8

EXPLORING YOUR WORLD WITH THE MAPS APP

When you need to determine the quickest route to an important business meeting; find your way back to the office from an unfamiliar location; circumvent traffic in order to make your next flight; locate the closest hotel, gas station, or ATM; or discover a new restaurant to impress an important client, the Maps app, in conjunction with its newly expanded Yelp! integration, can help with all this and more.

With iOS 7, not only does the Maps app have a new look, it has been redesigned to provide new functionality, more detail, and improved accuracy. This latest version of Maps is more seamlessly integrated with other apps, including Contacts and Yelp! (as well as iPad functions, like Siri), plus it offers detailed, turn-by-turn directions that can be combined with real-time traffic notifications (if you turn on this feature).

> **TIP** For the Maps app to function properly, your iPad must have continuous Internet access. If you have a Wi-Fi + Cellular model, it's possible to use this app from anywhere. When you do, turn on both the cellular and Wi-Fi connectivity for improved accuracy.
>
> If you're using a Wi-Fi–only iPad model, the Maps app is useful but can be used only while you're within the radius of a Wi-Fi hotspot. Thus, you won't be able to fully utilize the app's turn-by-turn directions feature while on the move.

The Maps app can be used as a standalone GPS device for navigation in a car or while walking. In addition, Maps can be used to display a detailed map of any location using a standard, hybrid, satellite, or 3D (flyover) view that fully utilizes the Retina display that's built in to the latest iPad models.

> **TIP** Even without using the turn-by-turn directions feature, it's possible to look up the address of any business, landmark, or airport, for example, while your tablet is connected to the Web and then save the directions to that location or print them using a compatible AirPrint printer before you leave. From within the Contacts or Maps app, you can also look up and map out any address that's stored within a Contacts entry.

> **TIP** To get the most use out of the Maps app, the main Location Services feature within your iPad (as well as Location Services for the app) must be turned on. To do this, launch Settings, tap on the Privacy option, and then tap on Location Services. From the Location Services submenu, turn on the virtual switch that's displayed near the top of the screen (associated with Locations Services), and then scroll down and make sure the virtual switch that's associated with the Maps app is also turned on.

> **CAUTION** Just as when using any GPS device for turn-by-turn directions, do not rely 100 percent on the directions you're given. Pay attention as you're driving and use common sense. If the Maps app tells you to drive down a one-way street or drive along a closed road, for example, ignore those directions and seek out an alternate route. Don't become one of those people who literally drives into a lake or over a cliff because their GPS told them to. Yes, this does happen.

In addition, real-time, color-coded traffic conditions can be graphically overlaid onto maps (which show traffic jams and construction, for example), and when you look up a business, restaurant, point-of-interest, or landmark, the Maps app seamlessly integrates with Yelp! in order to display detailed information about specific locations.

The Yelp! information screens in the Maps app are interactive, so if you tap on a website URL, Safari launches and the related website is automatically loaded and displayed.

> **TIP** To enhance the capabilities of the Yelp! integration, download and install the optional (and free) Yelp! app from the App Store. Without the Yelp! app, when appropriate, the Maps app transfers you to the Yelp! website.

> **TIP** Another companion app that's worth installing is Open Table (free). It allows you to find restaurants by location, price range, or food type, for example, plus view menus, read detailed reviews, and then make reservations online, directly from your iPad.

> **NOTE** Yelp! is a vast online database that contains more than 30 million reviews related to local businesses, stores, restaurants, hotels, tourist attractions, and points-of-interest. Reviews are created by everyday people, who share their experiences, thoughts, and photos. However, beyond user-provided reviews, Yelp! also offers details about many businesses and restaurants.

Don't forget, Maps is fully compatible with Siri, which allows you to utilize voice commands and requests. For example, regardless of what you're doing on the iPad, it's possible to activate Siri and say, "How do I get home from here?" or "Where is the closest gas station?" and then have the Maps app provide you with the directions and map you need.

Anytime you're viewing a map within the Maps app, tap on the My Location icon (which looks like a northeast-pointing arrow) that's displayed near the bottom-left corner of the screen to pinpoint and display your exact location on the map. Your location is displayed using a pulsating blue dot. If for some reason the Maps app loses its Internet signal temporarily, tap on this My Location icon again to reestablish your location.

OVERVIEW OF THE MAPS APP'S SCREEN

Displayed in the top-left corner of the main Maps app screen (shown in Figure 8.1) is the Directions option. Tap on it to enter a Start and End location and then obtain detailed driving, walking, or public transportation directions between those two points.

> **NOTE** Depending on the two points you enter, walking directions may not be applicable or viable. Currently, if you request public transportation directions between two addresses, you're redirected to the App Store in order to seek out an alternate app. Thus, if you're relying on public transportation to get around a popular city, such as New York, the District of Columbia, Boston, London, or Paris, download an app specifically designed for that public transportation system. Use the Search option within the App Store to find one of these apps. For example, enter the search phrase "London Tube Map" to find a variety of interactive apps to help you navigate your way around London's subway/train system.

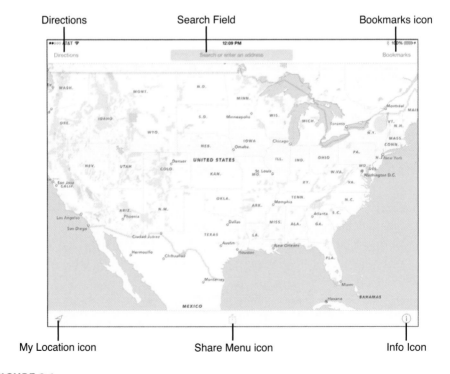

Directions   Search Field   Bookmarks icon

My Location icon   Share Menu icon   Info Icon

FIGURE 8.1

The first time you launch the Maps app, by default, a map of The United States is displayed if you have this set as your home country or region.

Displayed at the top-center of the screen is the Search field. Use it to find and map out any address. Here, you can enter a complete address (house/building number, street, city, state) or provide less specific information, such as just a city, state, or country. For example, within the Search field, enter United States to see a map of the entire country. Or, enter California to view a map of the state. You also have the option to enter Los Angeles, California, to view a more detailed map of the city, or enter a specific street address located within Los Angeles to view it on a detailed map that shows specific streets (and street names).

Once the Maps app finds the location you're looking for, you can zoom in or zoom out manually on that map to see more or less detail. Plus, you can change the Map view and switch between the Standard, Hybrid, Satellite, 3D, and/or Flyover view (each of which is explained shortly).

> **TIP** Within the Search field of the Maps app, enter the name of any contact within your Contacts database to find and display an address for that contact. As you perform a search, the contents of your iOS device (including the Contacts app) are searched, followed by a web-based search, if applicable.

Anytime a particular location is specified on the map, such as results of a Search, those results are displayed using virtual red push-pins. Tap on a push-pin to view more details about that location and to access a separate Location window.

As you're looking at the main Maps screen, however, look to the upper-right corner to find the Bookmarks option. Just like Safari, the Maps app allows you to store bookmarks for specific locations. When you tap on the Bookmarks option, three command tabs are displayed near the bottom of the window. They're labeled Bookmarks, Recents, and Contacts (shown in Figure 8.2).

Tapping on the Bookmarks tab reveals a list of previously saved locations. Tap on the Edit button to edit, delete, or reorder this list, or swipe your finger from left to right across a Bookmark listing to delete it.

Tap on the Recents tab to view a list of recently searched or viewed locations. To clear this list, tap on the Clear button that's displayed near the top-left corner of the window.

When you tap on the Contacts tab, the All Contacts listing is displayed. This shows a comprehensive list of all entries stored within your Contacts database. Whether you're looking at the Bookmarks, Recents, or All Contacts list, tap on one of the listings to view that location on a map.

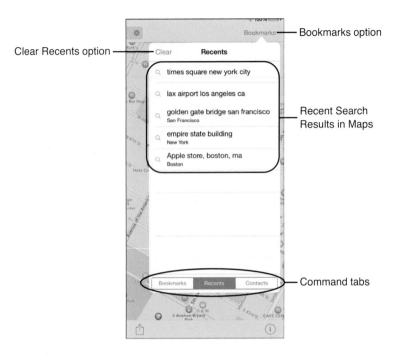

Clear Recents option

Bookmarks option

Recent Search Results in Maps

Command tabs

FIGURE 8.2

Near the bottom of the Bookmarks window are three tabs, labeled Bookmarks, Recents, and Contacts.

Again, as you're looking at the main Maps screen, the center area of the display is used to showcase maps. Remember, in most cases, you can zoom in or zoom out on the map you're looking at. You can also use your finger to move around within that map and see other areas of it.

Displayed near the bottom-left corner of the screen is the My Location icon (it looks like a northeast-pointing arrow). At anytime a map is displayed, tap on this icon to locate and display (or update) your current location on the map. This feature is useful if you look up another destination and then want to quickly see where you're currently located in comparison to that other location. However, when you're using the Maps app for turn-by-turn directions, your iPad keeps track of your location in real-time and displays this on the map as you're in motion.

NOTE As you're viewing a Standard, Hybrid, or Satellite map, tap on the 3D button that's displayed near the bottom-left corner of the screen to switch to a 3D view. Many people find the 3D view more visually interesting, although it doesn't reveal any new onscreen information that could not be seen using the Maps app's Standard, Hybrid, or Satellite view.

> **TIP** When you're viewing a map of a popular city or metropolitan area, the 3D button is automatically replaced by the Flyover icon. The Flyover feature offers a true, 3D-looking map of a city from the perspective of an airplane cockpit. From this view, use your finger to move around on the screen and see a bird's-eye view of a city, which is visually impressive and highly detailed.

The Info icon is now displayed near the bottom-right corner of the main Maps screen. When you tap on this circular "i" icon, a new window pops up that allows you to quickly switch between the Standard, Hybrid, or Satellite map view. Simply tap on one of the labeled tabs that are displayed near the top of this window (shown in Figure 8.3).

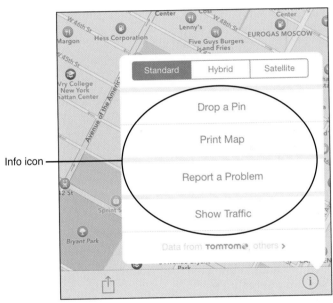

FIGURE 8.3
Tap on the Info icon to reveal this newly designed Info window.

Displayed to the left of the Info icon, along the bottom of the main Maps screen is a Share icon. Tap on this icon to share map details you're currently viewing with others via the Message, Mail, Twitter, or Facebook app. The Share menu of the Maps app is shown in Figure 8.4.

> **TIP** The newly redesigned Share menu includes an Add Bookmark button. Tap on this to save the currently viewed location as a Maps bookmark for later reference.

Share icon

FIGURE 8.4

The Share menu within the Maps app allows you to quickly share details about a location with others, plus create a bookmark for a specific location for later reference.

THE MAPS APP'S INFO SCREEN

The Maps app's Info screen displays several command buttons and command tabs. The command buttons are labeled Drop A Pin, Print Map, and Show (or Hide) Traffic.

THE DROP A PIN COMMAND

When you tap on the Drop A Pin option, the full Maps screen returns. Now, tap anywhere on that map to place a virtual push-pin. The new push-pin is displayed in purple, instead of red. Once a push-pin is placed, it's possible to view detailed information about that particular location, including its exact address. You can then tap on the displayed Info icon to view a Location Menu that offers a handful of menu options, including: Directions To Here, Directions From Here, Transit Directions, Create New Contact, Add To Existing Contact, Remove Pin, Add Bookmark, or Report A Problem.

THE PRINT MAP COMMAND

If you have a wireless printer linked to your tablet via AirPrint, tap on the Print button to create a print-out of whatever is displayed on the screen, whether it's a detailed map, a text-based list of turn-by-turn directions to a destination, or a listing of search results (such as restaurants or gas stations in a particular area).

When you tap on the Print button, the Print options window is displayed. Select an AirPrint-compatible printer and the number of copies you want printed; then tap on the Print button. If you have a color printer linked to your iPad, you can print maps (or color-coded directions) in full-color.

> **NOTE** If you encounter a serious problem with the Maps app or an error in the mapping, use the Report A Problem feature to contact Apple. When you do this, a menu appears with a handful of options relating to different types of Maps-related problems. Choose one and then follow the onscreen prompts to further explain the problem you've encountered. Tap the Send option to email your correction to Apple. This does not guarantee, however, that Apple will quickly fix the error or problem you've encountered.

THE SHOW/HIDE TRAFFIC OPTION

Regardless of which map view you're looking at, you can have color-coded, real-time traffic information superimposed on the map. This feature can help you avoid traffic jams and construction and allows you to seek an alternate route before you get stuck in the traffic.

> **NOTE** Mild traffic is showcased on a map using yellow, while heavy traffic is depicted in red. When construction is being done on a roadway, separate construction icons (displayed in yellow or red) are displayed on the map.

> **TIP** The Show Traffic feature works much better when you're viewing a zoomed-in version of a map that shows a lot of street-level detail. Figure 8.5 shows moderate traffic conditions (a dashed orange line) near the famous intersection of Hollywood Blvd. and Highland, in Hollywood, California.
>
> Use the Show Traffic feature to help plan your route in advance, and seek out an alternate route if necessary, to avoid being late for an important meeting or flight, for example.

FIGURE 8.5

An orange line along a roadway indicates moderate traffic when you have the Show Traffic feature turned on within the Maps app.

THE STANDARD, HYBRID, AND SATELLITE TABS

Displayed along the top of the Maps Info window are the three map view command tabs—Standard, Hybrid, and Satellite. The Standard map view (shown in Figure 8.6) displays a traditional-looking, multicolored map on the screen. Street names and other important information are labeled and displayed on the map.

The Satellite view uses high-resolution and extremely detailed satellite imagery to show maps from an overhead view, while the Hybrid map view showcases the same satellite imagery but overlays street names and other important information, similar to the information you'd see using the Standard view.

> **TIP** Anytime you're viewing a map, you can switch between Map views. Then from the main Maps screen, tap on the My Location icon to display your exact location on the map and/or tap on the 3D icon to add a three-dimensional element to the map. If a Flyover view is available, the Flyover icon is displayed instead of the 3D icon.

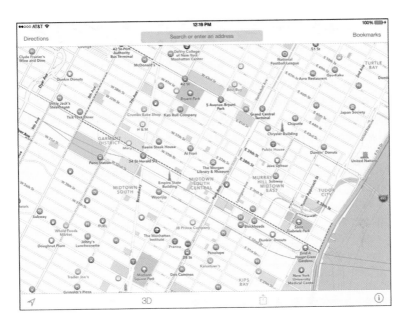

FIGURE 8.6

The Standard map view shows a traditional, multicolored map with street names and other points-of-interest listed on it. Shown here is part of midtown Manhattan.

OBTAINING TURN-BY-TURN DIRECTIONS BETWEEN TWO LOCATIONS

The turn-by-turn directions feature of the Maps app is not only easy to use, it's also extremely useful. Tap on the Directions option that's displayed near the top-left corner of the screen. The Start and End fields, as well as the reverse directions, driving, walking, and public transportation icons, are displayed (shown in Figure 8.7). Within the Start field, the default option is your Current Location. However, to change this, tap on the field and enter any starting address. Then tap on the End field and enter any ending address.

> **TIP** Displayed below the Start and End field are recent locations you've utilized within the Maps app. Scroll up or down this list using your finger, or tap on any entry to use it as your Start or End location.

FIGURE 8.7
Fill in the Start and End fields to obtain detailed, turn-by-turn directions between any two locations that you choose.

> **TIP** Within the Start and End fields, you can enter a Contact entry's name, a full address, a city and state, just a state, or just a country. You can use two-letter state abbreviations, and you don't have to worry about using upper- and lowercase letters. The app understands what you're typing either way. For example, you can type "New York, NY"; "new york, ny"; "ny, ny"; or "New York, New York" and get the same result. This goes for contacts or business names as well.

When the Start and End fields have been filled in, tap on the car-shaped icon near the top-center of the screen to access detailed driving directions. Or, tap on the person-shaped icon to obtain walking directions between those two locations.

Next, tap in the Route option that's displayed near the upper-right corner of the screen. There's also a Route button displayed on the virtual keyboard. A route overview map (shown in Figure 8.8) is displayed. The green push-pin represents your starting location, and the red-push pin represents your ending location. If you selected Driving directions, the Maps app displays between one and three possible routes between the Start and End locations.

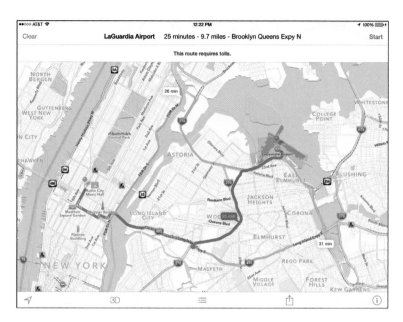

FIGURE 8.8

A sample route overview map shows your Start and End locations on one map, plus up to three possible driving routes to get there.

The primary route (Route 1) is outlined on the route overview map with a dark blue line. If you see a 3 Routes flag along your main route, tap on it to reveal up to two alternate routes. Then, if available, one or two alternate routes are outlined with light blue lines and labeled Route 2 and Route 3.

> **TIP** Turn on the Show Traffic option to display current traffic conditions along the three routes, and then choose the one with the least congestion or construction. Tap on the Route 1, Route 2, or Route 3 flag to select your route. Route 1 is the default selection.

Tap on the Start button that's displayed near the upper-right corner of the screen to begin the real-time, turn-by-turn directions. Just like when using a standalone GPS device, a voice guides you through each turn, while also displaying related information on the main map screen (shown in Figure 8.9).

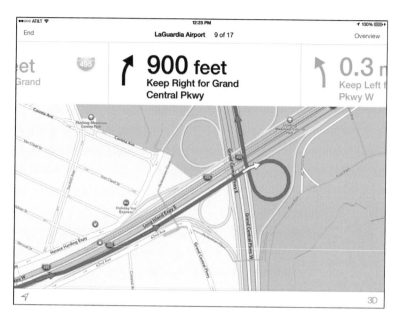

FIGURE 8.9

The Maps app shows detailed, turn-by-turn directions on the map screen, plus speaks to you as you're driving.

While the turn-by-turn directions are being displayed, the Standard map view is used. Your ETA, as well as how much time is left in your trip and the distance from your destination, is displayed near the top-center of the screen. Tap the Overview option to return to the route overview map or tap the End option to exit out of the turn-by-turn directions feature and return to the main Maps screen.

Follow the voice and onscreen prompts until you reach your destination. If you press the Home button, you can return to the Home screen and launch another app while the Maps feature is still running and then return to the turn-by-turn directions by tapping on the blue bar at the top of the screen that says Touch To Return To Navigation. This also works when you launch another app.

VIEWING A LISTING OF TURNS TO YOUR DESTINATION

After entering Start and End locations using the Directions feature of the Maps app, before tapping Start to obtain real-time turn-by-turn directions, tap on the Listing option that's displayed near the bottom-center of the screen to view text-based directions to your destination.

Use your finger to scroll up or down on this list or tap on one of the individual directions to jump to the map that shows that step.

LOOKING UP CONTACT ENTRIES, BUSINESSES, RESTAURANTS, LANDMARKS, AND POINTS-OF-INTEREST

One of the other primary uses of the Maps app is to find and display addresses, contacts, businesses, points-of-interest, or landmarks on a map screen. To do this, from the main Maps screen, type what you're looking for into the Search field. In Figure 8.10, Gillette Stadium in Foxboro, MA (home of the New England Patriots), was entered into the search field.

FIGURE 8.10

Gillette Stadium in Foxboro, MA, is shown here using the hybrid and 3D map.

Here are some examples of what you can enter into the Search field:

- A full address for almost any location in the world. This displays a map of that specific location.
- An intersection (such as 42nd street and Broadway or Hollywood and Highland).
- A city and state. This displays a map of that area.
- A state. This displays a state map.
- A country. This displays a country-wide map.
- A person or business name from your Contacts database. This displays the corresponding address on a map.

- The name of a business, restaurant, or point-of-interest followed by the city and state.

- Just the name of a business, restaurant, or point-of-interest. The Maps app looks in the most recent search area for what you're looking for, or if it's a known landmark (such as The White House or the Empire State Building), for example, the app finds and displays it.

- The type of business or service you're looking for. For example, type gas station, hospital, seafood restaurants, or post office.

> TIP   If you're looking for businesses or services in your immediate area, tap on the My Location icon first, so the iPad pinpoints your location, and then enter what you're searching for. No city or state needs to be entered. If you don't tap on the My Location icon first, you need to enter what you're looking for, followed by the city, a comma, and the state in order to find local search results. Otherwise, the Maps app defaults to the last search location.

USING THE INTERACTIVE LOCATION SCREENS TO FIND MORE INFORMATION

Once search results are displayed on the map, in the form of virtual push-pins, tap on any push-pin to view an information banner for a location on a map. In Figure 8.11, a search for Apple Store locations in Los Angeles was performed and displayed on the map.

Tap on one push-pin and then tap on the left side of the information banner to obtain "quick" turn-by-turn directions from your current location. Or, tap on the Info icon on the right side of the listing to view an interactive Location screen.

A separate Location window (shown in Figure 8.12) displays details about that search result using details from the Maps app, the Internet, and Yelp!. Tap on the Info tab on the Location window to view the phone number, address, website URL, and/or other information for that search result. What information is displayed depends on whether it's a business, restaurant, point-of-interest, or tourist attraction, for example.

> TIP   When looking at multiple search results on a map, tap on Listing icon to view a text-based, interactive listing of the search results.

FIGURE 8.11

A search for Apple stores in the Los Angeles area was performed. The results are shown as red virtual push-pins on this hybrid view map.

FIGURE 8.12

A detailed Location window combines location information with details about that location obtained from Yelp!. Information about the Apple Store at The Grove shopping center in Los Angeles is shown here.

Scroll down on the Location window to see the Directions To Here and Directions From Here options (as well as a Transit Directions option). Tap on any of these to obtain directions to or from your current location to the address listed on the screen.

Tap on the More Info On Yelp! option to launch the Yelp! app or visit the Yelp! website to view more detailed information about that location.

The Create New Contact, Add To Existing Contact, Add Bookmark, and Report A Problem options are available by scrolling down within the Location window as long as you have the Info tab at the top of the window highlighted.

Within the Location window, tap on the Reviews tab to view Yelp!-related star-based ratings and text-based reviews from other Yelp! users, or tap on the Photos tab to view photos of that location, including photos uploaded by other Yelp! users. You can also contribute your own star-based rating, review, or photos for a location.

> **TIP** If you look up information about a restaurant, for example, the Location screen includes Yelp!-related information, such as the type of food served, the menu price range (using dollar sign symbols), the hours of operation, and potentially a website link that allows you to view the restaurant's menu. You can also determine if the restaurant delivers or accepts reservations.
>
> If reservations are accepted, use the optional Open Table app to make reservations online. You can also activate Siri and say, "Make a reservation for [number of people] for [day and time]."

THE MAPS APP'S FLYOVER VIEW

While the 3D feature makes looking at Standard, Hybrid, and Satellite maps more interesting, the Flyover map view that's available for many major cities is just plain cool, although it doesn't really serve a navigation purpose. This feature, however, can be used to help you get acquainted with the layout of a city and allow you to take a virtual tour of its skyline from your iPad.

When it's available (from the Hybrid or Satellite view), the 3D icon that's normally displayed near the lower-left corner of the Maps screen is replaced with the Flyover icon (which looks like a building). Tap on it to switch to a stunning Flyover map view (shown in Figure 8.13).

> **TIP** When using the 3D or Flyover view, you can zoom in or out on the map, plus change the perspective by placing two fingers (side-by-side) on the screen and moving them up or down together. You can also use just one finger to move up, down, left, or right to view a different area of the map and scroll around.

FIGURE 8.13
The Flyover view of New York City.

THE MAPS APP INTEGRATES NICELY WITH OTHER APPS

Just like before, the Maps app works nicely with other apps on your iPad. For example, from the Contacts app, as you're viewing a specific entry, tap on any address to launch the Maps app and view that location on a map. This also works from within Safari as you're surfing the Web (if an address is displayed as part of a web page) or while using the Mail app, if an address is displayed in an email message.

USING SIRI WITH THE MAPS APP

Of course, the Maps app also works with Siri, enabling you to access directions, look up maps, and pinpoint locations using verbal commands.

For directions, simply activate Siri (press and hold the Home button for about 2 seconds). When you hear the tone, say something like, "How do I get to [location]?" or "Look up the address for [contact name]."

You can also ask, "Where is [person from your Contacts database or any business name] in [city and/or state] located?" or say, "Show me the address of [landmark or destination, such as The Lincoln Memorial in Washington, DC]."

Thanks to Siri's integration with Yelp! and other services, you can also say something like, "Find me a Chinese restaurant in Boston, MA," or "Where's the nearest coffee shop?", and then look at a pop-up window that shows your search results with Yelp!-related information. You can then view the search results in the Maps app with a single tap.

> **TIP** You can always activate Siri and ask, "How do I get home?" or "How do I get back to work?" Siri will activate the Maps app and promptly display detailed directions from your current location. For this to work, you must first associate your own information with Siri by creating a detailed entry for yourself in the Contacts app and then linking it to Siri from within Settings. To do this, Launch Settings; tap on Mail, Contacts, Calendars; scroll down to the My Info option on the right side of the screen; then link your personal Contacts entry.
>
> By linking relatives in your Contacts entry using the Related People field, you can then use Siri and ask questions like, "How do I get to my mom's office?" or "Where does my brother live?"

MAPS APP ALTERNATIVES

As a business person on-the-go, you may rely on the iPad's navigation capabilities often (especially if you have an iPad Wi-Fi + Cellular model) to help you make your way more efficiently around your home city or to easily find your destination when traveling in an unfamiliar location.

If the Maps app doesn't offer the features and functionality you need, consider visiting the App Store and installing either the free Google Maps app or the BringGo app ($49.00–$59.99), which transforms your tablet into a full-featured GPS system that's ideally suited for the needs of business travelers.

> **TIP** To find these and other navigation apps, launch the App Store app, tap on the Categories option, and choose Navigation or use the App Store app's Search field.

> **CAUTION** Keep in mind, the Maps app relies heavily on Internet access. If you're using a cellular data connection, which is necessary to use turn-by-turn directions while on-the-go, and have a monthly usage allocation, using the Maps app often could quickly use a significant portion of this allocation.

DIGITAL PHOTOGRAPHY ON YOUR iPAD

The latest iPad models have two powerful, high-resolution cameras built in that, when used with the Camera app, make snapping detailed, clear, and vibrant photos as easy as tapping on the device's screen.

When it comes to viewing, organizing, enhancing, printing, and sharing digital photos on your iOS device, you have a multitude of options. The Photos app that comes preinstalled on the iPad offers decent photo-organizing and basic photo-editing features. However, available from the App Store is Apple's iPhoto app. It dramatically enhances your ability to view, organize, edit, enhance, share, and print images.

When using your iPad as a business tool, there are many situations in which being able to snap photos of people, places, or things can be beneficial. The photos you take, edit, or store on your iPad can then be imported into various apps, such as Contacts, Pages, Numbers, or Keynote, as well as database apps, such as FileMaker Go.

Many other apps also enable you to import or somehow utilize digital photos. For example, the Square app that's used for credit card processing allows photos to be imported as part of its virtual cash register functionality, so you can tap an item's photo that someone is about to purchase to create a detailed receipt.

Of course, if you're active on Facebook, Twitter, Instagram, YouTube, and/or Vine, for example, and use your iPad to manage your online social networking accounts, it's possible to easily share photos taken with (or that are stored on) your tablet.

Plus, if you manage a website or blog, this too can easily be done from your tablet (using the WordPress app, for example), and you can publish photos or videos clips taken and edited on your iPad.

> **NOTE** The iOS 7 edition of the Camera app features three shooting modes—still, video, and square—which are explained shortly, plus eight special effect filters that you can incorporate into your photos after-the-fact when editing them on your tablet.

Meanwhile, the Photos app offers new ways to enhance your images and then organize, view, and share them. Both the Camera and Photos apps have a redesigned look.

LOADING DIGITAL IMAGES ONTO YOUR iPAD

Before you can view, edit, print, and share your favorite digital images, you first must shoot them using the Camera or Photo Booth app that comes preinstalled on your iPad or transfer images into your tablet. You can also use many other optional third-party photography apps to take, edit, and manage your digital images via your tablet.

Aside from shooting images using one of your iPad's built-in cameras, there are several ways to import photos into your iOS device and then store them within the Photos app:

- Use the iTunes sync process to transfer photos to your device. Set up iTunes to sync the image folders or albums you want, and then initiate an iTunes sync or wireless iTunes sync from your primary computer.
- Load photos from My Photo Stream or a Shared Photo Stream (via iCloud).
- Receive and save photos sent via email. When a photo is embedded within an email, as shown in Figure 9.1, hold your finger on it for a second or two until a menu appears giving you the option to Save Image. This menu can also offer other options, based on how your tablet is configured. For

example, you can print, copy, mail, tweet, or publish the incoming image directly to Facebook. If you copy the image to your device's virtual clipboard, you can then paste it into another app.

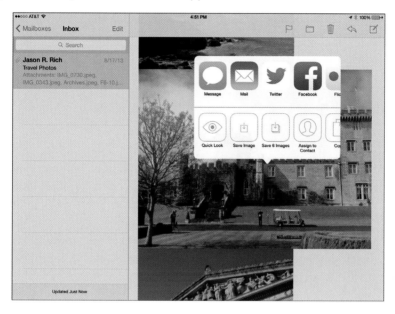

FIGURE 9.1

When you receive a digital photo attached to an incoming email (via the Mail app), save that image within the Photos app by holding your finger on the image thumbnail (within the email) and then tapping the Save Image option when it appears.

> **TIP** If an incoming email has several images attached to or embedded in it, you're given the option to save just the selected image or save all the images in the email at once. Whether you tap on the Save Image or Save [#] Images option, the incoming images are saved in the Camera Roll album in the Photos app.

■ **Receive and save photos sent via instant message.** Tap the image you receive using the Messages app, and then tap the Copy command to copy the image to your device's virtual clipboard (after which you can paste it into another app).

■ **Save images directly from a website as you're surfing the Web.** Hold your finger on the image you're viewing in a website. If it's not copy-protected, after a second or two, a menu appears enabling you to Save Image or Copy it to your device's virtual clipboard (after which you can paste it into another app).

■ Use the optional Camera Connection Kit ($29.00, available from Apple Stores or Apple.com) to load images from your digital camera's memory card directly into your iPad.

> **NOTE** When you use the Save Image command, the image is stored in the Camera Roll album of Photos. You can then view, edit, enhance, print, or share it using the Photos app or another app, such as iPhoto or Adobe's Photoshop Touch.

THE REDESIGNED CAMERA APP

The Camera app that comes preinstalled with iOS 7 has been redesigned, yet it still remains very easy to use if you want to snap a photo or shoot a video clip. In fact, you can now launch the app and begin snapping photos faster. To begin using the Camera app, launch it from your device's Home screen.

The main camera viewfinder screen (shown in Figure 9.2) appears as soon as you launch the Camera app. The main area of the screen serves as your camera's viewfinder. In other words, what you see on the screen is what you photograph or capture on video.

Along the right margin of the screen are several command icons and options. In the lower-left corner is a thumbnail image of the last photo or video clip you shot. Tap on it to view that image or video clip and use some of the Photo app's viewing and editing functions without leaving the Camera app.

On middle-right side of the screen is the camera's round shutter button. Tap on this to snap a photo or to start and stop the video camera. In Video mode, the shutter button icon transforms from a bright red circle into a red square (pause button) when you tap on it to begin shooting a video clip.

Displayed just below the shutter button icon are the shooting mode options—Video, Photo, and Square. Use your finger to scroll up or down and then tap on your selected option. Video is for shooting video. Photo is used to snap regular digital (still) images. Square allows you to pre-crop images to be compatible with services such as Instagram. You wind up with already cropped square images.

The latest iPad models each have two built-in cameras—one in the front and one on the back of the device. The front-facing camera makes it easier to snap photos of yourself or participate in videoconferences, for example. The rear-facing camera (which allows you to take higher-resolution photos or video) allows you to photograph whatever you're looking at that's facing forward. Tap on the camera-shaped icon located in the upper-right corner of the screen to switch between cameras.

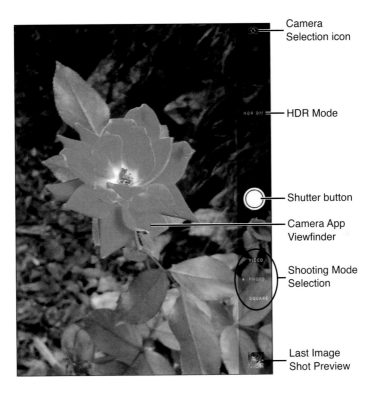

Camera
Selection icon

HDR Mode

Shutter button

Camera App
Viewfinder

Shooting Mode
Selection

Last Image
Shot Preview

FIGURE 9.2

From the Camera app's main screen, you can snap digital photos or shoot video.

When applicable, displayed just above of the shutter button is the HDR button.
Tap on it to turn on/off HDR mode when taking digital photos.

> **NOTE** HDR mode stands for High Dynamic Range. It can be used with the
> rear-facing camera only. When turned on, this feature captures the available light
> differently and can help you compensate for bad lighting with a photo that would
> otherwise be over- or underexposed.
>
> When HDR mode is turned on, your iPad saves two images each time you tap
> the shutter button to snap a photo. One utilizes HDR mode and the other does
> not. You can later view the images, choose which you like best, and discard the
> other one. The drawback to using HDR mode is that it takes several extra sec-
> onds to store both images each time you snap a photo, and this slows down the
> Camera app.

HOW TO SNAP A PHOTO

Snapping a single digital photo using the Camera app is simple. Follow these steps:

1. Launch the Camera app from the Home Screen.

2. Make sure the shooting mode is set to Photo or Square. Swipe the photo mode selector to choose the desired option.

3. Choose which of your tablet's two built-in cameras you want to use by tapping on the camera selection icon.

4. Compose or frame your image by holding up your iPad and pointing it at your subject.

5. Select the main subject of your photo, such as a person or an object. Tap your finger on the screen where your subject appears in the viewfinder. An auto-focus sensor box appears on the screen at the location you tap. Where this box is positioned is what the camera focuses on (as opposed to something in the foreground, in the background, or next to your intended subject).

> **TIP** To activate the auto exposure/auto focus lock feature, press and hold your finger over your subject within the viewfinder for two or three seconds. Once this feature kicks in, you can take multiple photos using the same autofocus lock without having to refocus on your subject(s).
>
> As you're holding your iPad to snap a photo or shoot video, be sure your fingers don't accidentally block the camera lens that's being utilized.

> **NOTE** If you're taking a group photo (up to 10 people), the camera app detects this and multiple autofocus sensors appear on all of your subjects' faces.

6. If you want to use the Camera app's zoom feature, use a pinch motion on the screen. A zoom slider (shown in Figure 9.3) appears along the bottom of the screen. Use your finger to move the dot within the slider to the right to zoom in or to the left to zoom out on your subject.

7. When you have your image framed within the viewfinder, tap on the shutter button to snap the photo. You see an animation of a virtual shutter closing and then reopening on the screen, indicating that the photo is being taken.

8. The photo is saved on your tablet within the Camera Roll album of Photos. You can now shoot another photo or preview the just-taken image using tools from the Photos app.

Zoom slider

FIGURE 9.3

As you're framing an image, you can zoom in (or out) on your subject using the onscreen zoom slider. Use a pinch finger gesture on the screen to make this slider appear, and then move the slider to the right or left to increase or decrease the zoom level.

HOW TO SHOOT VIDEO

From the Camera app, it's also possible to shoot video. Follow these steps for shooting video using your iPad:

1. Launch the Camera app.

2. Swipe to the Video shooting mode option.

3. Choose which camera you want to use. You can switch between the front- and the rear-facing cameras at any time.

4. Hold your iPad up to the subject you want to capture on video. Set up your shot by looking at what's displayed on the screen.

5. When you're ready to start shooting video, tap on the shutter button. The red dot turns into a red square. This indicates you're now filming. Your iPad captures whatever subject(s) you see on the screen, as well as any sound in the area.

6. As you're filming video, notice the timer displayed on the screen (shown in Figure 9.4). Your only limit to how much video you can shoot is based on the amount of available memory within your iOS device and how long the battery lasts. However, this app is designed more for shooting short video clips, not full-length home movies.

Video Timer

Shutter button

FIGURE 9.4

When shooting video on your iPad, make sure the timer is counting upward. This indicates you're actually recording.

7. Also as you're filming, tap anywhere on the screen to focus in on your subject using the app's built-in autofocus sensor. Be sure to hold your tablet as steady as possible to ensure a clear video image.

8. To stop filming, tap again on the shutter button. Your video footage is saved. You can now view, edit, and share it from within the Photos app or the optional iMovie app, for example.

> **TIP** Although the Photos app enables you to trim your video clips as well as view and share the videos, if you want to edit your videos, or add titles and special effects, use Apple's feature-packed iMovie app, which is available from the App Store ($4.99). For more information about iMovie, visit www.apple.com/apps/imovie.

> **TIP** iCloud's Shared Photo Stream feature now allows you to include video clips shot on your iOS mobile device (up to five minutes in length) within a Shared Photo Stream that you ultimately share with others.

TIPS FOR SHOOTING EYE-CATCHING PHOTOS USING YOUR iPAD

To generate the best possible, in-focus, well-lit, and nicely framed images when shooting with your iPad, follow these basic shooting strategies (many of which also apply when shooting video):

- Pay attention to your light source. As a general rule, the light source (such as the sun) should be behind you (the photographer) and shining onto your subject. When light from your primary light source shines directly into your camera's lens (in this case your iPad), you wind up with unwanted glare or an overexposed image.

- As you look at the viewfinder screen, pay attention to shadows. Unwanted shadows can be caused by the sun or by an artificial light source. When shadows show up in your images, they can be distracting, so make sure they aren't covering your subjects.

- As you get ready to tap the shutter icon and snap a photo, hold your iPad perfectly still. Even the slightest movement could result in a blurry image, especially in low-light situations.

- When shooting portraits of people or specific objects, make sure you use the Camera app's autofocus sensor box to focus in on your subject. As you look through the viewfinder, tap the main subject's face, for example. This ensures that the Camera app focuses in on the person and not something in the foreground, background, or to the side of your subject.

> **TIP** As you're shooting, instead of holding the camera head-on, directly facing your subject, try shooting from a different perspective, such as from slightly above, below, or to the side of your subject. This allows you to create more visually interesting images.

- As you're framing your subjects in the viewfinder, pay attention to what's in the foreground, background, and to the sides of the subject. These objects can often be used to frame your subject and add a sense of multidimensionality to a photo. Just make sure the autofocus sensor of the Camera app focuses in on your intended subject, and not on something else in the photo, to ensure clarity.

> **TIP** When shooting a digital photo, hold the iPad as still as possible. This is also important when shooting video. However, when shooting video, if you choose to pan up, down, left or right, for example, use slow, fluid motions.

ADJUSTING CAMERA AND PHOTOS APP OPTIONS FROM WITHIN SETTINGS

From within Settings, it's possible to adjust a handful of settings related to the Camera and Photos app. To do this, launch Settings and then tap on the Photos & Camera option that's displayed on the left side of the screen. The options available from the Photos & Camera submenu include:

- **My Photo Stream**—Turn on this iCloud-related feature to automatically upload and store 1,000 of your more recently shot images for up to 30 days. You can then almost immediately view the images on any Mac, Apple TV, or iOS mobile device that's linked to the same iCloud account. This feature only needs to be turned on and set up once. To activate My Photo Stream, turn on the virtual switch associated with this feature.

- **Photo Sharing**—Turn on the ability for you to create Shared Photo Streams, which can be stored online within your iCloud account; accessed from all Macs, Apple TV, and iOS mobile devices linked to your iCloud account; plus shared with other people via the Internet. To activate iCloud's Shared Photo Stream feature, turn on the virtual switch associated with the Photo Sharing feature.

- **Summarize Photos**—Determine how images are "summarized" when displayed as thumbnails as you're using the Photos app to organize and view them as Collections or Years.

- **Play Each Slide For**—When using the Photos app to create Slide Shows in order to showcase your images, this option sets the default for how long each slide is displayed.

- **Repeat**—When using the Photos app to create Slide Shows in order to showcase your images, this option allows images to automatically repeat during the presentation.

- **Shuffle**—When using the Photos app to create Slide Shows in order to showcase your images, this option allows the app to randomize the order in which photos are displayed. When the feature is turned off, photos are displayed in the order they were shot and saved.

- **Grid**—When turned on, a grid is displayed on the viewfinder screen as you're taking pictures using the Camera app. This grid makes it easier to use the Rule of Thirds photography technique. However, the grid does not actually appear in your photos.

- **Keep Normal Photo**—When HDR more is turned on, by default two images are stored—one that uses HDR mode to adjust lighting and contrast and one that does not. When turned off, only the HDR version of each photo will be stored.

HOW TO USE THE RULE OF THIRDS WHEN SHOOTING

It's a common mistake for amateur photographers to hold their camera directly up to their subject, point it at the subject head-on, center the subject in the frame, and snap a photo. The result is always a generic-looking image, even if it's well lit and in perfect focus. Instead, as you look at the viewfinder screen to compose or frame your image, utilize the Rule of Thirds. This is a shooting strategy used by professional photographers, but it's very easy to take advantage of, and the results are impressive.

Take advantage of the Grid feature within the Camera app or imagine a tic-tac-toe grid being superimposed on your camera's viewfinder. The center box in the tic-tac-toe grid corresponds to the center of the image you're about to shoot as you look at the viewfinder screen. Instead of framing your subject in this center box, reframe the image so your subject is positioned along one of the horizontal or vertical lines of the grid, or so the main focal point of the image is positioned at one of the grid's four intersection points.

Using the Rule of Thirds when framing your images takes a bit of practice, but if you use this shooting technique consistently and correctly, you'll discover the quality of your images will vastly improve. Of course, you also want to take into account lighting, as well as what's in the foreground, background, and to the sides of your main subject. And be sure to tap your creativity when choosing your shooting angle or perspective for each shot.

> TIP   When you're shooting a subject in motion, capture the subject moving into the frame, as opposed to moving out of it, while also taking into account the Rule of Thirds.

USING THE PHOTOS APP TO VIEW, EDIT, ENHANCE, PRINT, AND SHARE PHOTOS AND VIDEOS

Launch the Photos app from your iOS device's Home screen. First and foremost, use the Photos app to view images stored on your iOS device.

> WHAT'S NEW   When viewing images in the Photos app, you can now auto-sort them based on when or where they were shot using the Collections, Moments, and Years options.
>
> Years displays thumbnails of all images shot within a particular year and includes details about where those images were shot. Collections breaks up images within a Years grouping and displays them based on when and where they were shot. Moments allow you to display thumbnails of images within a Collection that represent one location or date.
>
> As you're viewing thumbnails, tap on one of them to view a single image. Or, at the bottom of the screen, tap on Photos, Shared, or Albums to view a different set of images stored on your mobile device.

To exit out of a Moments, Collections, and Years thumbnail view, use the options displayed near the top-left corner of the screen. As you're viewing thumbnails grouped together when using one of these views, tap on the Select option that's displayed near the top-right corner of the screen to choose one or more thumbnails. Once selected, tap the Share icon to manage those images or tap the Trash icon to delete them.

Each group of photos that are shot at the same place and in the same time frame are automatically grouped together into an event. As you're viewing these events, tap on the Share button associated with it to quickly share all images in that event or select and share specific images from it via email, Message, or iCloud.

VIEWING AN IMAGE IN FULL-SCREEN MODE

When viewing thumbnails of your images, tap on any single image thumbnail to view a full-screen version of it. As you're then viewing an image, tap on the Edit option to make the various command icons for editing and sharing the image appear on the screen (as shown in Figure 9.5).

FIGURE 9.5

When viewing an image in full-screen mode, tap anywhere on that image to reveal the command icons you'll use to ultimately edit, enhance, and share that image.

To exit the single-image view and return to the multi-image thumbnail view, tap anywhere on the screen to make the command icons appear, and then tap on the left-pointing arrow-shaped icon that's displayed in the upper-left corner of the screen.

As you're viewing a single image in full-screen mode, along the bottom of the screen is a filmstrip depiction of all images stored in the current album, or all images stored on your iOS device if you were previously in Photos viewing mode. The Edit command is displayed in the upper-right corner of the screen, the Share command icon is displayed in the lower-left corner of the screen, and the Trash icon is displayed near the lower-right corner of the screen (as shown in Figure 9.6).

Edit icon

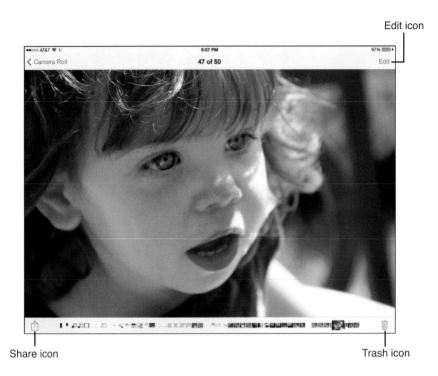

Share icon   Trash icon

FIGURE 9.6
The Edit, Share, and Trash icons are displayed when viewing a single image on your iPhone or iPad's screen.

EDITING PHOTOS AND VIDEOS

After selecting a single image to view in full-screen mode, tap on the Edit button to access the Edit commands for photos.

> TIP When you tap on the thumbnail for a video clip, you have the option to play that clip in the Photos app or you can tap anywhere on the screen (except for the Play icon in the center of the screen) to access the video trimming (editing) feature, as well as the Share icon and the Trash icon (used to delete the video clip from your iOS device).

> TIP To trim a video clip, look at the filmstrip display of the clip located at the top of the screen and move the left or right editing tabs accordingly to define the portion of the clip you want to edit. The box around the filmstrip display turns

yellow, and the Trim command icon appears on the right side of the screen. Before tapping on Trim, tap on the Play icon to preview your newly edited video clip. If it's okay, tap on the Trim icon to save your changes. Two additional command icons appear, labeled Trim Original and Save As New Clip. Trim Original alters the original video clip and replaces the file, whereas the Save As New Clip option creates a separate file and keeps a copy of the original clip.

COMMANDS FOR EDITING PHOTOS

When you tap on the Edit command icon while viewing a single image in full-screen mode, the following command icons are displayed along the bottom of the screen (refer to Figure 9.5).

These icons provide the tools for quickly editing and enhancing your image. They include:

- **Rotate**—Tap on this icon once to rotate the image counterclockwise by 90 degrees. You can tap the Rotate icon up to three times before the image returns to its original orientation.

- **Enhance**—Tap on the Auto-Enhance feature to instantly sharpen the photo and make the colors in it more vibrant. You should notice a dramatic improvement in the visual quality, lighting, detail, and sharpness of your image. Once you tap the Auto-Enhance feature, it works automatically. If you don't like the enhancement, tap the option again to remove it.

- **Filters**—Add one of the new special effect filters available to you after an image has been shot. These filters include Mono, Tonal, Noir, Fade, Chrome, Process, Transfer, and Instant. Each filter gets applied to an entire image and dramatically alters its appearance. After selecting the desired filter, tap Apply to use it.

- **Red-Eye**—If any human subject in your photo is exhibiting signs of red-eye as a result of your using a flash, tap on the Red-Eye icon to digitally remove this unwanted discoloration in your subject's pupils.

- **Crop**—Tap on this icon to crop the image and reposition your subject in the frame. If you forgot to incorporate the Rule of Thirds while shooting a photo, you can sometimes compensate by cropping a photo. You also can cut away unwanted background or zoom in on your subject, based on how you crop it. When the crop grid appears, position your finger in any corner or side of the grid to determine how to crop the image. When you're done, tap on the Crop icon to confirm your changes.

> TIP As you're cropping an image, tap on the Aspect Ratio option (displayed near the bottom-center of the screen) to select an image size, such as Original, Square, 3" x 2", 3" x 5", 4" x 3", 4" x 6", 5" x 7", 8" x 10", or 16" x 9". Unless you need the image in a specific size, choose the Original option.
>
> If you're cropping an image by moving around the cropping grid using your finger, if you first tap on the Aspect Radio icon, this forces the basic dimensions of your image to stay intact. This allows you to make perfectly sized prints later without throwing off the image dimensions.

- **Undo**—If you tap Undo (when applicable), the last edit you made to the image is undone but any other edits remain intact.
- **Save**—After you've used the various editing commands to edit or enhance your image, tap on the Save command to save your changes.
- **Cancel**—Tap on this icon to exit the photo-editing mode of the Photos app without making any changes to the photo you're viewing.
- **Revert To Original**—After making edits or enhancements to an image, if you don't like the results while still in editing mode, tap on the Revert To Original option to return the image to its original appearance.

PRINTING PHOTOS

iOS 7 is fully compatible with Apple's AirPrint feature, so if you have a photo printer set up to work wirelessly with your iOS device, you can create photo prints from your digital images using the Print command in the Photos app. Follow these steps to print an image:

1. Launch the Photos app from the Home screen.
2. From the main View Images screen, tap on any thumbnail to view an image in full-screen mode. You might need to open an album first by tapping on the Album's thumbnail, if you have the Albums viewing option selected.
3. Tap on the full-screen version of the image to make the various command icons appear.
4. Tap on the Share icon.
5. From the Share menu, select the Print option.

6. When the Printer Options submenu appears, select your printer, determine how many copies of the print you'd like to create, and then tap on the Print icon.

> **NOTE** To print wirelessly from your iOS device using the AirPrint feature, you must have a compatible printer. To learn more about AirPrint, and to configure your printer for wireless printing from your iPad, visit http://support.apple.com/kb/HT4356.

> **TIP** Many one-hour photo processing labs within pharmacies and stores like Wal-Mart or Target allow you to email photos directly from your iPad to their lab and then pick up prints that same day, often within an hour.
>
> There are also photo lab services that have special apps which allow you to select photos stored on your iOS mobile device, upload them to a lab, and then have prints mailed to you within a few days. Walgreens for iPad, RitzPix, FreePrints, SnapFish, and Kodak Kiosk Connection are among the apps that allow you to order prints directly from your iPad.
>
> When emailing a photo to a lab (or someone who will be printing them on their home photo printer), to achieve the best possible prints, send the images in Full Size mode from your iOS device. To do this, after filling in the Email fields tap on the Images option that's displayed to the right of the From field and then, when the Image Size options appear, tap on the Actual Size tab.

SHARING PHOTOS AND VIDEOS

The iOS 7 version of the Photos app offers an expanded Share menu (shown in Figure 9.7). Once you have selected one or more images, tap the Share icon to access the Share menu.

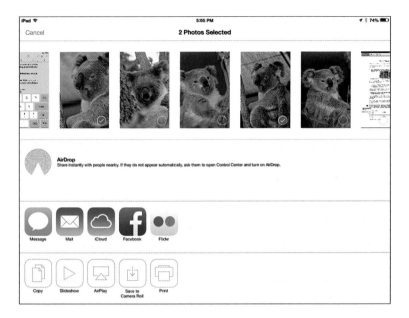

FIGURE 9.7

The Share menu within the iOS 7 version of the Photos app has been expanded.

SENDING IMAGES WIRELESSLY VIA AIRDROP

If you're within close proximity of another iPhone, iPad, or iPod touch user, and you both have the AirDrop featured turned on, you can wirelessly send people images from within the Photos app using the AirDrop for iOS feature. This feature only becomes active when others nearby can receive an AirDrop transmission.

NOTE   Currently, iOS 7's AirDrop feature only works with the more recent iPad and iPhone models, and not with the AirDrop feature built in to the Mac's operating system.

When someone sends you a digital photo via AirDrop, a pop-up window will display on your tablet's screen (shown in Figure 9.8). Tap on the Accept button to receive the photo and store it within the Camera app's Camera Roll folder.

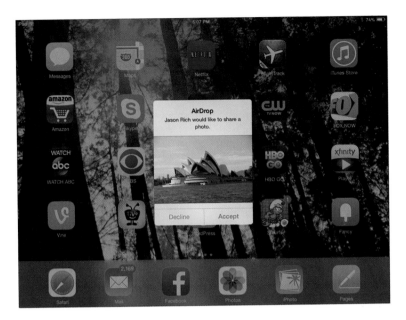

FIGURE 9.8

When someone sends you a photo, for example via AirDrop, a pop-up window will appear on your device's screen giving you the option to accept or decline it.

SENDING IMAGES VIA TEXT/INSTANT MESSAGE

Tap this option to send images using the Message app via instant message. When the New Message window appears, fill in the To field with the recipient's cell phone number or iMessage account username. Tap the plus-sign icon to send the same message to multiple recipients.

Add a text message to the photo(s) that is attached to the message. To add more images to the outgoing message, tap on the Camera icon. When you're ready, tap the Send option to send the photos and message.

EMAILING FIVE IMAGES AT A TIME

When looking at thumbnails for images within an Album, tap on the Edit button to select between one and five images and then tap on the Share icon.

Select the Mail option and fill in the To field when prompted. If you want, edit the Subject field and/or add text to the body of the email, and then tap the Send button.

When viewing a single image, tap on the Share button; select Mail; fill in the
To field; edit the Subject; and, if you want, add text to the body of the message
(shown in Figure 9.9); then tap the Send button.

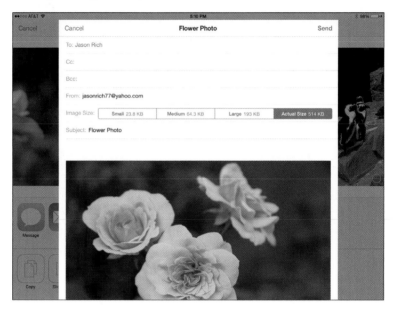

FIGURE 9.9
You can send an email with one to five photos attached to it from within the Photos app.

UPLOADING IMAGES TO AN iCLOUD SHARED PHOTO STREAM

See the section called "Create and Manage a Shared Photo Stream via iCloud,"
found later in this chapter.

TWEETING A PHOTO TO YOUR TWITTER FOLLOWERS

To tweet a photo, after tapping the Share icon while viewing a single photo in full-
screen mode, select the Twitter option. Compose your tweet message (which will
already have the selected image attached), and then tap the Send icon.

It's also possible to tweet photos from the official Twitter app or from a third-party
Twitter-related app, such as Twitterific (available from the App Store).

PUBLISHING PHOTOS ON FACEBOOK

To publish one or more photos to Facebook with an optional text-based message, tap the Facebook button within the Share menu. From the Facebook window (shown in Figure 9.10), tap on Album option to choose to which existing Facebook Photos Album you want to publish the image(s).

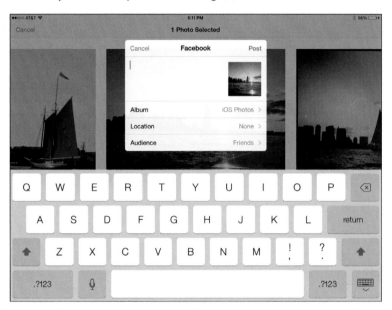

FIGURE 9.10

From the Photos app, you can send an image directly to your Facebook page as part of a Status Update.

Next, tap the Location option to publish the location the image was shot on Facebook in conjunction with the photo. Tap on the Audience option to decide who will be able to view the image(s) on Facebook. Your options include Public, Friends, Friends Except Acquaintances, Only Me, Close Friends, or people within a specific Facebook group you've created.

To the left of the photo thumbnail, use the virtual keyboard to enter a caption for the image(s) you're about to upload and then tap the Post option (displayed near the top-right corner of the Facebook window) to publish the photos online from the Photos app.

> **TIP** An alternative to using the Photos app to publish photos to Facebook is to use the official Facebook app. This gives you additional options, such as the ability to tag photos with the names of the people who appear within them.

UPLOADING IMAGES TO FLICKR

Flickr is an online-based photo-sharing service and photo lab operated by Yahoo!. To upload selected images to your existing Flickr account, select the images from within the Photos app, tap the Share icon, and then tap the Flickr option. You're then able to choose which Album you want to send the images to or create a new online-based Album for your images.

The first time you use this feature, you need to access Settings when prompted and enter your Flickr username and password and then tap Sign In to access the service. It's also possible to use the official Flickr app to upload and manage your online-based Flickr account from your iPhone or iPad.

COPYING AN IMAGE TO ANOTHER APP

From within the Photos app, you can store a photo in your iOS device's virtual clipboard and then paste that photo into another compatible app. To copy a photo into your device's virtual clipboard, follow these steps:

1. Tap on the Share icon.

2. Tap on the Copy option. The photo is stored in the virtual clipboard.

3. Launch a compatible app and hold your finger down on the screen to use the Paste option and paste your photo from the clipboard into the active app.

CREATING A SLIDESHOW

To create and display an animated slideshow featuring images stored within your iOS mobile device that you select, select a group of images, tap the Share icon, and choose the Slideshow option. From the Slideshow Options screen, choose to display the image on the or iPad or via Apple TV. Also, select your Transition effect from the menu and decide whether or not you want music to accompany the presentation. By turning on the virtual switch associated with Play Music, you're able to choose music that's stored within the Music app of your iOS mobile device. To begin the Slideshow, tap on the Start Slideshow option.

SHOWING IMAGE ON A TELEVISION VIA AIRPLAY

Instead of viewing an image in full-screen mode on your tablet, tap the AirPlay option, which is part of the Share menu, to wirelessly transmit the image to your HD television set or Mac screen. To use this feature with an HD TV, you need the optional Apple TV device. To use the feature with a Mac, be sure AirPlay on your Mac is turned on.

SAVING THE IMAGE TO YOUR CAMERA ROLL FOLDER

If you're viewing images stored within your Photo Stream or a Shared Photo Stream, tap on the Save To Camera Roll option (which only appears when it's available) to store the image within the Camera Roll folder of the Photos app.

ASSIGNING AN IMAGE TO A CONTACT

To link an image stored in the Photos app to a specific contact in the Contacts app, follow these steps:

1. Tap on the Share icon.

2. Tap on the Assign to Contact option.

3. An All Contacts window, displaying the names associated with all your contacts, is displayed. Scroll through the listing, or use the Search field to find the specific entry with which you want to associate the photo.

4. Tap on that person's or company's name from the All Contacts listing.

5. When the Move and Scale window opens, use your finger to move or scale the image. What you see in the circle is what is saved.

6. Tap on the Use option to save the photo and link it to the selected contact.

7. When you launch Contacts and access that person's entry, you see the photo you selected appear in that entry.

USING AN IMAGE AS WALLPAPER

As you're viewing a photo, it can be assigned to be the wallpaper image used on your Home screen or Lock screen by tapping on the Share icon and then choosing the Use As Wallpaper option. When the image is previewed on the screen, tap on the Set button. From the Set Lock Screen, Set Home Screen, or Set Both menu, choose where you want the selected image displayed.

PRINTING AN IMAGE WIRELESSLY

If you have an AirPrint-compatible printer that's linked to your iOS mobile device, from the Share menu, tap on the Print icon to wirelessly send the selected image(s) to the printer.

DELETING PHOTOS STORED ON YOUR iOS DEVICE

To delete one image at a time as you're viewing them in full-screen mode, simply tap on the Trash icon that's displayed near the bottom-right corner of the screen.

To select and delete multiple images at once, as you're looking at thumbnails of images, tap on the Select button. Tap on each thumbnail that represents an image you want to delete. A checkmark icon appears within each selected thumbnail. Tap on the Trash icon to delete the selected images.

WORKING WITH iCLOUD'S PHOTO STREAM IN THE PHOTOS APP

If you have your iPad set up to work with iCloud, the Photo Stream feature is turned on, and your tablet is connected to a Wi-Fi Internet connection, the Photo Stream tab is displayed along the top center of the main Photos screen.

The My Photo Stream feature automatically stores, syncs, and displays up to 1,000 of the most recently shot or imported digital photos.

> **TIP**   A Photo Stream can include up to 1,000 images and store them for up to 30 days online. By default, this is the most recent 1,000 you shoot or transfer to your Photo Stream. However, you can manually edit the collection of images that are part of your Photo Stream. Beyond the 1,000 images stored on iCloud (or after the 30 days), all your digital images are automatically backed up and stored on your primary computer's hard drive (or on a hard drive connected to your primary computer) if you have My Photo Stream set up to sync with iPhoto or Aperture running on your Mac or if you enable Photo Stream on Windows.

When viewing My Photo Stream on your iPad from within the Photos app, thumbnails representing the images are displayed. To view these images as a slideshow, tap the Slideshow icon.

To share, copy, or delete any of the Photo Stream images, tap the Edit button. A new Share button, along with a Delete button, appears near the upper-left corner of the screen. Tap one or more image thumbnails to select them, tap on the Share button, and then choose which Share command you'd like to utilize from the pop-up menu that appears. Depending on how your iPad is set up, your options include Mail, Message, Facebook, Print, Copy, and Save to Camera Roll.

NOTE When you delete photos from your Photo Stream, not only are the images deleted from your iPad, they also are erased from the Photo Stream stored on iCloud and on the Photo Stream you can view from your primary computer and/or iPhone that's linked to the same iCloud account.

Unlike other images stored in albums, photos viewable from your Photo Stream are not permanently stored on your iPad. To move one or more images from the Photo Stream to an album, tap the Edit button, tap the thumbnails for the images you want to store on your tablet, and then tap the Save icon displayed near the upper-right corner of the screen.

TIP To utilize iCloud's Photo Stream feature, launch Settings, tap the Photos & Camera option, and then turn on the My Photo Stream option. To utilize this feature and be able to upload and download photos to and from your iOS devices, a Wi-Fi Internet connection is required.

NOTE If you're a Windows PC user, you can install the iCloud Control Panel on your computer and use it to transfer photos to and from your Photo Stream. To download this free Windows software from Apple's website, visit http://support.apple.com/kb/DL1455.

CREATING AND MANAGING A SHARED PHOTO STREAM

The My Photo Stream feature is a tool designed to make it easy for you to sync your latest digital photos between your own computer(s), Apple TV device, and iOS mobile devices that are linked to the same Apple ID/iCloud account.

The iCloud Shared Photo Stream feature, however, is a tool that allows you to share groups of photos with other people via the Internet (and iCloud). Once you have the Shared Photo Stream feature turned on, as well as an active iCloud account, select the images you want to share from the Photos app.

Next, tap on the Share icon and select the iCloud option. From the iCloud window, add a Comment to the image(s) you're about to upload and then tap on the Stream option to choose the Shared Photo Stream folder you want to add the selected images to.

To create a new Shared Photo Stream folder, tap on the Stream option and then tap on the New Shared Stream option. You're prompted to enter a Stream Name, which is the title for the Shared Photo Stream. Tap the Next option. You're then prompted to enter the email addresses (or names) of the people you want to share the photo stream with (shown in Figure 9.11).

FIGURE 9.11

As you're creating a Shared Photo Stream, decide who can see it and send an email people that contains a special URL to access the photos to those people.

If the invitees already have entries within your Contacts database, type their names. Otherwise, enter their email addresses into the To field. Tap the Next option to continue.

Tap the Post option to upload the images to an iCloud Photo Stream so that they can be viewed by the people you've selected.

If the recipients are iPhoto '11 (Mac) users, they can view your images or download them into their iPhoto '11 software. If they're iOS mobile device users, they can use the Photos or optional iPhotos app. Otherwise, they're only able to view the photos online by visiting the unique URL assigned to your Shared Photo Stream.

> **TIP** For Windows-based users to be able to view your Shared Photo Stream(s), they need to use their web browser to view each Shared Photo Stream as an online gallery. For this to work, be sure to turn on the Public Website option when creating the Shared Photo Stream, or after the fact by launching the Photos app, tapping on the Shared option, tapping on a Shared Photo Stream listing, and then tapping on the People tab. Turn on the virtual switch associated with Public Website.

You can create and edit as many Shared Photo Streams as you desire and make each available to different people, if you choose to. A Shared Photo Stream can also have any number of pages within it, so it's great for sharing collections of images.

Delete a Shared Photo Stream at anytime by tapping on the Photo Stream button within the Photos app, opening a Shared Photo Stream, tapping the Edit button, and then selecting which photos you want to delete. Tap the Delete button to continue. From the Select Photos screen, however, you can also add photos to an existing Shared Photo Stream.

MANAGING WHO HAS ACCESS TO YOUR SHARED PHOTO STREAMS

After a Shared Photo Stream is created, to edit or add to the list of invitees who can view it, launch Photos and tap on the Shared icon (near the bottom-center of the screen). From the Shared Streams menu, tap on one of the listed Shared Photo Stream listings. Thumbnails for the images within that Shared Photo Stream are displayed. Near the bottom of the thumbnail screen, tap on the People tab.

To remove access for people already invited to view the Shared Photo Stream, tap on their names. To the right of their names, the Invited status is displayed. From the Info screen for that person, tap on the Remove Subscriber option. They will no longer be able to view your Shared Photo Stream.

To add people (subscribers) who can view an already existing Shared Photo Stream you've created, after tapping on the People tab, tap on the Invite People option, and then add the names (or email addresses) to the To field of the Invite People screen.

UPGRADING TO APPLE'S iPHOTO APP

If you want photo organization, editing, viewing, and sharing options that are beyond what the free Photos app is capable of, visit the App Store and download a copy of Apple's iPhoto app.

Not only does the iOS version of iPhoto offer similar functionality to iPhoto '11 for the Mac, it includes a handful of enhanced features, such as Journals and Smart Browsing, plus it makes syncing or transferring images between iOS devices, Macs, and iCloud's Photo Stream a straightforward process. Journals offers a new way to sort and view images in an interactive collage-like format, while Smart Browsing offers additional options for organizing and finding your images.

UTILIZING POWERFUL PHOTO-EDITING CAPABILITIES WITH THIRD-PARTY PHOTOGRAPHY APPS

If you want even more powerful photo-editing tools available to you from your iPad, check out one or more of the third-party photography apps available from the App Store.

When you launch the App Store from your iPad, tap on the More command tab located along the top of the screen, and then choose the Photo & Video category. You'll discover hundreds of third-party photography apps that add or supplement functionality that's built in to the Camera, Photos, and iPhoto apps.

In addition to the photography apps, you can find specialized apps that make it easy to manage specific types of online social networking accounts, through which you can publish and share your digital photos and video clips. For example, official apps for Instagram, Google+, YouTube, and Vine, as well as Flickr, SmugMug, and many other online-based photo sharing services, are available from the App Store. Cloud-based file sharing services, like Dropbox, when used in conjunction with their proprietary apps, can also be used to store and share digital images and albums.

IN THIS CHAPTER

- Accessing the App Store from your iPad
- Discovering why some apps are free and some are not
- Finding and downloading the best apps for you

10

FINDING AND INSTALLING APPS FROM THE APP STORE

Yes, the iPad is a sleek piece of hardware with lots of capabilities, but it's ultimately the iOS 7 (or later) operating system and the collection of apps on your tablet that make it capable of doing so much.

In the past two years or so, tremendous strides have been made in terms of the capabilities of third-party apps, particularly those used by business professionals. Thanks to optional apps, the iPad can be used for many different work-related tasks, such as word processing, spreadsheet management, time management/scheduling, credit card processing, online banking, database management, online social networking, brainstorming, videoconferencing, project/task management, managing emails, and much more.

From the App Store, you can find, download, and install optional apps for your iPad that greatly expand its capabilities. However, with literally hundreds of thousands of third-party apps available, the task of finding the right app(s) to meet your

personal or professional needs can be daunting. For every task the iPad can perform using an app, there are most likely at least a handful of app choices, from different developers, that offer very similar functionality.

The pricing for apps varies greatly. Plus, a growing number of apps allow for or require in-app purchases or a paid subscription to fully utilize them.

> **NOTE** After you purchase an app from the App Store, all future updates to that app are free. However, some developers have begun renaming apps when a major revision is done, requiring users to repurchase the app.

APPLE'S APP STORE: ONE-STOP SHOPPING FOR iPAD APPS

If you want to add apps to your iPad, the only way to do this is to acquire them from Apple's App Store. There are two ways to access the App Store to find, purchase, download, and install apps onto your tablet.

First, you can use the App Store app, which comes preinstalled on your iPad. To use it, your tablet must have access to the Internet.

> **NOTE** Some apps that have a large file associated with them cannot be downloaded and installed using the App Store app if you're connected to the Internet via a cellular data connection. Either a Wi-Fi connection is necessary or you'll need to download certain apps using the iTunes software on your primary computer (to access the App Store) and then transfer those apps to your tablet using the iTunes sync process. The majority of apps, however, can be downloaded and installed directly onto your iPad using a 3G, 4G (LTE), or Wi-Fi connection via the App Store app.

The second option for finding, purchasing, downloading, and installing apps is to access the App Store through the iTunes software on your primary computer and then transfer the acquired apps to your tablet using the iTunes sync process or iCloud.

Regardless of how you visit the App Store, you first need to set up an Apple ID account and have a major credit card or debit card linked to the account to make purchases.

> **TIP** If you don't have a major credit card or debit card that you want to link with your Apple ID account so you can purchase apps from the App Store, it's possible to purchase prepaid iTunes gift cards from Apple or most places that sell prepaid gift cards, such as convenience stores, supermarkets, and pharmacies.
>
> iTunes gift cards can be used to make app purchases or in-app purchases, plus buy content (music, TV shows, movies, audiobooks, etc.), from the iTunes Store. Prepaid iTunes gift cards are available in many different denominations.

UNDERSTANDING THE APP STORE

When you open the App Store app (shown in Figure 10.1), a handful of command icons and tabs are displayed along the top and bottom of the screen that are used to navigate your way around the online-based store.

App Store search field

App category tabs   Wish List icon

App Store command icons

FIGURE 10.1

The main App Store screen.

If you already know the name of the app you want to find, tap the Search field, which is located in the upper-right corner of the App Store app's screen. Using the virtual keyboard, enter the name of the app. Tap the Search key on the virtual keyboard to begin the search.

> **TIP** You also can perform a search based on a keyword or phrase that describes an app or app category, such as word processing, to-do lists, time management, credit card processing, or photo editing.

When you perform a search in the App Store, the search results are displayed using app preview boxes. Each preview box contains the name of the app, the name of its developer, its average star-based rating, the number of ratings it has received (the number in parentheses), a logo or icon for the app, and one sample screen shot from the app (shown in Figure 10.2).

FIGURE 10.2

After performing a search within the App Store, related search results are displayed within individual app preview boxes.

As you're looking at an app's preview box, tap on the app's title or logo to view a detailed description for the app, or tap on the Price icon to acquire and download the app immediately. When you access the App Store from your iPad (using the App Store app), by default, iPad-specific and hybrid apps are listed. When you tap on the iPad Only pull-down menu that's displayed near the top center of the screen, it's possible to select the iPhone Only option in order to see previews of iPhone apps (that also run on the iPad). These apps, however, are not formatted for the iPad's larger screen.

TIP In each app description screen, its price is listed in a price button. If you notice a plus sign icon displayed in the upper-left corner of the price button, this indicates that the app you're looking at is designed for both the iPad and iPhone and adapts accordingly, based on the device it's being used on.

In general, when choosing apps for your iPad, look for iPad-specific apps first and then look for hybrid apps that are designed for both iPad and iPhone. Apps that are iPhone-specific run fine on an iPad, but the app's graphics and user interface are formatted for the iPhone's smaller screen.

NOTE Within an app's Price button, if you see a price listed that is the one-time purchase price for the app. If the word Free appears within the box, the app is free of charge to download, but it may still have in-app purchases associated with it. If you see the word Open within the Price button, this means the app is already installed on your tablet. If the word Install appears within the Price box, this means you have previously purchased the app and it's stored within your online-based iCloud account, but it is not currently installed on your tablet. In this case, tap Install to download and (re)install the app, for free.

Displayed along the bottom of the main App Store screen are five command icons: Featured, Top Charts, Near Me, Purchased, and Updates. If you don't know the exact name of an app you're looking for, some of these icons can help you browse the App Store and discover iOS mobile device apps that might be of interest to you.

DISCOVERING FEATURED APPS

Tap the Featured icon to see a listing of what Apple considers to be new or note-worthy apps or "Hot Apps." The apps displayed on this screen are divided into several categories, including New and Noteworthy and What's Hot. Also on this screen are ever changing "featured" categories that Apple creates. When back-to-school season was upon us in August, for example, the theme for a "featured" category was Back To School.

Under the New and Noteworthy heading within the Featured screen, a handful of app listings are displayed. Use a horizontal swipe motion with your finger to scroll through all of the listings in this section. You can also tap the See All command that's displayed next to the New and Noteworthy heading to see more of the relevant listings presented on one screen.

> **TIP** As you're looking at the Featured page in the App Store, tap on one of the app category tabs that are displayed along the top center of the screen to narrow down your search. Be sure to tap on the More tab to view a comprehensive listing of app categories, including Finance, Lifestyle, News, Productivity, Reference, Travel, and Utilities.

CATEGORIES: FINDING APPS BY TOPIC OR GENRE

As you're viewing the main Featured screen in the App Store, tap on one of the Categories tabs displayed along the top of the App Store screen to access all the apps that fall into any one of the App Store's more than 20 main categories. When you tap the More icon, a menu of all app categories is shown (see Figure 10.3). Tap the category that most interests you to browse through listings of apps in that category.

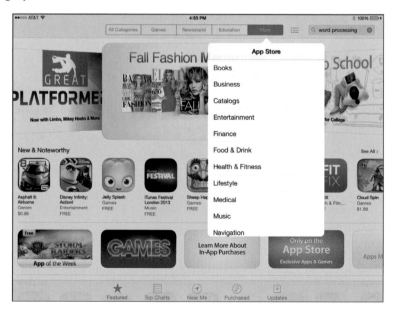

FIGURE 10.3

Browse apps in the App Store that fit into a specific category by first selecting a category that's of interest.

When you select a category, the apps for that category are displayed under several different headings. Once again, tap on the See All option displayed next to each heading to see more of the related app listings. As you're looking at the app listings, you can learn more about a particular app by tapping on its graphic icon or title. Then, you can purchase, download, and install the app by tapping its price button. (For free apps, when you tap the Free button, the app automatically downloads and installs.)

TOP CHARTS: SEEING WHAT APPS OTHER iPAD USERS ARE USING

Tap the Top Charts icon near the bottom of the App Store app's screen to access listings of the most popular Paid, Free, and Top Grossing iPad apps (shown in Figure 10.4). This is a general listing of all currently popular apps, so it constantly changes.

FIGURE 10.4

The Top Charts screen shows three separate listings: Paid, Free, and Top Grossing apps. Tap on the Categories option (in the upper-left corner of the screen) to narrow down the Charts list to select a specific app category.

> **TIP** While looking at the Top Charts screen, tap on the Categories option (found in the top-left corner of the screen) and select a specific app category. The Top Charts now displays only popular apps from the selected category, such as Business or Finance.

NOTE Use your finger to swipe several times (in an upward direction) along each of the three Charts listings to view the entire list. Each listing begins with the number-one most popular app and then displays the next 299 apps in order based on their sales or popularity. Keep in mind that these lists are comprised of apps from all categories.

NEAR ME: DISCOVERING WHAT APPS PEOPLE LOCATED IN YOUR GEOGRAPHIC AREA ARE USING

Thanks to the Location Services feature built in to iOS 7, your tablet always knows where you are. By tapping on the Near Me feature, it's easy to discover what apps iPad and iPhone users who are in close geographic proximity to you are shopping for. This feature is particularly useful for finding apps from local news and media outlets when you're traveling.

TIP As you browse through various apps, if you find one that's of interest, instead of purchasing it, it's possible to add it to your Wish List. To do this, tap on the Share icon that's displayed on the app's Description screen and then select the Add To Wish List option (shown in Figure 10.5).

From the Share menu, it's also possible to purchase a non-free app and send it to someone else as a gift. To do this, tap on the Gift icon. To share details about the app with others, tap the Messages, Mail, Twitter, or Facebook icon.

To view your Wish List, tap on the Wish List icon that's displayed to the immediate left of the Search field when accessing the main App Store screen (refer to Figure 10.1).

NOTE To manage your App Store account or redeem iTunes Gift Cards, when you scroll to the very bottom of the main Featured screen of the App Store (as well as several other subsection pages in the App Store), you see three buttons: Account [Your Apple ID Username], Redeem, and Send Gift.

Tap the Account icon to manage your Apple ID account and update your credit card information, if necessary. Tap the Redeem icon to redeem a prepaid iTunes Gift Card. Tap on the Send Gift option to send someone else a prepaid iTunes Gift Card via email.

FIGURE 10.5

Access the Share menu from any app's Description screen to add it to your Wish List or send it to someone else as a gift.

ACCESSING YOUR PURCHASED APPS

When you tap the Purchased icon displayed near the bottom of the App Store screen, a complete listing of all apps you've purchased to date using your Apple ID is displayed. Near the top of this screen are two command tabs. Tap on All to see a listing that includes all apps you've previously acquired (including free apps). Tap on the Not On This iPad tab to view only apps you've previously acquired that are not currently stored on your tablet.

Any of the listed apps, which are now stored online within your iCloud account, can be downloaded and installed onto your tablet, including your previous iPhone or iPod touch app purchases. To do this, simply tap the Install button (which looks like a cloud-shaped icon with a downward-pointing arrow) that's displayed with an app's listing.

> **TIP**   If you also own and use an iPhone or iPod touch that's linked to the same iCloud account, anytime you purchase an iPad/iPhone hybrid app, you can install it on any or all of your iOS devices without having to purchase the same app multiple times.

HOW TO ACQUIRE AN APP FROM THE APP STORE

To purchase an app (or download and install a free app), tap on the Price icon that's associated with its listing or that's displayed within its description screen. Upon doing this, the price button changes from blue and white to green and white and says Buy. If it's a free app, this new button is labeled Install. Tap the Buy or Install button to confirm your purchase and/or download and install decision.

An Apple ID Password window displays on the screen next. Your Apple ID username is already displayed, but you must manually enter your Apple ID password. Type your Apple ID password, and then tap the OK button. The app automatically downloads and installs itself on your iPad. This process can take between 15 seconds and several minutes. When the app is installed, the app icon for the new app appears on your tablet's Home screen. Within the App Store, the Price icon associated with the app now says Open.

CAUTION Some free apps are, in fact, free. However, they might ultimately require you to pay for a content subscription or make in-app purchases to fully utilize the app. When looking at an app's description screen, if in-app purchases are possible (or required), this will be mentioned when you tap on the Top In-App Purchases option, which displays only if applicable.

LEARNING ABOUT AN APP BEFORE MAKING A PURCHASE

Before committing to a purchase, as you're looking at an app's listing or preview box from within the App Store, tap its title or graphic icon to reveal a detailed description window for that app.

An app's description page (like the one shown in Figure 10.6) displays the app's title, logo, and average star-based rating (along with the number of ratings it has received) near the top of the screen, along with a detailed description of the app when you tap on the Details tab and scroll downward. Several sample screen shots from the app are also displayed on the main description page.

TIP When viewing an app's description page, tap on the Details tab to view a detailed description of the app and see sample screen shots from it. Tap on the Reviews tab to see its star-based ratings chart and read detailed reviews of the app that were written by your fellow iPad users. Tap on the Related tab to view a listing of apps offered by the same developer and/or that are somehow related to the app you're viewing.

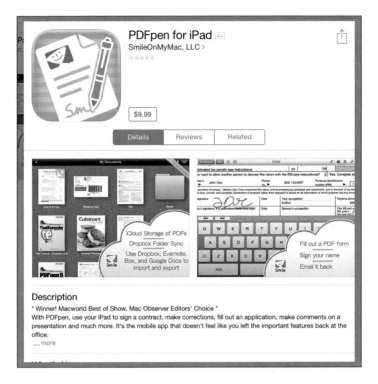

FIGURE 10.6

From an app's description page, you can learn all about a specific app. This information can help you decide whether it's of interest to you or relevant to your needs.

When the Details tab is selected, displayed below the command tabs are sample screen shots from the app. Using your finger, swipe along the screen shots in a right-to-left motion to view all of the images. Tap on an image to view it in full-screen mode. Then, tap on the Done button to exit out of full-screen mode and return to the description page.

> **TIP** Take a look at an app's sample screen shots to get a firsthand look at the graphics quality and user interface of the app. This is one way to determine the overall quality of the app, based on its visual layout and appeal. When you visit an app developer's website, however, you can sometimes watch demo videos of the app in use.

Below the screen shots is a detailed, text-based description of the app. It was written and submitted to Apple by the app's developer or publisher. To read the entire description for an app, you might have to tap on the More option associated with it.

As you scroll down on an app's description page, the What's New heading displays information about the newest features added to the app. Periodically, apps get updated with new versions. The What's New section informs you about new features, as well as any problems with the app that have recently been fixed.

After the What's New section, as you again scroll downward, the Information section for the app (shown in Figure 10.7) displays the app's developer, category, the date it was last updated, the current version number, the file size, the app's rating, and the system requirements for the app.

The Information section of an app's Description screen

FIGURE 10.7

The Information section of an app's description page provides additional details about the app, including its file size and system requirements.

If in-app purchases are available (or required), you'll discover this by tapping on the Show In-App Purchases option that's displayed in conjunction with the In-App Purchases section within an app's Description page (if applicable). What in-app purchases are available, as well as their prices and descriptions, are listed.

> **TIP** Tap on the Developer Website option near the bottom of an app's description page to launch Safari and visit the app developer's own website or the promotional website created by the app developer for the particular app you're looking at.
>
> To learn about an app's update history, tap on the Version History option.

When you tap on the Reviews tab that's part of every app's description page, you'll have the option to "Like" the app on Facebook, plus view a star-based ratings chart, and be able to read text-based reviews of the app written by people who have already purchased and used it.

The App Store Ratings are based on a five-star system. Anyone who purchases or downloads an app has the option to rate it. A top rating is five stars. From the Ratings Summary chart (shown in Figure 10.8), you can see how many people have rated an app; discover the app's average rating; and then see a breakdown of how many one-star, two-star, three-star, four-star, and five-star ratings the app has received.

Obviously, an app with a large number of five-star ratings is probably excellent, and an app that consistently earns three stars or less is probably not so great or is loaded with bugs.

Keep scrolling down to read full reviews that your fellow iPad users have written about that app. These reviews often describe the best features of the app and/or its worst problems.

While reviewing an app's description page, if you want to be reminded of the app's existence (without downloading it), or you want to tell a friend about the app, tap the Share icon that's displayed near the upper-right corner of the description page and then tap on one of the icons that are displayed in the Share pop-up window (such as Mail, Message, Twitter, Facebook, or Copy Link) that appears.

To exit an app's description page and continue browsing the App Store, tap anywhere outside the description window that contains the app information (such as the left or right margin of the screen) or tap on one of the command icons that's displayed near the top or bottom of the screen.

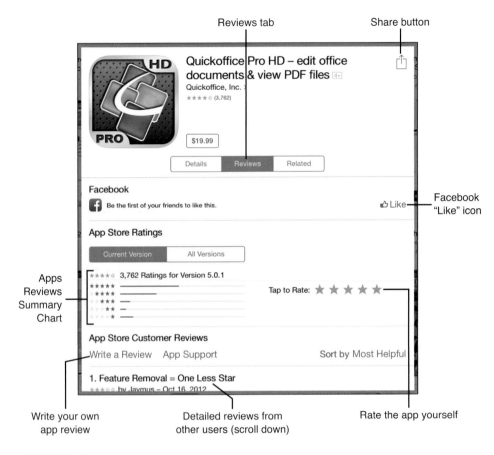

Reviews tab

Share button

Facebook "Like" icon

Apps Reviews Summary Chart

Write your own app review

Detailed reviews from other users (scroll down)

Rate the app yourself

FIGURE 10.8

Every app description contains an average rating and a rating summary chart. Use it to quickly see what other iPad users think about the app you're currently looking at.

VISITING THE APP STORE FROM iTUNES ON YOUR COMPUTER

The second method of finding, purchasing, downloading, installing, and updating apps is to use the latest version of the iTunes software on your primary computer to access the iTunes Store. Click the iTunes Store option displayed on the left side of the screen, under the Store heading. Your computer must be connected to the Internet to access the iTunes Store.

When the main iTunes Store launches within iTunes, click the App Store tab displayed near the top of the screen. You see a screen that's similar to the Featured page of the App Store when you access it from your iPad using the App Store app.

HOW APP PRICING WORKS

Here's a summary of the different types of apps from a pricing standpoint.

FREE APPS

Free apps cost nothing to download and install on your tablet. Some programmers and developers release free apps out of pure kindness and to share their creations with the iPad-using public. These are fully functional apps.

There are also free apps that serve as demo versions of paid apps. These are scaled-down versions of apps, or they have some type of limitation. For example, in some cases, basic features or functions of the app are locked in the free version but are later made available if you upgrade to the paid, premium, or "pro" version of the app.

A third category of free apps is fully functional apps that display ads as part of their content. In exchange for using the app, you must view ads, which offer the option to click on offers from within the app to learn more about the product or service being advertised.

A fourth category of free apps serves as a shell for premium (paid) content that must be loaded into the app to make it fully functional.

A fifth category of free apps relates to those offered by retailers and online merchants who offer a specialized shopping app used to access their own online store.

The final type of free app is fully functional, but it enables the user to make in-app purchases to add features or functionality to the app or to unlock premium content. The core app, without the extra content, is free.

PAID APPS

After you purchase an app, you own it and can use it as often as you like without incurring additional fees. You simply pay a fee for the app upfront, which is typically between $.99 and $9.99. All future upgrades of the app are free of charge. In some cases, paid apps also offer in-app purchase options to access premium content.

SUBSCRIPTION-BASED APPS

Apps based on subscriptions, such as monthly magazines, are typically free, but you pay a recurring subscription fee for content, which is automatically downloaded into the app. Many digital editions of newspapers, such as *The New York Times* and *The Wall Street Journal*, utilize a subscription app model, as do hundreds of different magazines.

IN-APP PURCHASES

The ability to make in-app purchases is a special function in some free and paid apps. The important thing to note is that, as you're actually using the app, you can purchase additional content or add new features and functionality to the app by making in-app purchases. The ability to make in-app purchases has become very popular and is being used by app developers in a variety of ways.

CAUTION The price you pay for an app does not translate directly to the quality or usefulness of that app. There are some free or very inexpensive apps that are extremely useful and packed with features that can really enhance your iPad experience. However, there are costly apps that are poorly designed, filled with bugs, don't live up to expectations, or don't offer the functionality promised in the app's Description page (which is content provided by the app's developer, not Apple).

The price of each app is set by the developer or programmer that created or is selling the app. Instead of using the price as a determining factor if you're evaluating several apps that appear to offer similar functionality, be sure to read the app's customer reviews carefully and pay attention to the star-based rating the app has received. The user reviews and ratings are a much better indicator of the app's quality and usefulness than the price of the app.

QUICK TIPS FOR FINDING APPS

As you explore the App Store, it's easy to become overwhelmed by the sheer number of apps that are available for your iPad. Spending time browsing the App Store introduces you to the many different types of apps that are available and provides you with insight about how you can utilize your tablet in your personal or professional life.

However, you can save a lot of time searching for apps if you already know the app's exact title, or if you know what type of app you're looking for. In this case, you can enter either the app's exact title or a keyword description of the app in the App Store's Search field to see a list of relevant matches.

If you're looking for vertical market apps with specialized functionality that caters to your industry or profession, enter that industry or profession (or keywords associated with it) in the Search field. For example, enter keywords such as medical imaging, radiology, plumbing, telemarketing, CRM, portfolio management, or sales.

As you're evaluating an app before downloading it, use these tips to help you determine whether it's worth installing onto your tablet:

- Figure out what type of features or functionality you want to add to your iPad.

- Using the Search field, find apps designed to handle the tasks you have in mind. Chances are that you can easily find a handful of apps created by different developers that are designed to perform the same basic functionality. You can then pick which is the best based on the description, screen shots, and list of features each app offers. Compare the various apps by reading their descriptions and viewing the screen shots.

- Check the customer reviews and ratings for the app. This is a useful tool to quickly determine whether the app actually works as described. Keep in mind that an app's description in the App Store is written by the app's developer and is designed to sell apps. The customer reviews and star-based ratings are created by fellow iPad users who have tried the app firsthand. When reading reviews, look for consistencies between many reviews by different people. Don't just rely on one or two positive reviews when there are a dozen or more negative ones, or vice versa.

- If an app has only a few ratings or reviews and they're mixed, you might need to try the app for yourself to determine whether it is useful to you. However, if an app has many reviews that are overwhelmingly negative (three stars or less), that's a strong indication that the app does not perform as described or that it's loaded with bugs.

- If an app offers a free (trial) version, download and test that version of the app before you purchase the premium version. You can always delete any app that you try but don't wind up liking or needing.

- Ideally, you want to install apps on your iPad that were designed specifically for the iPad, so if you have a choice, opt for the iPad-specific edition of an app first.

- As a business professional, browse specific Categories of the App Store that are more apt to offer apps you can utilize on-the-job. Some of the app Categories to focus on include Business, Finance, News, Productivity, Reference, and Utilities.

- Many of the businesses and financial institutions you already work with may have their own proprietary app. In addition, many popular PC and Mac software packages now have related apps that allow for the wireless exchange of data between a primary computer (or network) and the iPad. Plus, there are many online-based applications and services that can also utilize a specialized iPad app in order to sync and share data.

TIP   If your business uses a FileMaker Pro database, for example, the FileMaker Go app can be used to access that database from a tablet. Or, if you're already using the QuickBooks software on your Mac or PC, an app-based version of QuickBooks (as well as other third-party financial apps) provides remote access to your financial data from your tablet.

While using the Mac version of VIPOrbit, you can sync contact and scheduling data with the iPad version of this software, or if you're an Evernote user, for example, the Mac or PC version of Evernote is fully compatible with the iPad version.

In terms of online-based apps, if you're a Google Docs user, for example, there are many iPad apps that allow you to work with your Google Docs data and files directly from your Internet-connected tablet.

Be sure to check the App Store to determine if an iOS app related to the PC or Mac software you frequently use is available.

KEEPING YOUR APPS UP-TO-DATE

Periodically, app developers release new versions of their apps. Thanks to iOS 7, as long as your iPad has Internet access, by default it will automatically check for new app updates regularly, and when updates are available, they'll be downloaded and installed for you.

From within Settings, you can turn on or off the auto-update feature and then decide whether or not a cellular data connection or just a Wi-Fi connection will work. To adjust this, launch Settings, tap on the iTunes & App Store option, and from the iTunes & App Store submenu turn on or off the Updates option (found under the Automatic Downloads heading). Then turn on or off the Use Cellular Data option.

If you have Updates turned off, you can manually check for and install app updates. To do this from within the App Store app, tap on the Updates icon that's displayed near the bottom-right corner of the screen. A listing of all apps that require an update, if any, are displayed. Tap on the Update icon associated with each app, or tap on the Update All option to download and install the necessary app updates.

IN THIS CHAPTER

- Using iOS 7's AirPrint feature
- Wireless printing options for non-AirPrint printers
- Scanning business cards and documents into your iPad

11

WIRELESS PRINTING AND SCANNING VIA YOUR iPAD

Unlike laptop or netbook computers, the iPad does not contain a USB port that can be used to directly connect a printer or scanner to your tablet. However, built in to iOS 7 are the AirPrint feature and Bluetooth, which are two separate technologies that allow printers or scanners to wirelessly communicate with your tablet.

As a result, any app that integrates the AirPrint feature or taps into the iPad's Bluetooth capabilities can be used to wirelessly access and utilize external peripherals, such as a printer or scanner. When it comes to wireless printing, Apple has teamed up with several printer manufacturers to incorporate AirPrint technology into a growing number of printer models. You can learn more about AirPrint functionality shortly.

However, if your home or office printer is not AirPrint compatible, there are options for making your iPad compatible with your existing laser, inkjet, or photo printer. You must use

third-party software, such as Printopia 2 ($19.95, http://ecamm.com/mac/Printopia), on your Mac that's connected to the same wireless network as your iPad, or you can connect a peripheral, such as the Lantronix xPrintServer ($99.95, http://xprintserver.lantronix.com/home-edition), to your home or office wireless network. The xPrintServer enables you to share printers currently being used by PCs or Macs with an iPad or other iOS mobile devices.

In addition to wireless printing functionality that's available from an ever-growing selection of iPad apps, including Contacts, Calendar, Safari, Mail, Photos, Pages, Numbers, and Keynote, several companies have released portable scanners that can be connected to the iPad, enabling you to take paper-based documents and photos and scan them into the tablet to create full-color digital files that can be viewed on the tablet's screen, manipulated using compatible apps, and then shared with others. Learn more about scanning options later in this chapter.

> **NOTE** From the App Store, you'll discover third-party apps that utilize the iPad's built-in camera as a mobile scanner. You can take photos of business cards or documents, for example; store them in a popular file format on your tablet; and then view, edit, print, or share the "scanned" documents with others. ScannerPro ($2.99) is an example of this.
>
> Meanwhile, the CamCard HD app ($7.99) allows you to photograph a business card and then automatically import the text from the card directly into the iPad's Contacts app. In this case, no external scanner accessory is required.

WIRELESS PRINTING FROM YOUR iPAD

Depending on your printer make and model, there are a variety of ways to establish a wireless connection between an iPad and a laser, inkjet, or photo printer. The option you ultimately choose is based on the printer make and model you use.

If your printer is AirPrint compatible, you do not need any additional software, apps, or hardware to establish a wireless connection between the printer and iPad as long as they're both connected via Wi-Fi to the same wireless network. If your printer is not AirPrint compatible, additional software and/or hardware is necessary to wirelessly print from your tablet.

In the past few years, printer manufacturers including Brother, Canon, Dell, Epson, Fiji Xerox, Hewlett Packard (HP), Lexmark, Kyocera, Lenovo, Sharp, and Samsung have released AirPrint-compatible laser, inkjet, and/or photo printers. Thus, there are currently approximately 200 printer models that are AirPrint compatible, starting in price at less than $100.

> **NOTE** Unlike a desktop or notebook computer, your iPad does not have the capability to connect directly to a printer using a USB cable connection. Thus, some type of wireless connection must first be established before you can utilize the Print command that's now built in to many iPad apps.

USING THE AIRPRINT FEATURE TO WIRELESSLY PRINT FROM YOUR iPAD

AirPrint is a wireless printing feature that enables you to connect your tablet to a compatible printer without using cables. The printer and iPad, however, must be connected (wirelessly via Wi-Fi) to the same network.

After the wireless connection is made, you can freely use the Print command that's built in to an ever-growing selection of apps. In most cases, the Print command can be found within the Share menu of an app (which you access by tapping on the Share icon). However, some apps, including the iWork for iOS apps, have a separate Print command.

If you're creating or editing a document using Pages, for example, and you're ready to print the document, follow these steps:

1. Tap the wrench icon displayed on the Pages screen.
2. Tap the Share and Print option.
3. Tap on the Print option.
4. Tap on the Select Printer option from within the Printer Options window, and choose which printer you want to utilize.
5. Determine the number of copies of the document you want to print.
6. Tap the Print command icon in the Printer Options window.

> **NOTE** Printing from the Numbers and Keynote apps is done in the same way as with Pages.

For many other third-party apps, the Print command can often be found within the Share menu that's part of the app. This is also the case for Safari and Photos, for example. After you set up the AirPrint feature once to establish the wireless connection between your tablet and an AirPrint-compatible printer, printing from your tablet is easy.

NOTE   The AirPrint feature works between an AirPrint-compatible printer and the iPad only when the two devices are connected wirelessly (via Wi-Fi) to the same wireless network. A printer that is connected to a wireless network using Bluetooth or a USB cable connection does not necessarily support the AirPrint feature.

To see an up-to-date list of compatible AirPrint printers, visit http://support. apple.com/kb/HT4356. Click or tap on each of the printer manufacturer names to view a listing of compatible inkjet, laser, and/or photo printer models from each manufacturer.

PRINTING FROM AN iPAD TO A NON-AIRPRINT–COMPATIBLE PRINTER

If your printer is not AirPrint compatible, there are three options for establishing a wireless connection between your tablet and printer. These options include:

■ Using the Printopia 2 software on your Mac (or similar software). The Mac can be connected to the printer using a Wi-Fi, Bluetooth, USB, or Ethernet connection, but the Mac must be connected to your network via a Wi-Fi connection.

■ Connect the Lantronix xPrintServer device to your home or office network's wireless router via an Ethernet cable. Up to 10 printers that are on a network (connected to other PCs or Macs within the network) instantly become AirPrint compatible and accessible from your iPad regardless of the printer make and model.

■ Download and install a third-party app on your iPad that enables you to connect wirelessly to your home or office's wireless network to print from your tablet to printers that are connected to that network.

USING THE PRINTOPIA 2 SOFTWARE VIA A MAC

Printopia 2 ($19.95, http://ecamm.com/mac/Printopia) is an easy-to-use program that enables an iPad to wirelessly access any printer that's already connected to a Mac, as long as the Mac is also connected via Wi-Fi to a home or office network and is turned on.

When Printopia 2 is installed on the Mac, the printers connected to that Mac are displayed on your iPad whenever you access the Print command from an AirPrint-compatible app. This works even if the printer itself is not AirPrint compatible.

> **NOTE** handyPrint for the Mac ($29.99, www.netputing.com/handyprint)
> is similar to Printopia 2 but is offered by another software developer. Using any
> search engine, enter the search phrase, "AirPrint using Windows" to find solutions
> for using a non–AirPrint-compatible printer with your iPad in conjunction with a
> Windows-based PC.

USING XPRINTSERVER TO ACCESS PRINTERS ON A NETWORK

Regardless of whether you utilize Windows-based PCs or Macs, if you have a home
or office wireless network, when you connect the xPrintServer device ($99.95 or
$149.95, depending on the model) to your wireless router, up to 10 different print-
ers that are also on that network (no matter how they're connected to the network)
instantly become AirPrint compatible, enabling you to access them from your iPad
as long as the iPad can connect wirelessly (via Wi-Fi) to the same network.

Developed by Lantronix (www.lantronix.com), the xPrintServer is a small device
(measuring 4.5" × 2.37" × .87") that connects directly to any network's wireless
router using a standard Ethernet cable connection (an RJ45 connector). When the
device is connected to a network, it seeks out all printers on that network and
instantly makes them AirPrint compatible. In seconds, each printer becomes accessible from an iPad that's running any AirPrint-compatible app (or an app with a
Print command). Absolutely no configuration, special printer drivers, or optional
software is required.

The xPrintServer works with laser, inkjet, or photo printers from more than two
dozen printer manufacturers (and supports hundreds of printer models), including
HP, Toshiba, Kodak, Lexmark, Canon, Brother, Xerox, and Epson. In some cases, the
printer must connect to the network via Wi-Fi or an Ethernet cable (as opposed to
a USB connection) to work properly from an iPad using the AirPrint feature.

> **NOTE** The xPrintServer device is available online, directly from the Lantronix
> website (800-422-7055, www.lantronix.com).

USING A THIRD-PARTY PRINTING APP ON YOUR iPAD

A variety of third-party apps are available from the App Store that enable the tablet
to connect wirelessly to specific printer makes and models that are connected to
the same wireless home or office network as the iPad. In some cases, these apps
first send the document, image, or file to a PC or Mac that's also connected to the
network and then print the desired content from that computer.

If you're interested in creating prints from digital images stored on your iPad (in the Photos app), there are also free apps available from the App Store, such as FreePrints, MotoPhoto, or RitzPix, that enable you to upload your images to a photo processing company via the Web and then have the prints shipped directly to you for a small fee.

> **TIP** To determine whether there's a specialized iPad app available that can facilitate wireless printing using your existing printer, visit the App Store. In the Search field, enter the manufacturer of your printer, such as Epson, Canon, or HP.

SCANNING DOCUMENTS ON-THE-GO INTO YOUR iPAD

Depending on the type of work you do, you might find it extremely useful to be able to scan paper-based documents directly into your iPad while you're on-the-go. This might include letters, documents, research materials, receipts, reports, photos, business cards, or other paper-based printed content.

Once receipts are scanned into your tablet, they can be imported into specialized apps (or software on your primary computer) that are used for expense tracking and/or creating expense reports. For example, the Shoeboxed Receipt and Mileage Tracker app (free), in conjunction with the fee-based Shoeboxed.com online service (www.shoeboxed.com), is designed for this.

> **NOTE** Some apps utilize the camera that's built in to the iPad and allow for receipts to be photographed (scanned) directly into the app, without needing a separate scanner.

Using one of several portable scanners currently available from Brookstone and Doxie, for example, you can scan any document or image into your iPad to save it, and then you can store, view, edit, annotate, print, and share it using a variety of third-party apps.

The iConvert Scanner for iPad ($79.99, www.brookstone.com) is an extremely lightweight and portable, 300-dots-per-inch resolution scanner that enables you to scan any full-color or black-and-white document or photo that's between 2" and 8.5" wide.

The scanned documents are then saved in a JPEG format, which is compatible with a variety of iPad apps. The iConvert Scanner works with the free iConvert Scan app that gets downloaded from the App Store. This app is used to scan and save the JPEG files. Then, you can use other apps to view, organize, store, edit, annotate, and share the digitally scanned files.

Unlike other scanners that are compatible with the iPad, the iConvert Scanner connects to the tablet via the tablet's built-in 30-pin Dock Connector port. This port is located on the bottom of the tablet. Thus, to use the scanner, simply set the iPad on top of the scanner and launch the iConvert Scan app.

> **NOTE** If you're using one of the newer model iPads with a Lightning Port, Apple's Lightning to 30-pin Adapter ($29.00) will be required. It's available from the Apple Store or Apple.com.

The scanner itself measures 12.1" × 4.4" × 2.8", and it weights 1.44 pounds. The iConvert Scanner is not battery powered, so you must plug it in to an AC power source to operate it.

Another portable scanning option is the Doxie Go + Wi-Fi portable scanner from Apparent Corporation ($229.00, www.getdoxie.com). This is a compact, battery-powered scanner that you can use anywhere.

After you scan paper-based documents (up to 8.5" wide) into the scanner, the scanner connects to any wireless network via Wi-Fi and transfers the scanned documents to the online (cloud-based) service of your choice, such as iCloud, Dropbox, Flickr, or Evernote. The files can also be sent directly to your own FTP site.

After being uploaded, you can access the scanned files using an iPad that's connected to the Internet so that you can view, save (in a choice of formats), edit, and share them using your tablet.

Unlike the iConvert Scanner from Brookstone, the Doxie Go + Wi-Fi can create searchable PDF files from scanned documents, so you can use optional third-party apps, such as PDFpen or Evernote, to edit or annotate the scans. Or, if the scanned file is a graphic or photo, you can save it in the JPEG format and use it with the iPad's Photos app (or any third-party photo-editing and sharing app).

The Doxie Go + Wi-Fi Scanner measures 10.5" × 1.7" by 2.2", weighs 14.2 ounces, and can easily be transported in a briefcase or computer bag, making it perfect for a mobile executive.

The Doxie Go + Wi-Fi scanner has a 600-dots-per-inch resolution and can scan an 8.5" × 11" page in eight seconds (in 300 dpi resolution). The scanner's internal memory holds up to 600 pages or 2,400 photos. You can connect an optional USB flash drive or SD card to the scanner to provide more internal storage until you can sync files with an iPad or computer.

The Neat Company (www.neat.com) also offers a portable scanning solution as well as a specialized iPad app that enable you to scan and work with scanned documents and images on your tablet.

In addition, the Neat app (free) transforms your iPad into a scanner using its built-in camera. The app itself then uses text recognition capabilities that enable you to work with and edit your scanned documents. The Neat app only works with the separate NeatCloud service (http://store.neat.com/NeatCloud.html), which is a fee-based service for managing and syncing scanned documents and files.

Using any of these scanning solutions with an iPad, it's easy to manage, access, and store documents, files, and photos from virtually anywhere. When combined with wireless printing capabilities and the functionality of various apps for viewing, editing, and sharing documents, photos, and files, the iPad gains capabilities that were once exclusive to desktop or notebook computers.

TIP Use a portable scanner with your iPad to create a more paper-free work environment for yourself while maintaining full access to your important documents, files, and photos on-the-go.

A scanner that utilizes OCR technology (Optical Character Recognition), such as the Doxie Go + Wi-Fi, can convert text-based information from a scanned document into data that can be manipulated or edited using a spreadsheet app, expense manager, word processor, or annotation app on your iPad.

In addition to scanning photos, these scanners can be used to import and store digital versions of drawings or other graphics on your tablet, which you can then view, edit, and share using various third-party apps related to photography.

UNDERSTANDING FILE FORMATS CREATED BY SCANNERS

A scanner that utilizes OCR technology can take a text-based paper document and transform it into an editable digital file accessible from your iPad. You can edit it using Pages, Evernote, Notes, or another word-processing app. A compatible word-processing or text-editing iPad app is required to view, edit, print, or share the scanned text-based document.

If the scanner can transform the scanned document into a PDF file, using a third-party app, such as PDFpen, iAnnotate PDF, or GoodReader for iPad (available from the App Store), you can annotate and edit any PDF file, as well as view, print, and share it from within the app.

The scanned documents or files created by a scanner that can only create JPG files are treated like digital photos by your iPad. You can view, print, or share them using the Photos app or another photography-related app that's available from the App Store. Some photography apps, such as Skitch for iPad (free), enable you to annotate digital images.

> **NOTE** Without using a portable scanner connected to your tablet, you can still create a scanned document using your desktop or notebook computer that's connected to any type of scanner. Then you need to transfer the file to your iPad to view, store, edit, print, or share it.

12

USING iCLOUD WITH YOUR iPAD TO BACK UP AND SYNC DATA

iCloud is an online-based service operated by Apple that's designed to offer a wide range of features and functions to iOS mobile device and Mac users. (Some iCloud functionality is also offered to Windows PC users.)

As an iPad user, iCloud can be used for a wide range of tasks, the majority of which are offered to you free of charge. To begin taking advantage of what iCloud offers, you need to set up a free iCloud account, which takes just minutes, and it can be done using your existing Apple ID username and password.

> **NOTE** Using iCloud in conjunction with your iPad (and other Macs and/or iOS mobile devices) is optional but recommended. However, if you're already taking advantage of a cloud-based service through your work, for example, and it's accessible from your iPad, you probably want to stick with that option and only use iCloud for specific tasks that don't overlap with the other cloud-based services you're using.

Just as the iOS operating system continues to evolve, so does iCloud. With the release of iOS 7, your iPad and the iCloud service can now be set up to:

- Sync app-specific data with your other iOS mobile devices (including your iPhone) and your Mac(s). This data also gets stored "in the cloud."
- Remotely store all of your iTunes Store, App Store, iBookstore, and Newsstand content purchases.
- Allow you to track the whereabouts of your iOS mobile devices and Macs.
- Sync data related to your web surfing activities using Safari, including your Bookmarks, Favorites Bar content, Reading List, as well as website-specific usernames and passwords.
- Maintain an online backup of your iPad.
- Create and store digital photos using My Photo Stream and Shared Photo Streams.
- Provide access to online versions of core iPad apps, including Contacts, Calendar, Reminders, Notes, Pages, Numbers, and Keynote through the iCloud.com website.

Once you set up a free iCloud account, the majority of iCloud's features and functions are designed to be turned on and activated once and then continue to work automatically and in the background.

An iCloud account includes 5GB of free online storage space for your backup files, iCloud-related email account data, app-specific synced data, and other content that you store online. However, all of the additional online storage space within your iCloud account that's needed for iTunes Store, App Store, iBookstore, or Newsstand purchases, or that's needed to maintain your My Photo Stream and/or Shared Photo Streams is automatically provided by Apple for free.

> **NOTE** If additional iCloud online storage space is required, it can be pur-
> chased and become instantly available from your iPad. To do this, launch Settings,
> tap on the iCloud option, and then tap on the Storage & Backup option. From the
> Storage & Backup submenu, tap on the Buy More Storage option. An additional
> 10GB of online storage (giving you 25GB total) is priced at $20.00 per year. For
> 20GB of additional online storage, the fee is $40.00 per year, or for 50GB of online
> storage, the auto-recurring fee is $100.00 per year.

For any iCloud-related function to work on your iPad, an Internet connection is
required. While most of the available functions will work using either a cellular
or Wi-Fi Internet connection, the iCloud Backup, My Photo Stream, and Shared
Photo Stream features work only with a Wi-Fi connection. Plus, accessing certain
types of past content purchases from your iCloud account that have large file sizes
associated with them, such as TV shows and movies, also requires a Wi-Fi Internet
connection.

> **TIP** If you're a Windows PC user, app-specific data can be set up to sync data
> with compatible Windows software on your PC. To do this, however, it's neces-
> sary to download the free iCloud Control Panel software for windows. For exam-
> ple, Contacts, Calendar, Reminders, and Notes data can be set up to sync with
> Microsoft Outlook on a PC, and some Safari-related information on your iPad can
> sync with Internet Explorer on your PC. To download the Windows version of the
> iCloud Control Panel from your PC, visit http://support.apple.com/kb/DL1455.

SET UP AN iCLOUD ACCOUNT

During the initial iPad activation and setup process, you'll be prompted to either
enter your existing iCloud information or create a new iCloud account using your
Apple ID and password (or another email address and a password you create). At
anytime, however, you can set up a free Apple ID/iCloud account from your tablet
when it's connected to the Internet.

To do this, launch Settings and tap on the iCloud option. Then, from the iCloud
submenu, tap on the Get a Free Apple ID option (shown in Figure 12.1). However,
if you already have an iCloud account set up for your Mac or iPhone, for example,
enter your existing account information within the Apple ID and Password fields
found near the top of the iCloud submenu within Settings, and then tap on the
Sign In option.

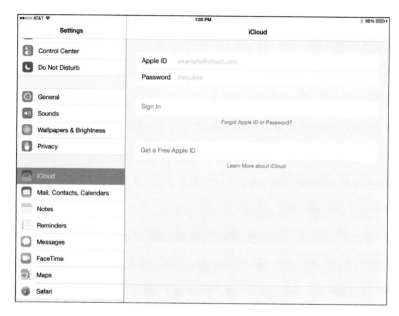

FIGURE 12.1

You can create a new iCloud account (with a new Apple ID) directly from your iPad. However, you only need one account which can be used with all of your Macs, iOS mobile devices, and Apple TV.

NOTE If you already have an iCloud account set up to sync Contacts, Calendar, Reminders, Notes, Mail, Safari, Pages, Numbers, and/or Keynote app-specific data from your iPhone and/or Mac(s), as well as your My Photo Stream and Shared Photo Stream content, as soon as you enter your Apple ID and password within the iCloud submenu within Settings on your iPad, all of your applicable app-specific data automatically loads into your tablet and becomes accessible from the various apps on it.

As soon as you create a new iCloud account or sign in using your existing Apple ID and password (or preexisting iCloud account information), the iCloud submenu within Settings displays the iCloud submenu (shown in Figure 12.2). From here, you can turn on or off individual iCloud features, and in some cases, customize specific options related to iCloud features.

FIGURE 12.2
From the iCloud submenu within Settings, it's possible to turn on or off specific iCloud features that relate to your iPad.

TURN ON iCLOUD FEATURES FROM THE iCLOUD CONTROL PANEL

The iCloud Control Panel within Settings displays your iCloud Account username (email address) near the top of the screen. Keep in mind, when you created your iCloud account, an iCloud-related email address was automatically set up for you.

Displayed below your iCloud account information is a series of virtual switches that allow you to turn on or off specific iCloud features, including Mail, Contacts, Calendars, Reminders, Safari, Notes, Photos, Documents & Data, and Find My iPad.

While the new iCloud Keychain feature directly relates to Safari and maintaining a secure database of the website-specific usernames, passwords, and credit card details you use to make online purchases, this feature needs to be turned on separately. This is done from the Safari menu screen within Settings. Tap on the

Passwords & AutoFill option and then turn on Names and Passwords and, if you choose, the Credit Cards feature as well.

> **NOTE** Once you turn on the Documents & Data option from the iCloud Control Panel, it's still necessary to turn on iCloud functionality within each compatible app, including Pages, Numbers, and Keynote. See Chapter 13, "Getting Work Done On-the-Go Using the iWork Apps," for details on how to do this.

Even once Find My iPad is turned on, to be able to locate a lost or stolen tablet, it must be turned on and have access to the Internet. Otherwise, you can set up the Find My iPad service to alert you when the tablet is turned on by someone else and then decide whether you want a custom message displayed on the screen, the tablet to be locked down, or the contents of your tablet to be erased.

SET UP iCLOUD TO SYNC APP-SPECIFIC DATA

From the iCloud submenu, you have the ability to turn on app-specific data and file syncing related to a handful of the core apps that come preinstalled with iOS 7. When the iCloud sync feature is turned on for an app, all of the content related to that app is automatically backed up "in the cloud," becomes accessible to you from the iCloud.com website. It can then automatically sync with all of your other Macs and iOS mobile devices that are linked to the same account.

Keep in mind, if you want your Contacts database to sync with the Contacts app running on your Mac(s), for example, it's necessary to turn on iCloud functionality on each of your Macs and link each Mac to the same iCloud account as your iPad (by logging in with the same iCloud username and password). Then, you must turn on the app-specific iCloud functionality for the Contacts app from the iCloud Control Panel on each of your Macs separately. Repeat this process for the other compatible apps, like Calendars, Reminders, and Notes.

> **TIP** On a Mac, the iCloud Control Panel is accessed by launching System Preferences and then by clicking on the iCloud icon.

Likewise, if you want your iPad to sync app-specific data with your iPhone, it's necessary to access the iCloud submenu from Settings on your iPhone, sign in using the same iCloud account username and password, and then turn on the setting for each separate (and compatible) app that you want to sync with your iPad (Contacts, Calendar, Reminders, Mail, Safari, Notes, Keychain, Photos, etc.).

> **CAUTION**   Simply turning on iCloud-specific features only on your iPad will result in the specific apps syncing data with your online-based iCloud account, but unless you also turn on this functionality on your other Macs or iOS mobile devices, the data will not automatically sync with those other computers or devices.

TURN ON THE iCLOUD BACKUP FEATURE

In addition to backing up and syncing app-specific data within your online-based iCloud account (which is definitely something you should do), it's possible to set up iCloud to automatically create and maintain a backup of your tablet's other content, personalized settings, and data.

To turn on and begin using the iCloud Backup feature, launch Settings, tap on the iCloud option, and then from the iCloud Control Panel scroll down toward the bottom of the screen and tap on the Storage and Backup option.

From the Storage and Backup submenu (shown in Figure 12.3), turn on the virtual switch associated with iCloud Backup. This only needs to be done once. Now, once per day, as long as your iPad is in sleep mode, has access to a Wi-Fi Internet connection (a cellular data connection will not work), and the tablet is plugged into an external power source, a backup of your tablet will automatically be created or updated and stored "in the cloud" within your iCloud account.

As long as you're maintaining a backup of your iPad, you can Restore your tablet using these backup files should something go wrong. The Restore process can be done on your existing iPad or on a replacement iPad, as long as a Wi-Fi Internet connection is present.

> **TIP**   Once the iCloud Backup feature is turned on, it's possible to manually create a backup (or update the existing backup). To do this, launch Settings, tap on the iCloud option, access the Storage and Backup submenu, and then tap in the Back Up Now option. Displayed below this option, you'll see the time and date when the last successful backup was created.

Back Up Now option

FIGURE 12.3

From the Storage and Backup submenu within Settings, it's possible to set up and activate the iCloud Backup feature, plus initiate a manual backup of your tablet.

Once iCloud Backup is turned on, to manually create an online backup of your tablet at anytime, launch Settings, tap on the iCloud option, and then tap on The Storage & Backup option. Next, tap on the Back Up Now option (refer to Figure 12.3). In addition, be sure you have iCloud set up to sync app-specific data from Contacts, Reminders, Notes, Safari, and so on.

> **NOTE** Unless you're using the iTunes Sync process to maintain a backup of your iPad (which is still a viable option), be sure to turn on the iCloud Backup feature and take advantage of it. One difference between iCloud Backup and iTunes Sync is that while the iCloud Backup files are stored online ("in the cloud"), iTunes Sync backup files are stored on your primary computer's hard drive. Thus, if you need to Restore the tablet, it will need to be connected to your primary computer. Whereas you can Restore an iPad using an iCloud Backup from almost anywhere.

SET UP AND USE THE FIND MY... FEATURE

To set up the Find My iPad feature on your tablet, launch Settings, tap on the iCloud option, and then from the iCloud Control Panel turn on the virtual switch that's associated with the Find My iPad feature.

Now, at any point, if your iPad gets lost or stolen, you have two options. From your iPhone (or another iPad), use the free Find My iPhone app to pinpoint the location of your tablet. Or, it's possible to access the iCloud.com website, log in using your iCloud account username and password, and then click on the Find My iPhone icon.

Whichever method you use, as long as your tablet is turned on (or in sleep mode) and it has access to the Internet (via a cellular or Wi-Fi connection), a detailed map will display the location of all Apple Macs and iOS mobile devices you have linked to your iCloud account.

The green dot(s) on the map indicate the locations of your devices. You can zoon in on the map to view more detail, select an alternate map view (Standard, Satellite, or Hybrid), or click on one of the dots to access additional features. From the banner that's displayed above the green dot you click on, you can see the name of the device and when it was last located. Tap on the Info ("i") icon to view a new menu window that offers three additional options (shown in Figure 12.4).

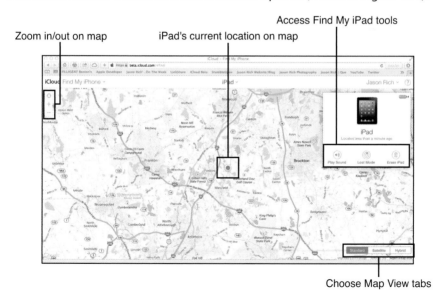

FIGURE 12.4

The Find My iPhone feature is shown here using Safari on a MacBook Air. It's tracking the location of an iPad.

Depending on the Apple computer or device that's being tracked by the Find My... feature, these options include: Play Sound, Lock (Mac), Lost Mode (iOS device), and Erase.

The Play Sound option will cause the missing computer or device to emit a sound to help you locate it. The Lock option (available for Macs) allows you to lock down your Mac with a password to keep unauthorized people from accessing it.

The Lost Mode option (available for iOS mobile devices) allows you to create and activate a Passcode feature, which will prevent anyone from using the device without the proper code. You'll also have the option to enter a phone number (which will be displayed on the phone's screen, so the person who finds it can contact you). A custom message (asking for the iPad to be returned, for example) can also remotely be set up to display on the tablet's screen.

The Erase option allows you to remotely erase all content on the lost or stolen computer or device. Once the iPad, for example, is recovered, you can then Restore it using iCloud Backup for the iTunes Sync process, assuming you've maintained a backup.

TAKE ADVANTAGE OF THE iCLOUD.COM WEBSITE

The newly designed iCloud.com website can be accessed for free by pointing any web browser to www.iCloud.com. Sign in to the service using your iCloud username and password. Then, from the iCloud website's main menu (shown in Figure 12.5), it's possible to use the online version of the Mail, Contacts, Calendar, Notes, Reminders, Pages, Numbers, or Keynote apps or access the Find My iPhone feature.

When you launch any of the online apps, all of your synced data from your iCloud account will be available to you. For example, if you launch the online version of Contacts, it will be populated with all of your Contacts database entries.

TIP You can access the iCloud.com website from any computer (a PC or Mac) that's connected to the Internet, whether or not that computer is linked to your iCloud account. However, if you're using someone else's computer to access your iCloud account and use the online apps that are populated with your data, be sure to sign off from the service when you're done. To do this, click on your username that's displayed near the top-right corner of the iCloud.com browser window and then click on the Sign Off option.

FIGURE 12.5

Online versions of Contacts, Calendar, Maps, Reminders, Notes, Pages, Numbers, and Keynote, as well as Find My iPhone, are available for free from the iCloud.com website.

One benefit of using the Pages, Numbers, and Keynote online apps is that you can literally drag and drop a Microsoft Office document or file into one of these apps, and it is automatically converted into a Pages, Numbers, or Keynote document of file and then become accessible using Pages, Numbers, or Keynote on your iPad (or any Mac or iOS mobile device that's linked to your iCloud account). So, if you use Microsoft Word on your PC or Mac and the Pages word processor on your iPad, you can easily export a Word document from your computer using the online edition of Pages, and it syncs with your iPad and is available as a Pages document. You can then view, edit, print, or share the document or export it back into Word format.

> **NOTE** The online editions of Mail, Contacts, Calendar, Notes, Reminders, Pages, Numbers, and Keynote work almost identically as their iOS 7 counterparts that run on the iPad.

ACCESS ALL iTUNES STORE CONTENT PURCHASES VIA iCLOUD

As soon as you create an iCloud account using your Apple ID and password, all previous, current, and future content purchases from the iTunes Store, iBookstore, App Store, and Newsstand are automatically saved within your iCloud account. This includes your music, TV show episodes, movies, audiobooks, ringtones, eBooks, apps, and digital publications.

Using the iTunes Store, App Store, iBooks, or Newsstand apps, you can then access previous purchases that were acquired using the same Apple ID, regardless of which of your Macs or iOS mobile devices originally accessed the content. The storage of your iTunes Store and related content purchases within your iCloud account happens automatically, and this does not utilize any of the 5GB of free online storage space that's provided to you by Apple.

From within Settings, it's possible to turn on the Automatic Downloads option, which allows your iPad to automatically download music, apps, and app updates, regardless of which Mac or iOS mobile device (that's also linked to your iCloud account) that the content was purchased on. To turn on this feature, launch Settings; tap on the iTunes & App Store option; and then from the iTunes & App Store submenu turn on the virtual switches associated with Music, Apps, and/or Updates that are displayed under the Automatic Downloads heading.

TIP   In addition to backing up and allowing you to sync your music that's purchased from the iTunes Store, if you upgrade to the iTunes Match service ($24.95 per year), your entire digital music collection, including music you've acquired from other sources or "ripped" from your audio CDs, can be stored online and synced between all of your Mac(s), iOS mobile devices, and Apple TV.

CLOUD-BASED ALTERNATIVES TO iCLOUD

The benefit to using iCloud in conjunction with your iPad is that the iOS 7 operating system, many of the core apps that come preinstalled with your tablet, as well as a growing number of other apps, all offer seamless iCloud integration. Plus, the iCloud service can be used to handle a wide range of tasks, many of which have been described in this chapter.

There are, however, many other cloud-based services in cyberspace that can be used in conjunction with an iPad. Some of these services have specialized apps available from the App Store. For example, there's Dropbox, which is a popular file sharing, backup, and syncing service that can also be used to store and share photos.

Amazon offers a cloud-based service that can be used for managing your music library online and on your iPad, while Microsoft offers its free SkyDrive service (and iPad app) that can be used for backing up, storing, and sharing certain types of Microsoft Office and related data and files, particularly if you're an Office 365 user.

If you utilize Adobe creative software on your Mac or PC, plus use the Photoshop Touch app on your tablet, it's possible to take advantage of Adobe's Creative Cloud service to sync, back up, and share Adobe-related files. Meanwhile, if you already use Google Docs, for example, there are a handful of apps (including Google Drive and GoDocs for Google Drive & Google Docs) for the iPad that allow you to access and utilize these popular online-based apps.

Moving forward, there's one thing that's certain, and it's that more and more features and functions of the iPad, as well as the apps you're using with your tablet, are sure to have greater reliance on cloud-based computing services and technologies. As a result, continued expansion and improvements to Apple's iCloud service, as well as other popular cloud services, should be expected in the months and years to come.

IN THIS CHAPTER

- Learning what the iWork for iOS apps can do
- Using Pages, Numbers, and Keynote with Microsoft Office documents and files
- Syncing iWork files with iCloud, your Mac, and your iPhone
- Using the iWork for iCloud apps in conjunction with the iWork for iOS apps

13

WORKING WITH PAGES, NUMBERS, AND KEYNOTE

For business users, three of the best designed, most versatile, and feature-packed apps available for the iPad are Pages, Numbers, and Keynote, which together make up Apple's trio of iWork for iOS apps. Each app, however, is available separately from the App Store. Although each has its own purpose, they all use the same basic user interface and menu structure. This design similarity reduces the learning curve for getting the most use out of them.

With iOS 7, Apple redesigned all three iWork for iOS apps, giving them an entirely new look, and adding many few features and functions. These additions include new themes and templates, AirDrop functionality (for wirelessly sharing app-specific documents and files), the ability to collaborate with others on documents and files, plus full integration with the iWork for iCloud versions of the apps. As a result, the versions of Pages, Numbers, and Keynote released for the iPad in late-October 2013 allow the tablet to become an even more powerful business tool than ever before—with enhanced cross-platform file and document compatibility.

If you're not familiar with what each app in the iWork for iOS trio is designed for, here's a quick overview:

- Pages is a full-featured word processor. It is Microsoft Word (for PC and Mac) compatible, as well as fully compatible with Pages for the Mac, and with the online-edition of Pages that's available on iCloud.com.

- Numbers is an extremely powerful spreadsheet management tool. Its capabilities rival Microsoft Excel running on a desktop computer. In fact, Numbers is compatible with Excel (for PC and Mac), as well as with the Numbers software for the Mac and with the online edition of Numbers that's available on iCloud.com.

- Keynote is a versatile digital slideshow presentation tool that enables you to create and showcase presentations on your iPad. After you create a presentation, you can connect your iPad to an HD television or LCD projector, for example, and share your presentation with a group. Or, you can take advantage of the iPad's Retina display to convey information graphically (using animated digital slides) to one or two people at a time. Keynote is compatible with Microsoft PowerPoint (for PC and Mac) and Keynote for the Mac, as well as with the online edition of Keynote that's available on iCloud.com.

In addition to enabling you to import Word, Excel, or PowerPoint documents or files into the appropriate app to view, edit, print, or share them, you also can create documents or files from scratch on your tablet, and then export them into Word, Excel, or PowerPoint format, as well as PDF format, before transferring them to your primary computer or another device.

> **NOTE** If you use iWork for Mac (Pages, Numbers, or Keynote), thanks to iCloud, files sync automatically between a Mac and iPad without requiring you to change file formats during the import or export process. Pages, Numbers, and Keynote are available for the Mac from the Mac App Store. You can also use the online edition of each app can for free by accessing www.iCloud.com and logging in using your iCloud (Apple ID) username and password.

> **NOTE** The iWork for iOS apps are all fully compatible with the iPhone as well. So, if you use both an iPhone and iPad, your documents and files can sync between these mobile devices automatically and in real-time as they're being used.

One of the most useful features of the iWork for iOS apps is that you have several options for easily importing and exporting files between your Mac or PC (or another iOS mobile device) and your tablet. You can email files as attachments to or from the iPad, or you can sync files using the iTunes Sync process. However, the easiest method of transferring files is to use iCloud or the AirDrop wireless file transfer feature that's built into iOS 7.

Unlike most other iPad apps, Pages, Numbers, and Keynote can be seamlessly integrated with iCloud, so your files and documents always remain synchronized (wirelessly) with your primary computer and other devices. Using this feature, if you make a change to a Pages document on your iPad, for example, within seconds, the revisions are transferred to iCloud and sent to all the computers and iOS mobile devices that are linked to the same iCloud account. The process happens in the background and is fully automated. Meanwhile, if you're collaborating on a document or file with others, everyone can work simultaneously on the same project with all edits and changes reflected in almost real-time on each person's respective computer or iOS mobile device.

You can also access and work with your most recent versions of documents and files through the online editions of these apps, which are available for free from iCloud.com.

> **TIP** Because Pages, Numbers, and Keynote require significant data entry, consider using these iPad apps with an optional external keyboard. In addition to making touch-typing easier, an external keyboard offers navigational arrow keys that make moving around within a document or file more efficient. All three apps, however, make excellent use of the iPad's virtual keyboard.
>
> You can also use the iPad's Dictation feature to quickly enter text into your tablet using your voice, as opposed to the virtual keyboard. This feature is most useful when using Pages to create large text-based documents.

Thanks to Pages, Numbers, and Keynote, the capability of your iPad or iPad mini to serve as a powerful business-oriented tool increases exponentially. Using these apps, many businesspeople find they can rely on their iPads for a much broader range of tasks while on-the-go, and they can often leave their notebook computer behind, in favor of being able to work directly from the iPad.

WORKING WITH PAGES

When you launch Pages, Numbers, and Keynote, the main Library screen showcases thumbnails for the documents or files stored in that app (shown in Figure 13.1).

Add Document icon

Create Document thumbnail

Share icon

Document thumbnails

Help icon   Edit button

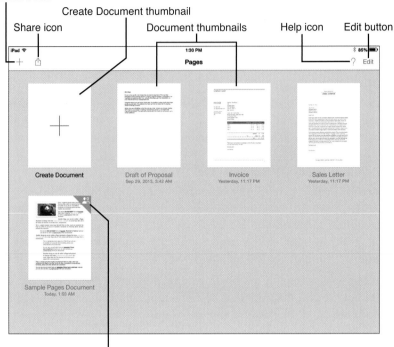

Shared document icon (using Collaboration)

FIGURE 13.1

The main Library screen of Pages. From here, you can manage, import, or export your document files. Similar functionality is offered by Numbers and Keynote.

WHAT'S NEW Displayed on almost every screen within Pages, Numbers, and Keynote is the new Help icon (the question mark). Tap on it for detailed descriptions of what each menu, option, or feature displayed on the screen is used for. Then, tap on the highlighted Help listing to view detailed information about how to use that specific feature or function.

From the Library screen, it's possible to create a new document or file from scratch; rename a document; or import a document or file manually by tapping on the plus-sign icon. Or, you can share a document by tapping on the Share icon. Tap on the Edit button to select, and then copy or delete a document or file from the app you're working with.

> **NOTE** When exporting a Pages, Numbers, or Keynote document or file from your iPad, you can keep it in its current format or export it in Word, Excel, or PowerPoint format (depending on which app you're using). All three apps also allow files to be exported as PDF files.

To open a document or file, tap on its thumbnail while viewing the Library screen. In the document editing mode of Pages (shown in Figure 13.2), several command icons and buttons appear at the top of the screen. At the top-left corner of the screen is the Documents option, which returns you to the app's Library screen. To the immediate right is the Undo icon, which enables you to undo your most recent actions in the app.

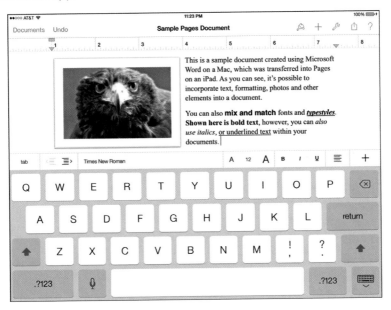

FIGURE 13.2

The main document editing mode screen of Pages.

Displayed near the top center of Pages' editing mode screen is the active document's filename. Near the top-right corner of the screen are five command icons that are used for accessing a variety of submenus.

WHAT'S NEW   The iOS 7 edition of Pages, Numbers, and Keynote now include dozens of professional-looking, Apple-designed templates that you can use to easily format a document or file. Select a template when you opt to create a new document or file. You also have the option to select a Blank template and format the document or file yourself from scratch.

When working with Pages, from the Library screen, tap on the Create Document thumbnail. When the Choose A Template screen appears, tap on the thumbnail that represents the template you want to work with. You're able to scroll downward on the Choose A Template screen to view all of the options for Basic documents, Reports, Letters, Resumes, Envelopes, Business Cards, Flyers & Posters, Cards, Miscellaneous, or Newsletters.

TIP   Both Numbers and Keynote also feature an all-new and expanded selection of easy-to-customize templates.

USING THE FORMATTING COMMANDS WITHIN PAGES

The Formatting icon (which looks like a paintbrush) is context sensitive and adapts based on what type of content you're working with in Pages. For example, if you're working with traditional text, tapping this icon reveals a pop-up window containing menu options for formatting text. Near the top of this window are three command tabs: Style, List, and Layout (shown in Figure 13.3).

Use the Style tab to easily apply a font, typestyle (bold, italics, underlined, and so on), paragraph style, or heading style, or add a bulleted or numbered list to a document. You also can create a header and footer.

After you tap on the List tab, you can adjust tabs and indents, or format a bulleted or numbered list. For example, it's possible to control the size of the bullet or opt to use letters or numbers to create an outline. Tap the Layout tab to create multiple columns within a document and control line spacing.

TIP   If you first select a photo or graphic in your Pages document and then tap on the Formatting icon, a different set of menu options appear in the pop-up window. By tapping on the Style tab, you can add a shadow, frame, or border around an image, plus add a reflection effect, for example, and then fully customize the appearance of the image in your document by adjusting each option.

After you tap on the Arrange tab when a photo or graphic is selected, you can rearrange the order of photos (from front to back), flip images, choose how text will wrap around the images, and make other adjustments.

In the actual document, use your finger to move the actual photo or graphic around, as well as to increase or decrease its overall size and shape (constraint).

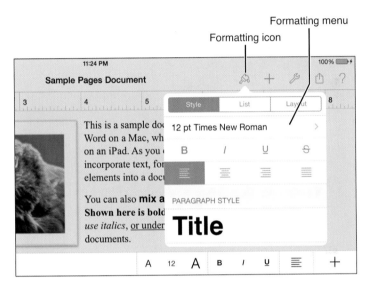

FIGURE 13.3
The formatting command icon reveals a pop-up menu window with three command tabs.

USING THE PLUS-SIGN ICON WITHIN PAGES

When you tap on the plus-sign icon displayed near the top-right corner of the Pages' editing mode screen, a pop-up menu window displays with five command tabs along the top. Each command tab reveals separate submenu options.

From left to right, tap the Media tab to import a photo that's stored on your iPad into the document you're working on. Tap the Tables tab to create and format a table within the document. When you tap the Charts tab, three additional command tabs appear that enable you to create fully customizable and colorful 2D, 3D or Interactive bar, line, area, or pie charts. As you're looking at this menu, be sure to scroll up, down, left, and right in the menu window to reveal all your chart options.

Tap on the Text ("T") tab to create a text box and place it within a document. You can then control the size and position of the box—either before or after you type or paste text into it. Menu options allow you to determine the color of the text box's frame, or you can choose to have no visible frame around the text box.

Tap the Shapes tab to import and customize colorful shapes into your document. You can resize these shapes and place them over or under text, or make the text wrap around the shapes.

ACCESSING THE TOOLS MENU WITHIN PAGES

By tapping on the Tools icon, which is the wrench-shaped icon displayed near the top-right corner of the Pages app's editing screen, the Tools menu is revealed (shown in Figure 13.4).

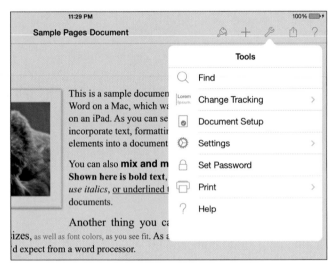

FIGURE 13.4

The Tools icon reveals a handful of submenu options for customizing documents in Pages. Similar functionality is offered when you access this menu in Numbers or Keynote.

The following options are available from the Tools menu:

- **Find:** Enables you to search for any keyword or phrase in the document you're using. When the Search field appears, tap the gear icon to access the Find, Find and Replace, Match Case, and Whole Words features. Or, if multiple results are found for your search, tap the left- or right-pointing arrow keys to scroll through and display each result in the document.

- **Change Tracking:** Just like in Microsoft Word, the iOS version of Pages allows users to keep track of changes made to a document or file. Tap on the Change Tracking option to reveal a sub-menu from which you can turn on or off the Tracking feature.

- **Document Setup:** Enables you to adjust the margins of the document you're working with, including the header and footer. For example, you can add and format page numbers or line breaks from the Document Setup screen. Tap on the Done button to exit out of this screen.

- **Settings:** Enables you to control the auto Check Spelling feature built into Pages, as well as the Word Count feature. You also can turn on or off the Comments, Ruler, Center Guides, Edge Guides, and Spacing Guides that can be displayed within a document. These guides are useful when sizing and placing photos, charts, or graphics into a document. Tap on the new Author Name option to associate your name (or initials) when adding comments or tracking changes within a document.

WHAT'S NEW   The Tracking and new Comments features built into Pages, Numbers, and Keynote make it much easier for multiple people to collaborate on documents and files. In addition to color-coding edits and comments, Pages can automatically insert the name or initials of the person who made the edits or added comments. For this feature to work, tap on the Tools icon, and then from the Tools menu, tap Settings. From the Settings menu, tap Author Name, and then in the Author Name field, insert your full name or initials.

TIP   Many of the document formatting commands available under the Style command tab are also part of the main toolbar that's now displayed above the virtual keyboard when composing or editing a document. To save onscreen real estate, you can remove the ruler by turning off the virtual switch associated with the Ruler option that's found by tapping on the Tools icon, and then tapping on the Settings option.

THE NEW SHARE ICON

As you compose or edit a document within Pages, a spreadsheet within Numbers, or a digital slide show presentation with Keynote, you can, at any time, tap on the newly expanded Share icon. There is also a Share icon near the top-left corner of the each app's Library screen.

Within Pages, as you're editing or working with a document, you'll find the Share icon near the top-right corner of the screen. The new Share menu (shown in Figure 13.5) offers several context-appropriate options that can include: Share Link via iCloud, View Share Settings, Send A Copy, and Open In Another App.

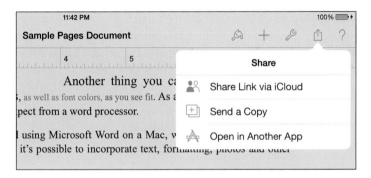

FIGURE 13.5

The new Share icon. Each option reveals a submenu with additional options for sharing or collaborating.

Tap on the Share Link via iCloud icon to upload the document or file you're working with to your online-based iCloud account. Upon doing this, the document or file is assigned a unique URL that you can then share with others. Anyone with a link to your document or file can view and edit it. As soon as anyone makes changes, those change almost immediately affect the version of the document or file stored on your iPad, iPhone or Mac.

TIP If you plan to share your iWork for iOS documents and files with others, and those people will be making changes to your work, you or your collaborators should turn on Tracking to make it easy to see who made what changes or edits. However, if you want to retain a copy of your original document or file, be sure to make a copy of it before sharing it. One way to do this is to return to the Library screen of Pages, Numbers, or Keynote. In Pages, tap on the Documents option that's found in the top-left corner of the screen, and then tap on the Edit option that's found in the top-right corner of the screen. Next, tap on the thumbnail for the document or file you want to copy and tap on the Copy icon that's found in the top-left corner of the screen. A copy of the document or file is created and a thumbnail for it is displayed on the Library screen of the iWork for iOS app. Added to the filename of the copied document is the word Copy.

You can now re-open the original version of the document or file (or the copy), tap on the Share option, and select the Share Link via iCloud option.

Keep in mind, you are also given the opportunity to create a copy of the document or file from within the Share menu after tapping on the Share Link via iCloud option.

Upon choosing the Share Link via iCloud option, the iOS 7 Share menu appears (see Figure 13.6). Depending on how you have your iPad configured, options for sharing your document or file include Message, Mail, Twitter, Facebook, or AirDrop. (Not all iPad models support the new AirDrop feature, however.)

FIGURE 13.6

Pages, Numbers, and Keynote offer a handful of new ways to easily share documents and files in order to collaborate with others, or simply send others a copy of your work.

After selecting how you want to share the document, the iWork for iOS app composes a message to your intended recipients, which contains the unique link to the document or file stored within your iCloud account. Only those people who know the link to your document or file can access it. If you're sending the link via Message or Mail, for example, fill in the To field with the desired recipients.

> **TIP** One new feature within Pages, Numbers, and Keynote is the ability to associate a unique password with each document or file. This feature gives you an added level of security to prevent unauthorized people from viewing your work.
>
> To set a password for a document or file, tap on the Tool icon to access the Tools menu. Next, tap Set Password. When prompted, create and enter a desired password, and then verify it by typing the same password again in the Verify field. Within the Hint field, you can add text to help remind you of the password.

Also available from the Share menu, once you begin collaborating with others on a document or file, is the View Share Settings option. From here, you can invite additional people to view, access, and collaborate on the iWork for iOS documents or files you're working with, or you can revoke access to one or more people who were previously granted access to your document or file.

NOTE   When you use the Share Link via iCloud option to share an iWork for iOS document or file, you determine who can view and collaborate on that document, and can revoke their access at anytime. This is done on a per-document or per-file basis. Thus, someone who is given access to one Pages document that's stored online within your iCloud account will not have access to any of your other Pages, Numbers, or Keynote documents or files.

CAUTION   Keep in mind, storing Pages documents as well as Numbers spreadsheets and Keynote files within your iCloud account uses some of your 5GB of free online storage space. Once you use up this free online storage space, you must pay an annual fee to expand your online storage space or delete files and documents stored within your iCloud account to make more room.

WHAT'S NEW   When viewing the Library screen, documents or files that are shared with others (for collaboration purposes) have a green and white Sharing icon displayed near the top-right corner of the document thumbnail. (Refer back to Figure 13.1.)

The Send A Copy option that's part of the Share menu allows you to send a copy of the document or file to someone else via Message, Mail, or AirDrop, but does not invite those people to collaborate with you when working with the file. They'll simply receive a copy of the document or file using the sending method you choose.

From the Send A Copy submenu, you can also opt to send the file to yourself via iTunes or send the file to a WebDAV compatible, cloud-based file sharing service with which you have an established account.

By tapping on the Open In Another App command that's part of the Share menu, you can export the document or file you're working with from Pages, Numbers, or Keynote, and then open it within a compatible app that's installed on your tablet. When you choose this option, a submenu appears, giving you the option to export the document or file in another file format.

For example, from within Pages, you can export the document in Pages, PDF, Word, or ePub format (see Figure 13.7). If you're using Numbers, it's possible to export the file in Numbers, PDF, Excel, or CSV format. When using Keynote, files can be exported in Keynote, PDF, or PowerPoint format.

FIGURE 13.7

Upon choosing the Open In Another App option, you can export the document of file you're working and choose a different file format.

Then, once you choose the file format, you can select a compatible app to open that document or file. The compatible app must already be installed on your tablet. For example, if you export a document or file in PDF format, you can then open and view it within iBooks, PDFpen, or Evernote.

USING THE DOCUMENT NAVIGATOR FEATURE

If you're working with a multipage document, to easily scan thumbnails of the entire document, use the Document Navigator (shown in Figure 13.8). As you're viewing, creating, or editing a document, hold your finger on the right margin of the document. An thumbnail version of the page you're viewing displays along with a vertical slider. Drag your finger up or down to scan the entire document.

> **TIP** Using the Document Navigator, scroll down in a document by dragging your finger. When you release your finger, you can continue viewing or editing the page you scrolled to in the document.

> **TIP** When working with the virtual keyboard in almost any app, you can split the keyboard by holding down the Hide Keyboard key and selecting the Split option. Or, you can move the keyboard up higher on the screen (reposition it) by selecting the Undock option, and then holding your finder on the Hide Keyboard key as you drag it up (or later, down).

Document Navigator

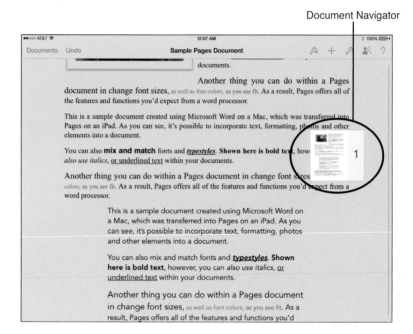

FIGURE 13.8

The Document Navigator feature is exclusive to Pages. It makes it easier to scroll through a long document to see thumbnails of each page or jump to a specific page in the document you're using.

WORKING IN FULL-SCREEN MODE

As you're proofreading a document, or if you're using an optional external keyboard for typing, position your iPad in portrait mode and take advantage of Pages' full-screen viewing mode to fully use the onscreen real estate to view your document (shown in Figure 13.9).

> **NOTE** When typing using the iPad's virtual keyboard, the individual keys appear larger on the screen when the iPad is positioned in landscape mode. The larger keys make it easier to touch-type; however, less of your document can be displayed on the screen at any given time.

In full-screen mode, most of the formatting buttons, the onscreen ruler, and the virtual keyboard disappear, giving you almost the entire screen to see and read your document.

FIGURE 13.9

When you position your iPad in a portrait position and use the full-screen viewing mode, you can see an entire page on the screen at once.

To remove the onscreen keyboard, tap the hide keyboard key on the virtual keyboard. It's the key located near the bottom-right corner of the keyboard.

Swipe your finger on the screen to scroll up, down, left, or right while in full-screen mode. Tap and hold your finger anywhere on the screen (in the document) for a second or two to exit out of full-screen mode.

> **TIP** All the iWork for iOS apps are compatible with the Select, Select All, Copy, Cut, and Paste commands built into iOS 7. To access these command options, hold your finger on a specific word, photo, or graphic. When the pop-up tab menu appears, you can also use the Insert command to insert a tab, page break, line break, column break, or footnote into your document.

USING THE FORMATTING TOOLBAR

When you're composing or editing a document within Pages, the formatting tool-bar is now displayed directly above the virtual keyboard (see Figure 13.10). From left to right, the one-tap options available from this toolbar include: the tab key; the paragraph indent option; font selection option (tap on it to display the full font menu); font size options (increase or decrease font size); typestyle options (choose from bold, italic or underline text); the left, right, or left/right paragraph justification option; and the More Options menu (the plus sign icon).

Tap on the More Options icon to display the Comment, Page Break, Line Break, Column Break, and Footnote options (also shown in Figure 13.10).

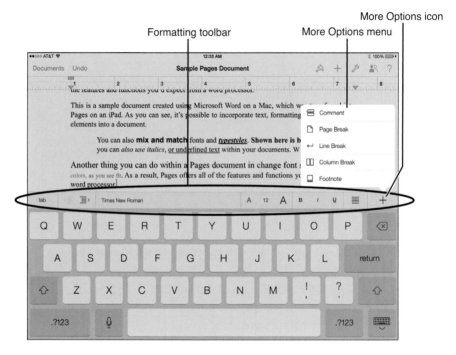

FIGURE 13.10

The new Formatting Toolbar within Pages appears just above the iPad's virtual keyboard.

> **TIP**   In Pages, at anytime while you're typing or editing a document, tap on one of the formatting icons to quickly adjust the appearance of the text you're working with.

Keep in mind, many of the options available from the Formatting toolbar are also accessible from the Formatting menu by tapping on the paintbrush-shaped icon that's displayed near the top-right corner of the app screen. If you're using an external keyboard with your iPad, you'll need to access formatting commands from the Formatting icon, since the toolbar above the virtual keyboard appears and disappears with the virtual keyboard.

As you're composing or editing a document, place and hold your finger on any word to reveal a row of additional commands, including: Select, Select All, Paste, Highlight, and Comment. Tap on an option, and then select text on which the option will be used. If you tap on Comment, for example, a Comment box appears that is associated with the selected word. You can then type your comment. Once a Comment is created, a yellow, square-shaped icon appears in the margin, to the immediate left of the selected word with which the Comment is associated. The selected word is automatically highlighted. See Figure 13.11 for an example of this.

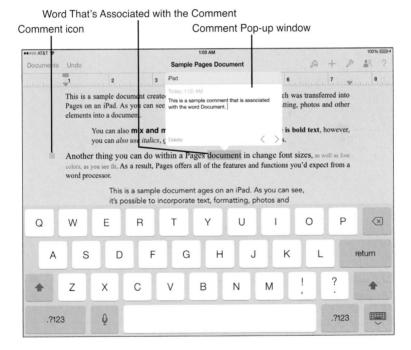

FIGURE 13.11

When you add a Comment to a Pages document, the word the Comment is associated with is highlighted and a Comment icon appears in the left margin.

WORKING WITH NUMBERS

Whereas Pages is for word processing, the Numbers app is used for organizing, analyzing, and crunching numbers and creating powerful spreadsheets. Numbers also enables you to create, display, and print customizable, 2D, 3D or Interactive bar, line, area, and pie charts in full color using spreadsheet data (as shown in Figure 13.12).

> **NOTE** When it comes to navigating your way around a complex spreadsheet, the app offers a series of highly intuitive sliders, steppers, and pop-up menus that make it easier to work with your numeric data on the tablet's screen.

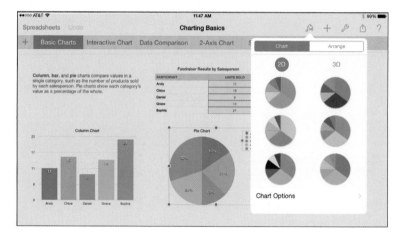

FIGURE 13.12

Create charts from spreadsheet data that look amazing. Charts created in Numbers can be cut and pasted into Pages documents or Keynote presentations.

> **WHAT'S NEW** Added to the iOS 7 edition of Numbers is the ability to create interactive charts in a variety of formats. This allows users to animate the depiction of data on the iPad's display to emphasize important information.
>
> Just as with Pages, it's now possible to collaborate with others when creating spreadsheets or share data with others in a variety of ways, including AirDrop. Plus, it's possible to export spreadsheet data in Numbers, Excel, CSV, or PDF format.

When it comes to performing complex mathematical calculations, Numbers has it covered. Built into the app is a calculations engine that can handle several hundred different functions. When numbers have been crunched, you can decide exactly how you want to view them in either a spreadsheet, table, or graphical form, and customize every aspect of the option you choose.

Like all the iWork for iOS apps, Numbers is fully AirPrint compatible. Before printing, however, you can see an onscreen preview of exactly what a spreadsheet, chart, table, or graph will look like. Then, you can format the printed page with headers, footers, and page numbers.

If you're already familiar with the Pages app, the Numbers app (and the Keynote app) offers a similar user interface and menu layout. When you launch the Numbers app, you see the Library screen. From here, you can create a new spreadsheet from scratch, rename an existing spreadsheet, open a spreadsheet file that's stored on your tablet, or manually import a spreadsheet from other sources or collaborators. (Remember, iCloud file syncing can be automatic.)

WHAT'S NEW Upon creating a new spreadsheet from scratch using Numbers on the iPad, the Choose A Template menu now offers dozens of professional-looking templates sorted by categories that include: Basic, Personal Finance, Personal, Business, and Education. Within the Business template category, you'll discover pre-created spreadsheets designed to handle employee scheduling, invoicing, break-even analysis, and other common functions. Each template can then be easily customized to fit your specific needs, or you can select the Blank template and format your spreadsheet yourself.

Tap on the Edit icon on the Numbers' Library screen to select a file, and then copy the file (to make a duplicate of it with a different filename), or delete the file altogether from your iPad. The ability to share and collaborate is now accessible as you're actually working with a spreadsheet. Select a file to open, and then tap on the Share icon that's now displayed near the top-right corner of the screen. The main Share menu is very similar to what's offered within Pages. Options include: Share Link Via iCloud, Send A Copy, and Open In Another App. Each of these main options reveals a submenu with additional sharing functions.

To open a spreadsheet file that's already stored within the Numbers app on your tablet, tap on its thumbnail on the app's Library screen. Just like in the Pages app, as you're viewing, creating, or editing a spreadsheet in Numbers, you see a handful of command icons displayed along the top of the screen.

Located near the top-left corner of the screen is the Spreadsheets option. Tap on it to return to the Library screen within Numbers. Next to the Spreadsheets icon is the Undo button. Tap on it to undo the last actions (or last several actions) you performed in the app.

Displayed near the top-right corner of the Numbers screen are five command icons (which are similar to what's offered in Pages). These icons include the Formatting icon (which is shaped like a paintbrush), the plus-sign icon (for inserting media or content into a spreadsheet), the Tools menu icon (which is shaped like a wrench), the new Share menu icon and the Help icon.

> **TIP** Anytime you're not sure what a specific command, function, option, or icon within Numbers (or any of the iWork for iOS apps) is used for, simply tap on the Help icon (which looks like a question mark). It's located in the top-right corner of the screen.

USING THE FORMATTING COMMANDS IN NUMBERS

When you tap the Formatting icon, it reveals a pop-up menu window. However, the command tabs and menu options displayed in this window vary based on the type of data you currently have selected in the spreadsheet. For example, if you have a headline or text highlighted, the command tabs displayed at the top of the menu window are Style, Text, and Arrange. When you tap on any of these command tabs, various formatting options are revealed. However, if you have a specific cell in a spreadsheet highlighted, the command tabs displayed are Table, Headers, Cells, and Format, and the command options relate to the number-crunching features of the app.

Likewise, if you have a chart or graph selected and you tap the Formatting icon, you see an entirely different selection of submenus, used for creating and editing 2D, 3D, or Interactive charts and graphics.

USING THE PLUS-SIGN ICON IN NUMBERS

When you want to import a photo or shape into your spreadsheet, or you want to create a table or chart from scratch, tap the plus-sign icon. The pop-up window that appears displays five command tabs at the top: Media, Tables, Charts, Text Box and Shapes. Each of these command tabs reveals a separate submenu. Tap the Chart tab (shown in Figure 13.13) to select a chart style and color scheme that you can fully customize.

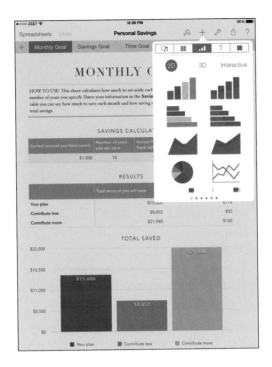

FIGURE 13.13
Choose between full-color 2D, 3D, or Interactive graphs.

ACCESSING THE TOOLS MENU IN NUMBERS

The Tools menu includes a handful of new options, including: Find, access to the Settings menu, the Set Password option, Print, and Help. Use the Set Password option, for example, to create a separate password for the spreadsheet. Each spreadsheet file can have a different password associated with it. This is separate from the Passcode Lock feature used to lock down your iPad. The Settings menu offers similar options to what's offered within Pages. From this menu, you can set up various tools used for collaborating with others, plus adjust formatting options.

WORKING WITH KEYNOTE

When it comes to creating, viewing, and giving presentations on the iPad, one of the most powerful tools at your disposal is the Keynote app. Using Keynote, you can create a digital slide show, complete with animated slides and eye-catching transitions. Or, you can import and use presentations created on a PC or Mac using Microsoft PowerPoint.

WHAT'S NEW The iOS 7 edition of Keynote features a selection of 30 new, professional-looking presentation templates, as well as an assortment of new slide transitions and animation options that you can use to visually enhance your presentations.

TIP To give presentations to groups, you might want to check out the Keynote Remote app ($0.99). It enables you to control a Keynote presentation on your Mac, iPad, iPhone, or iPod touch from another iPad, iPhone, or iPod touch in the room as long as both devices are connected to the same Wi-Fi network.

In addition to creating and showcasing basic text-based slides, Keynote enables you to create, animate, and display visually impressive 3D bar, line, area, and pie charts in your presentations. You can use the app's built-in templates to create professional-looking presentations with minimal formatting on your part.

The functionality available from the Library screen of the app is pretty much the same as the other iWork for iOS apps. You can create a new presentation from scratch; rename an existing presentation; import a presentation; share a presentation; export a presentation; copy a presentation; save a presentation file using a new filename; or delete a presentation from your iPad altogether.

CAUTION If you delete a document or file from Pages, Numbers, or Keynote, not only is the file deleted from your tablet, the version of the same file that's been synced with your iCloud account is also deleted almost immediately. There is no undo option.

From the Library screen, you also can load an existing presentation to view or edit it. Tap any presentation thumbnail to load it from the iPad's internal storage into the app.

NOTE Just as with Pages and Numbers, iCloud integration is built in to Keynote. After you initially set it up, the integration works automatically, in the background, to make sure all of your presentation files are synchronized between your iPad, other iOS devices, and the Mac(s) that are linked to the same iCloud account. You can also access your Keynote presentations using the online edition of Keynote which is available from the iCloud website (www.iCloud.com).

After you begin creating or editing a Keynote presentation, the now-familiar command icons from the other iWork for iOS apps are displayed along the top of the Keynote screen.

Tap the Presentations option to return to the Library screen of the app. Use the Undo button (displayed to the immediate right of the Presentations button) to undo the last action you took using the app. The presentation's filename that you're working with is displayed near the top center of the screen.

Near the upper-right corner of the Keynote screen are six command icons, including the Formatting, plus-sign, Tools, Share, Play and Help icons. As you can see in Figure 13.14, the thumbnails for each slide in your presentation are displayed along the left margin of the screen while you're creating or editing slides.

Slide thumbnails

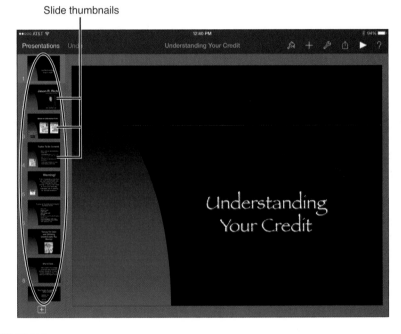

FIGURE 13.14

You can change the order of slides by using your finger to drag their thumbnails (displayed along the left margin of the screen) up or down.

USING THE FORMATTING COMMANDS IN KEYNOTE

When you tap the Formatting icon (the paintbrush) in Keynote, you see three command tabs: Style, Text, and Arrange. Each reveals a separate submenu you can use to format text in slides. For example, from the Style command tab, you can change the appearance of text, including font and background colors, borders, shadows, and other effects.

The Text command tab offers menu options for choosing a font, type size, typestyle, and justification, among other things. Tap the Arrange tab to access the Move to Back/Front feature to create layers within a slide. You can also adjust text alignment, adjust spacing, or add multiple columns to a slide.

However, if a graphic or photo is selected within a slide, the Formatting icon reveals the Style and Arrange tabs, which offer commands used to customize the appearance of graphics and photos.

USING THE PLUS-SIGN ICON IN KEYNOTE

Just like in the other iWork for iOS apps, tapping the plus-sign icon enables you to import photos or shapes into a slide; create or modify tables; add text boxes; or use 2D, 3D, or Interactive charts, depending on which command tab you tap.

ACCESSING THE TOOLS MENU IN KEYNOTE

From the Tools menu in Keynote, you can access a new menu that offers a handful of options, including: Transitions and Builds (used to add animations to your presentations), Find, Presenter Notes, Presentation Tools (used to add interactive links, a soundtrack and other functions to a presentation), the Settings menu, the Set Password option, Print, and Help. Many of these options are similar to what's found in Pages and Numbers.

From the Tools pop-up, you can access the Transitions and Builds submenu. These tools allow you to add animations to individual slides or to incorporate slide transition effects for the presentation (see Figure 13.15). There's also a Presenter Notes feature that enables you to compose and later view notes to yourself as you're giving the presentation.

WHAT'S NEW   Just as with Pages and Numbers, Keynote now offers a variety of tools that allow you to collaborate with others on the creation or editing of a digital slide presentation. To customize these options, tap on the Tools icon and then select the Settings option. From the Settings submenu, turn on Comments and add your name to the Author Name field. Then, to share you work with others and begin collaboration, use the Share Link via iCloud option that's accessible by tapping on the Share icon.

When you collaborate on a Keynote presentation with others, those other people can use Keynote for iOS on their iPad or iPhone, the Mac version of Keynote, or the online edition of Keynote (available from the iCloud.com website). Thus, even a Windows PC user can access and work with Keynote files, in Keynote format, without you first having to export the file to PowerPoint format.

> **TIP** Using an optional cable, it's possible to connect your iPad directly to a high-definition television set, monitor, or LCD projector when making a presentation to a crowd. Using the AirPlay feature, this can be done wirelessly if you also use an Apple TV device ($99.99, www.apple.com/appletv) and have access to a wireless network.

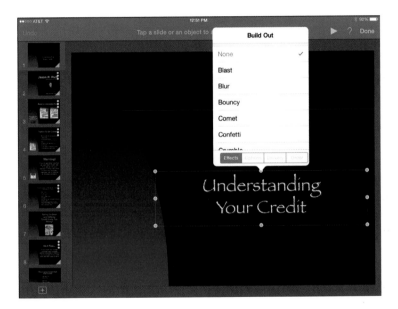

FIGURE 13.15
Keynote includes many slide animations and transitions. You can adjust these animations for individual elements of a slide (shown here), or an entire slide.

From the Tools menu, tap on the Presentation Tools option to incorporate interactive hyperlinks into slides, set up a presentation type, turn on and off the Loop presentation or self-playing features, and turn on or off the Enable Remotes feature (also used when giving a presentation). From the Settings submenu (which you can also access by tapping on the Tools icon), you can turn on or off slide numbering, guides, and the spell check feature.

IT'S SHOWTIME: USING THE PLAY ICON IN KEYNOTE

The Play icon (the right-pointing arrow) is used to transition the Keynote app from the slide creation and edit mode to the app's presentation mode. Tap it to display your presentation in full-screen mode. You can use the iPad's AirPlay feature (or optional cables) to showcase the presentation on an HD television, monitor, or LCD projector.

> **TIP**   To exit out of the Play mode, use a pinch figure gesture on the iPad's screen.

USING THE iWORK FOR iOS APPS WITH iCLOUD

After you set up a free iCloud account, be sure to set up Pages, Numbers, and Keynote to automatically sync documents and files with your other Mac and iOS devices via iCloud.

For each of the iWork for iOS apps, the iCloud functionality must be set up separately; however, after you've set it up, as long as your iPad has access to the Internet, changes you make to a document or file are reflected almost instantly on your Mac and other iOS devices (as well as within the online editions of the iWork apps).

> **NOTE**   Most other apps that are compatible with iCloud have a manual sync feature. Pages, Numbers, and Keynote are among the few apps that offer automatic iCloud integration and file synchronization that works behind the scenes.

To set up Pages, Numbers, and Keynote on your iPad to work with iCloud, follow these steps:

1. After installing Pages, Numbers, and Keynote onto your iPad, launch Settings from the tablet's Home Screen.

2. From the main Settings menu, tap the iCloud option.

3. At the top of the iCloud Control Panel screen, turn on iCloud functionality, and enter your Apple ID and password.

4. Also from the iCloud Control Panel screen, tap the Documents & Data option.

5. When the Documents & Data menu is displayed, tap the virtual switch associated with Documents & Data to turn it on.

6. If you have Pages installed on your iPad, on the left side of the Settings screen, scroll down in the main Settings menu to the Pages option, and tap it.

7. When the Pages menu appears in Settings (shown in Figure 13.16), tap the virtual switch that's associated with the Use iCloud feature to turn on the auto file-syncing feature with iCloud that kicks in each time the Pages app is launched. Repeat steps 6 and 7 for the Numbers and Keynote apps, if applicable.

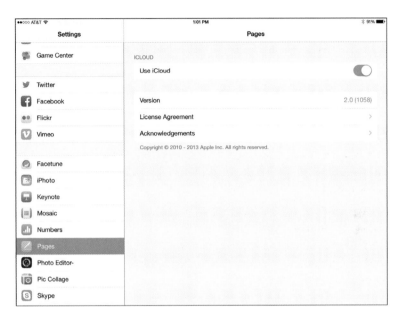

FIGURE 13.16
Turn on the iCloud feature for Pages, Numbers, or Keynote separately.

8. Repeat this process on each of your other iOS mobile devices on which you have Pages, Numbers, and Keynote installed, including your iPhone and iPod touch.

9. On your Mac, launch System Preferences.

10. From the System Preferences menu, click the iCloud icon.

11. When the iCloud window appears, make sure you sign in to iCloud using the same account username and password you used on your iPad (and other iOS mobile devices).

12. On the right side of the iCloud window (on your Mac), add a check mark to the checkbox associated with the Documents & Data option.

13. In the Pages, Numbers, and Keynote software running on your Mac, turn on the iCloud functionality for each program.

WORKING WITH THE iWORK FOR iCLOUD APPS

In conjunction with the release of iOS 7 and the latest revisions to the iWork for iOS apps, Apple simultaneously launched fully-functional online editions of Pages, Numbers and Keynote, which anyone (including Windows PC users) can access and use for free (assuming they have an iCloud account).

The online editions of Pages, Numbers and Keyword look and function almost identically to their iPad counterparts. Plus, once you set up app-specific syncing for these apps from your iPad, all of the latest versions of your Pages, Numbers and Keynote documents and files automatically become accessible to you from the online edition of these apps.

From within Pages, Numbers, or Keynote, however, you can also access the Share menu, select the Share Link Via iCloud option, and then invite others to access that specific document or file in order to collaborate on it with you. Alternatively, from the Share menu, you can now use the Send A Copy option to simply send someone else your document or file via the Message app, Mail or AirDrop.

To access the online edition of Pages, Numbers or Keynote from any computer (PC or Mac) that's connected to the Internet, point its web browser to www.iCloud.com. Log into the service using your iCloud (Apple ID) username and password, and then click on the app icon for Pages, Numbers or Keynote to launch that app (see in Figure 13.17).

iWork for iCloud App icons

FIGURE 13.17

From the iCloud.com website, you can run online versions of Pages, Numbers, or Keynote from any PC or Mac computer that's connected to the Internet and that has a compatible web browser.

The computer you use to access the iWork for iCloud apps does not otherwise need to be linked to your iCloud account. Thus, you can securely access these online apps (as well as online editions of Contacts, Calendar, Reminders, Mail and Notes), from a hotel's business center, Internet café, or from a coworker or friend's computer.

To keep your documents and data safe, however, be sure to log out of the iCloud.com service when you're done using the online-based apps.

> **TIP** To log out from the iCloud.com service, click on your username that's displayed near the top-right corner of the browser window, and then click on the Sign Out option.

One useful feature of the iWork for iCloud apps is that they run within the web browser window on your computer (or the computer you're using). Thus, the Pages, Numbers, or Keynote software does not need to be downloaded and installed.

As you're using any of the iWork for iCloud apps, it's possible to drag-and-drop a Microsoft Office (Word, Excel, or PowerPoint) file directly into one of them, and begin working with it within the online edition of Pages, Numbers or Keynote.

When you drag-and-drop a Microsoft Word document into the online edition of Pages, for example, the online app automatically converts the file into a Pages document, and then stores it within your iCloud account ("in the cloud"). As a result, almost instantly, it becomes accessible using the Pages app on your iPad as well.

As soon as you're done working with the document (either online or on your iPad), it's possible to export it back into Microsoft Word format. This is an easy way to insure document and file compatibility between Pages and Word, Numbers and Excel, and/or Keynote and PowerPoint, regardless of on what type of computer or mobile device these documents or files are being accessed from.

> **NOTE** If you're a Mac user, you can use the Mac versions of Pages, Numbers, or Keynote, or use the online versions of these apps available from iCloud.com. Windows PC users need to use the online editions of the app, or first export the iWork document or file into a Word, Excel, PowerPoint or PDF file to ensure compatibility.

THIRD-PARTY APPS THAT ALSO OFFER MICROSOFT OFFICE COMPATIBILITY

When you begin experiencing the word-processing capabilities of Pages, the number-crunching functionality of Numbers, and the digital-slide creation and viewing tools offered by Keynote on your iPad, and combine these capabilities with your iPad's 10-hour battery life and other functionality, you'll see why so many businesspeople are incorporating the iPad into their daily work lives instead of using a notebook computer.

Available from the App Store, you also have other options, including Documents To Go Premium—Office Suite, Quickoffice Pro HD, Documents Unlimited for iPad, and Smart Office 365 HD, that offer Microsoft Office document and file compatibility as well as file-sharing options, plus other features that are not offered by the iWork apps.

One of the key features that enables many business people to use their iPads as a powerful tool in their everyday work lives is the ability to view, create, edit, print, and share Microsoft Office documents and files on their iPad. This includes using the iPad to access documents and files created on a PC or Mac using Microsoft Word, Microsoft Excel, and Microsoft PowerPoint, and sharing documents and files created from scratch on the tablet with a PC or Mac.

In addition, when an iPad is connected to the Internet, third-party apps enable you to easily connect to and take control of your PC or Mac computer and actually run software remotely from it. So, while you're on-the-go, you can use your iPad to control Microsoft Word on your desktop computer and see everything from your tablet's screen. Thus, file compatibility is no longer an issue, and you have full access to all the Microsoft Office features and functions you need because you're actually controlling the Microsoft Office software from your iPad.

NOTE If you're a Microsoft Office 365 user, available from the App Store is the SkyDrive Pro for Office 365 Subscribers app (free). This app enables you to use your iPad in order to access, view and share Word, Excel and PowerPoint documents and files on your tablet that are stored within your Microsoft SkyDrive online account.

It's also believed that Microsoft is working on iPad versions of Microsoft Office applications, but this rumor has been circulating now for several years. An iPad version of Microsoft OneNote is currently available from the App Store.

WORKING WITH MICROSOFT OFFICE DOCUMENTS AND FILES USING THE DOCUMENTS TO GO PREMIUM—OFFICE SUITE APP

The Documents To Go Premium—Office Suite app ($16.99) from DataViz, Inc. (www.dataviz.com) offers document and file compatibility with Microsoft Office. This single app offers the same core functionality and features you'd get using Microsoft Office on a desktop or notebook computer, but it's designed for the iPad. This includes the ability to create, view, edit, print, and share Word, Excel, and PowerPoint documents and files.

This app also makes it easy to share (import/export) Office-compatible documents and files via email or one of several popular cloud-based file sharing services, including Google Docs and Dropbox. Documents To Go Premium—Office Suite comes with free software for a PC or Mac to make file syncing and transfers within a wireless network easy.

Documents To Go Premium—Office Suite has a unique user interface and menu layout. In other words, the available editing and formatting tools are similar to what's available from Microsoft Office running on a PC or Mac, but the app's menu structure and layout are vastly different.

> **NOTE** Documents To Go Premium—Office Suite also offers the proprietary InTact Technology feature, which helps automatically compensate for formatting incompatibility (font or type style incompatibility) when a file or document is transferred from a computer to an iPad (or from an iPad to a computer).

There are several versions of the Documents To Go app available from the App Store. Only the Documents To Go Premium—Office Suite edition enables you to create, edit, and view Word, Excel, PowerPoint, and PDF documents and files, as well as use a handful of cloud-based file-sharing services. The less-expensive version of the app does not enable you to edit or create PowerPoint-compatible files, for example, and has other limitations. Both versions, however, are compatible with Apple's iWork software.

> **CAUTION** Whether you're using the iWork apps, or another third-party iPad app to create, view, edit, print or share Microsoft Office files and documents, unless your iPad has the same library of fonts as your primary computer, you might discover minor font-compatibility issues as you're working.

Likewise, you might discover page-formatting issues or incompatibility with PowerPoint slide transitions and animations when you're using an iPad and attempting to work with files created on a PC or Mac (or you transfer an iPad-created file or document to a PC or Mac).

The Office-compatible app you're using often automatically compensates for minor compatibility issues. However, be sure to review documents or files carefully to make sure they've been handled correctly by the app. For example, after transferring a PowerPoint presentation to your iPad, review it carefully yourself before presenting it to an audience. When you import or export PDF files created from Office documents or files, all formatting and fonts are preserved perfectly, but your ability to edit the document or file in PDF format is limited based on which PDF reader app you're using.

WORKING WITH MICROSOFT OFFICE DOCUMENTS AND FILES USING THE QUICKOFFICE PRO HD APP

The Quickoffice Pro HD app ($19.99) from Quickoffice, Inc. (www.quickoffice.com/quickoffice_pro_hd_ipad) offers a comprehensive file and document creation and editing tool that is compatible with Word, Excel, and PowerPoint, as well as a handful of cloud-based file sharing services and online-based software tools, such as Google Docs.

Using this app, it's possible to import, view, edit, print, or share Microsoft Office–compatible files and documents with ease. You also can create documents or files from scratch on your tablet and then share them with other computers or mobile devices that are running Microsoft Office software.

Quickoffice Pro HD is one app with several distinct modules, used for word processing, managing spreadsheets, and working with digital slide presentations. The word processing module, however, is compatible with Microsoft Word (.doc and .docx) files, and the spreadsheet module is compatible with Excel (.xls and .xlsx) files. The digital slide presentation tools built in to the app are compatible with PowerPoint (.ppt and .pptx) files.

All three Quickoffice Pro HD modules can export files or documents into PDF format, and all offer AirPrint wireless printing capabilities. You can also use the app as a PDF file viewer.

When it comes to creating or editing Microsoft Office–compatible files and documents, the Quickoffice Pro HD app offers robust formatting tools that enable you to easily control fonts, typestyles, page and paragraph formatting, and other elements of a file or document. The app also works nicely when the iPad is in either portrait or landscape mode, and it supports a variety of iOS features, such as select, copy, cut, and paste.

When using Quickoffice Pro HD on an iPad, you'll discover that the app offers many of the same features and functions built in to Microsoft Office, but the user interface and menu layout of the app are vastly different from what running Microsoft Office software on a laptop or desktop computer looks like. However, when you get used to working with Quickoffice Pro HD, you'll find that it offers the features and functionality you need to get work done while on-the-go, yet still be able to maintain file compatibility with other Windows PC or Mac OS X Microsoft Office users.

Like its competitors, Quickoffice enables you to import or export documents and files via email or sync documents and files using a handful of cloud-based file sharing services, including Evernote, Dropbox, and Google Docs. You can also publish content to Facebook, Twitter, LinkedIn, and other online social networking sites directly from the app.

> **TIP** Beyond Documents To Go and Quickoffice are a handful of other third-party apps available from the App Store that offer Microsoft Office compatibility. To find these apps, visit the App Store and search for "Microsoft Office."
>
> One difference between these apps is how you can share documents and files with other computers or users. All the apps enable you to email documents and files (or receive documents and files via email), but each works with a different selection of cloud-based file sharing services. They are not all compatible with iCloud, Dropbox (www.dropbox.com), or Microsoft's SkyDrive (http://explore.live.com/skydrive-mobile), for example.
>
> Be sure to choose a solution that not only enables you to create and/or edit the Microsoft Office–compatible documents and files you need, but also choose one that meets your needs in terms of wireless file syncing and sharing with your primary computer and your co-workers.

ACCESSING YOUR PRIMARY COMPUTER REMOTELY WITH YOUR iPAD

When you use Apple's iWork apps or a third-party app to view, create, edit, print, or share Word, Excel, PowerPoint, and PDF files and documents, you need to worry about minor font and formatting compatibility issues. You also must successfully sync or transfer files and documents between your computer and tablet.

If your iPad has continuous Internet access, another option for working with truly compatible Microsoft Office files and documents is to use a remote desktop app, which enables you to wirelessly access and control your PC or Mac directly from your tablet via the Internet or a wireless network.

After establishing a remote connection between your iPad and PC or Mac, whatever would be seen on your computer's monitor is displayed in almost real time on your tablet's screen.

From the App Store, you can find a handful of remote desktop apps for the iPad, such as GoToMyPC (a free app, but there's a monthly fee), Remote Desktop ($6.99), Splashtop Remote Desktop for iPad ($4.99), and Jump Desk ($14.99).

Not only does a remote desktop app make it easy to use your iPad to access and work with any Microsoft Office file or document that's stored on your computer, you can create documents or files from scratch, run any other software that's installed on your PC or Mac, and access data that's stored on your other computer.

This solution requires your iPad to have a Wi-Fi Internet connection. Most of the remote desktop solutions typically do not function with a cellular Internet connection. Also, each of these remote desktop apps displays content from the primary computer to which it's connected in a slightly different way. However, viewing the content of a full-size monitor on your iPad's smaller screen is an intuitive process.

NOTE When you install a remote desktop app on your iPad, additional software (supplied for free) must also be installed and run on your PC or Mac whenever you want a secure connection to be made between your computer and tablet. Plus, for this solution to work, your primary computer must be left turned on while you're away. After the remote desktop software is set up (a process that takes just minutes), taking control over your PC or Mac from your iPad is an easy process that enables you to access documents, files, and data, plus run software on your computer with very little lag time.

WHAT'S NEW If you're a Windows 8 (PC) user (including Windows 8.1) and you want to remotely access your computer using your tablet in order to run Windows software via your iPad, or use your tablet to access documents, files, data, or photos stored on your PC, another free option that's available to you is the Microsoft Remote Desktop app that's available from the App Store.

IN THIS CHAPTER

- Using your iPad for video conferencing via the Web
- Learn about FaceTime, Skype, GoToMeeting, and WebEx

14

CONDUCTING VIDEOCONFERENCES AND VIRTUAL MEETINGS

Although the iPad isn't designed to work as a cell phone, when it's connected to the Internet, you can use the iPad as a Voice over IP (VoIP) telephone or speakerphone when you use a third-party app, such as Skype or Line2. These and other apps like them enable you to make and receive free or low-cost phone calls directly from your tablet.

Thanks to the tablet's built-in camera, microphone, and speaker, you can also use the iPad as a video calling or video-conferencing tool when an Internet connection is available. The FaceTime app that came preinstalled on your iPad is designed specifically for video calling (for free) with other Mac, iPad, iPhone, and iPod touch users.

> **NOTE** FaceTime is referred to here as a video calling app because it allows two people to communicate using a video connection. Videoconferencing apps, however, allow two or more people to simultaneously communicate.

To easily videoconference with PCs, Macs, or other web-enabled mobile devices, the Skype or ooVoo apps offer easy alternatives that are also free, unless you utilize either service's premium features.

Designed more for use in business, it's also possible to use your tablet for video-conferencing and to attend virtual meetings using GoToMeeting or WebEx, for example, when you download apps that enable you to connect to these fee-based services.

> **NOTE** In some cases, it's possible to participate in video calls or videoconferences using a cellular Internet connection. However, to experience the highest quality HD video and the clearest possible connections without quickly using up your monthly cellular data allocation, you should use a Wi-Fi Internet connection. In fact, a Wi-Fi connection is required for using certain services.

USING FACETIME FOR VIDEO CALLS

The first time you launch the FaceTime app, you must set up a free Apple ID account or enter your existing Apple ID username and password. You are also asked to enter an email address that will be associated with your FaceTime account (which can be the email account associated with your Apple ID or iCloud account, but does not have to be).

> **TIP** If you're also an iPhone user, it's possible to set up FaceTime to accept your iPhone's phone number and Apple ID as your unique FaceTime identifier when using FaceTime on your iPad (and/or Mac). To do this, on your iPad, log in to the same FaceTime account as you use with your iPhone.

Your Apple ID or the email address you provide becomes your unique FaceTime identifier (which acts just like a phone number), so others can initiate connections with you when you both have FaceTime running on your devices.

When you want to call another FaceTime user, you must know the other person's email address (the one associated with his or her FaceTime account) or their iPhone phone number.

After you complete the initial FaceTime setup process (it takes less than a minute), as long as you have FaceTime running on your tablet and it's connected to the Internet, you are able to participate in videoconferences.

After your iPad is connected to the Internet, launch the FaceTime app. As soon as it's launched, the tablet's front-facing camera turns on automatically and you should see yourself on the iPad's screen.

> **NOTE** FaceTime works with either a Wi-Fi or cellular Internet connection; however, some cellular data service providers have either blocked FaceTime use or require a special service plan. If this is the case, you can still use FaceTime, on an unlimited basis, using a Wi-Fi Internet connection.

On the right side of the screen is a window requesting that you sign in with your Apple ID username and password. Enter this information, and then tap the Sign In button.

You're now ready to initiate or receive FaceTime calls and participate in a video-conference via the Web. Displayed near the lower-right corner of this app screen are three options: Favorites, Recents, and Contacts.

CREATING A FACETIME FAVORITES LIST

A Favorites list in FaceTime is a list you can customize to include the people with whom you plan to FaceTime video chat the most. In essence, this Favorites option serves as a one-touch speed dial list.

To add a contact, tap the Add Contact (plus sign) icon that's located near the upper-right corner of the Favorites window and then select people from your established Contacts app database.

> **TIP** In the Contacts entry for each person, if the person is an iPhone user, be sure to associate their mobile phone number with the "iPhone" label rather than the "Mobile" phone label. Doing so helps the FaceTime app easily identify and connect with that person.

USING FACETIME'S AUTOMATIC RECENTS LIST

When you tap the Recents option while using FaceTime, you see a list of people with whom you've already communicated using this app. Tap any of the contacts within this list to videoconference again with that person.

If this is the first time you're using the FaceTime app, this window is empty except for the All and Missed tabs displayed near the top of the window.

After you begin using the app, the All tab displays all FaceTime videoconferences you've participated in, as well as any incoming missed calls. Tap the Missed tab to see a list of only the incoming FaceTime calls you didn't answer.

CHOOSING PREFERRED FACETIME CONTACTS

The Contacts icon that's displayed near the lower-right corner of the FaceTime screen enables you to select any person listed in your Contacts database to call using this app.

To initiate a call with someone who also has FaceTime installed and operating on their computer or iOS mobile device, select that person from your Contacts list and tap on the email address or iPhone phone number that was used to register with FaceTime. If a connection can be made, a FaceTime icon automatically appears next to the person's name within the FaceTime app.

When you initiate a call, near the bottom center of the screen, the FaceTime With message and the person's name are displayed. Next to this label is the End button, which you can tap at any time to terminate the connection.

PARTICIPATING IN A FACETIME CALL

If the person you're calling with the FaceTime app answers, your own image that was displayed in full-screen mode on the tablet's screen shrinks. It is now displayed as a thumbnail image on the screen. Meanwhile, the rest of the iPad's screen displays the person you're connected with using FaceTime.

NOTE   If you initiate a FaceTime call but the person you're calling does not answer after 30 seconds or so, you see the "FaceTime Unavailable. [Name] is not available for FaceTime." message.

TIP   While you're engaged in a FaceTime call, you can move the thumbnail-size video window that contains your image around on the screen using your finger. To help line up your eyes so you're looking into the iPad's camera, position this video window near the tablet's front-facing built-in camera. That way, when you look at yourself, it appears as if you're looking into the camera directly at the person you're conversing with.

As you participate in a video call, notice that near the bottom of the FaceTime screen are three command options: Mute, End Call, and Switch Camera. Use them for the following purposes:

- Tap the Mute button to continue the video connection, but mute the iPad's built-in microphone so the person you're communicating with is able to see you but not hear you.
- Tap the End Call button to terminate the FaceTime connection and promptly end the call.
- Tap the Switch Camera button to alternate between the two cameras built in to your iPad. The front-facing camera is facing toward you, whereas the camera on the back of the iPad shows off whatever it's pointing at.

The FaceTime app is pretty simple to use, and it is a powerful tool for video calls. The best thing about using FaceTime is that it's free, and you can communicate with anyone in the world who also uses the FaceTime app or software. In other words, you never have to pay long-distance phone charges, international calling fees, or cell phone roaming charges when using FaceTime. Nor do you have to worry about using up your cell phone minutes. (If you're using it with a cellular Internet connection, you do, however, need to consider your monthly wireless data usage allocation, if applicable.) The biggest benefit to using FaceTime is that you can actually see *and* hear the person you're communicating with.

TIP The ooVoo app and service works very much like FaceTime but is also available to Windows-based PC users and Android mobile device users, as well as Mac and iOS mobile device users. In addition, ooVoo allows for groups of up to 12 people to simultaneously videoconference in a conference call-like situation. To learn more, visit www.oovoo.com or download the ooVoo app from the App Store.

PARTICIPATING IN VIRTUAL MEETINGS FROM ANYWHERE

If your company uses a fee-based virtual meeting service, such as GoToMeeting or WebEx, there are apps that enable you to participate in these meetings using your iPad from anywhere an Internet connection is available (such as from your home, hotel room, poolside at a resort, or from a client's office).

Web conferences or virtual meetings involve using the Internet to connect people at different locations, enabling them to talk (or videoconference) while simultaneously sharing information on their computer screens in real time. This capability has changed the way many companies do business.

GOTOMEETING OFFERS VIRTUAL MEETING CAPABILITIES

One of the pioneers in the virtual meeting field is Citrix Systems, Inc., with its GoToMeeting software for PCs and Macs (www.citrixonline.com). For iPad users, a free iPad app that enables people to attend online-based virtual meetings that are hosted by others using GoToMeeting or GoToWebinar is available from the App Store.

> **TIP** The host of a virtual meeting who utilizes GoToMeeting or GoToWebinar pays a flat monthly fee, starting at $49.00 per month, to host an unlimited number of meetings with up to 25 attendees each. More attendees can be accommodated if the host subscribes to a higher-priced service plan. You cannot host virtual meetings from an iPad, but you can attend them.

Attendees using a PC or Mac to participate in a meeting can utilize audio conferencing via Voice over IP (VoIP) service, using their computer's microphone and speakers, while simultaneously being able to view whatever the meeting host is showcasing on his computer screen, such as a PowerPoint presentation or a spreadsheet report. People can also collaborate on Word documents, for example.

Thanks to the GoToMeeting app for iPad, tablet users can do everything a meeting attendee using a PC or Mac can do, such as see who is presenting, who's talking at any given moment, and who else is attending the meeting. Videoconferencing with multiple meeting participants is also possible.

The GoToMeeting app was designed to utilize some of the tablet's key features, such as its touch-screen interface, so you can zoom in on content being showcased during a meeting.

If you're a mobile executive who wants or needs to "attend" meetings or webinars from a location outside your office, this app is ideal. When you're invited to a virtual meeting via email, from the iPad simply tap the link embedded in the invitation email to connect to a meeting and automatically launch the GoToMeeting app. From within the app you can manually enter a meeting ID and your username to be connected to a meeting within seconds.

ANOTHER VIRTUAL MEETING OPTION: THE WEBEX PLATFORM

In addition to utilizing Citrix's GoToMeeting software and iPad app, similar functionality is provided by Cisco Systems, via its popular WebEx virtual meeting solution (www.webex.com).

For businesses, consultants, or entrepreneurs who already use WebEx to host meetings, the company offers a free iPad app that enables people to attend virtual meetings from their Apple mobile devices. Users connect via a Wi-Fi hotspot or through a cellular data connection.

> **CAUTION**   Participating in a virtual meeting requires a significant amount of wireless data use, and it quickly depletes your monthly cellular wireless data allocation. To avoid surcharges for additional wireless data use, consider using a free and unlimited Wi-Fi connection to participate in virtual meetings using the GoToMeeting or WebEx app.

To schedule and host a meeting using Cisco's WebEx, the host must be using the WebEx software from a Mac or PC and be a paid subscriber to the service. Pricing starts at $24.00 per month to host an unlimited number of meetings that can be attended by up to eight people. For $49.00 per month, you can host meetings with up to 25 attendees. A free account can also be set up that allows you to host non-high-definition-quality meetings, with fewer available features, with up to three attendees.

Attending meetings, however, is free and does not require a WebEx membership (but the free WebEx software for the PC, Mac, iPhone, or iPad is required). You can download WebEx for iPad free from the App Store.

MAKING AND RECEIVING PHONE CALLS OR VIDEOCONFERENCING WITH SKYPE

Skype is a VoIP phone service, as well as a videoconferencing and text/instant messaging service that enables you to make and receive phone calls over the Web (as opposed to a cellular phone network or traditional telephone landline). When used with the iPad, a smartphone, or a computer with a built-in camera, it also allows for free videoconferencing using a cellular or Wi-Fi Internet connection.

In addition to being a powerful and cost-effective communications tool for PC and Mac users, thanks to the Skype for iPad app, the service is fully functional on the iPad for worldwide VoIP phone calls, text/instant messaging, and videoconferencing.

The Skype app uses your iPad's built-in microphone, speaker, and camera(s) to enable you to hear and be heard during calls and be heard and seen during video-conferences. A Bluetooth headset or corded headset can also be used with the app to improve audio quality.

Making unlimited Skype-to-Skype VoIP or videoconferencing calls is always free. However, there is a very low per-minute fee to make calls to a landline or cellular telephone from your iPad using Skype. This per-minute fee is typically only pennies per minute, even if you're traveling overseas and make a call to the United States. You can also save a fortune on international calling from the United States when making calls to any other country.

The videoconferencing functionality of Skype is similar to using FaceTime, but it is compatible with Skype software or apps running on any other devices, including PCs, Macs, and iOS or Android Smartphones and tablets.

Through Skype, you can obtain your own unique telephone number (for an additional fee of $6.00 per month), which comes with call forwarding, voice mail, and other calling features.

With your own phone number, you can manage incoming calls whether or not Skype is activated and your iPad is connected to the Web. You also can receive calls on your iPad from people calling from a landline who do not use Skype.

Thus, people are able to reach you inexpensively by dialing a local phone number regardless of where you're traveling. However, you can initiate calls (and receive calls from fellow Skype users) without paying for a unique local phone number.

When traveling abroad, making and receiving calls on a cell phone (such as an iPhone) costs anywhere from $.50 to $3.00 per minute because international roaming fees apply. With Skype, that same call (made via an Internet connection) costs just a little more than $.02 per minute. Alternatively, you can pay a flat fee of less than $20.00 per month to make and receive unlimited domestic and international calls from your iPad.

In terms of call quality, as long as you're within a cellular data coverage area or Wi-Fi hotspot and your iPad has a strong Internet connection, calls are crystal clear. The Skype app is easy to use, and it enables you to maintain a contact list of frequently called people; dial out using a familiar telephone touchpad display; and maintain a detailed call history that lists incoming, outgoing, and missed calls.

If you opt to establish a paid Skype account (to have your own unique phone number and be able to make non-Skype-to-Skype calls), setting up the account takes just minutes when you visit www.Skype.com. All charges are billed to a major credit card or debit card.

15

DISCOVERING "MUST-HAVE" BUSINESS APPS

Right out of the box, the iPad is a powerful tool that includes a handful of useful, preinstalled apps, like Contacts, Calendar, Reminders, Mail, and Safari. However, by finding, purchasing, and installing third-party apps, you can truly customize the tablet and add additional functionality.

This chapter showcases a handful of business/work-related apps and describes some special-interest apps that can save you time and money; boost your productivity; and enhance your organization when traveling, participating in meetings, or juggling the many tasks and responsibilities you handle throughout your day.

> **TIP** The apps featured here have general appeal among business professionals, salespeople, freelancers, and consultants, but this is just a small sampling of the apps available from the App Store within the Business, Finance, Productivity, Reference, and Social Networking categories.
>
> Even if some of the apps described in this chapter are not directly relevant to your needs, they might help you understand the many different ways you can use your tablet for handling tasks you might not otherwise have realized were possible.

To find any of the apps described in this chapter, launch the App Store app on your tablet and enter the app's title in the Search field that's displayed near the upper-right corner of the screen (see Figure 15.1).

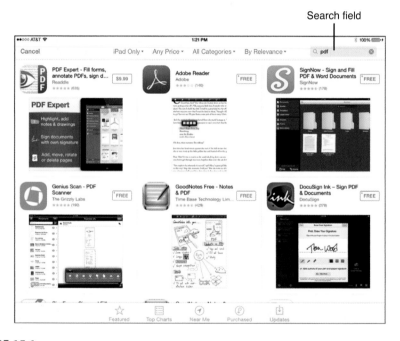

FIGURE 15.1

Use the Search field in the App Store to find specific apps based on their title or a keyword. In this example, a search for apps that can view PDF files was done using the keyword "PDF".

After entering the app's title, tap the Search key on the virtual keyboard. When the selection of search result preview boxes is displayed, tap the result that matches the specific app you're looking for. Tap the Price button to acquire the app, or tap the app's title or logo to view a detailed description of the app (shown in Figure 15.2).

FIGURE 15.2

Tap any app's title or logo within its preview box to reveal its detailed description.

> **NOTE** For more information about how to use the App Store app on your iPad, refer to Chapter 10, "Finding and Installing Apps from the App Store."

25 BUSINESS APPS THAT ENHANCE THE CAPABILITIES OF YOUR iPAD

The following is just a sampling of the business/work-related apps available from the App Store. Many of these apps, listed in alphabetical order, introduce you to new tasks above and beyond what's possible using the preinstalled apps that come with iOS 7.

Often, as you browse the App Store, you'll discover multiple apps that are designed to handle the same functions or tasks but that offer slightly different features or a unique user interface. For example, PDFpen is one of several dozen apps that enable you to view, edit, annotate, print, and share PDF files on the iPad.

With each app described in this section, similar apps are also listed. As you review an app's description when browsing the App Store, pay attention to its average rating, detailed reviews, listing of features, and sample screen shots to help you choose which app is best suited to meet your needs.

> TIP If a free version of an app is available, consider downloading it on a trial basis before you invest in the paid version of the app.

> TIP Whenever possible, choose the iPad-specific version of an app because it is designed to fully utilize your tablet's features. Remember, however, that iPad-specific apps do not run on iPhones or other iOS devices. If you also use an iPhone, unless you want to purchase two different versions of the same app, select the hybrid or iPhone version of the app to install on both your tablet and phone.

1PASSWORD—PASSWORD MANAGER AND SECURE WALLET

One of the many challenges people face is the need to memorize dozens of passwords, ID numbers, usernames, and other confidential pieces of information related to their personal identification, banking, favorite websites, and group or association memberships.

While the new iCloud Keychain feature that's built in to iOS 7 solves some of these problems, using an app such as 1Password for iPad ($7.99), it's possible to create and manage an easily accessible but secure database that contains all of your usernames, passwords, ID numbers, back account details, credit card numbers, and related information.

What's useful about 1Password Pro is that your personalized database can be synced with a PC or Mac (using optional Windows or OS X software). You also can customize the database to store specific types of information, such as website URLs and their related usernames and passwords or credit cards with their related account numbers, PINs, expiration dates, and contact information for the issuing bank or financial institution.

Using iPassword, it's possible to set up separate sections within the database to store bank account details, credit card information, personal ID information (driver's license, passport, Social Security, and so on), membership information, and frequently visited websites, for example.

1Password Pro uses a simple and intuitive user interface, plus it encrypts and password-protects all data. The app includes a nice collection of features designed to make it easy to keep track of important, highly confidential information. The app also offers iCloud and Dropbox integration for data backup and syncing data.

Similar apps available from the App Store: My Secret Folder, mSecure, oneSafe, eWallet, Password Wallet, Private Photo Vault, My Secret Apps, and Keeper Password & Data Vault

DROPBOX

As an iPad user, you may already be familiar with Apple's iCloud service and the tasks that a cloud-based file-sharing service can be used for, such as backing up or synchronizing app-specific data or photos wirelessly with other computers, mobile devices, and users.

In addition to iCloud, many other cloud-based file-sharing services provide similar functionality and offer free accounts with a predetermined amount of online storage space. These services make it easy for iPad users to share data, documents, photos, and files; back up information remotely; collaborate with other users; and transfer important information between a tablet and other computers or mobile devices.

Many of the popular cloud-based services now support the iPad, including Dropbox. Dropbox functionality has also been seamlessly incorporated into hundreds of third-party iPad apps. The Dropbox app, however, enables an iPad that's connected to the Internet to easily import files from a cloud-based Dropbox account or export files to a Dropbox account with a few taps on the tablet's screen. The app is also designed to help back up and share digital photos.

Dropbox is fully compatible with PCs, Macs, and most other mobile devices that can access the Internet. It's excellent if you want or need to securely share data and/or files with other people.

Similar apps available from the App Store: Box, Evernote, Amazon Cloud Drive, and Microsoft SkyDrive

EFAX MOBILE

Your iPad is capable of helping you communicate with other people in many ways. For example, use the Mail app to send and receive email or the Messages app to send and receive instant messages. You can use FaceTime, Skype, or WebEx for iPad for videoconferencing or make and receive telephone calls via Voice over IP (VoIP) using the Skype, Line2, Talkatone, or CallTime apps.

In addition, it's possible to transform your iPad into a feature-packed fax machine that sends and receives faxes wirelessly via the Internet. The eFax app nicely integrates with Contacts and enables you to add a digital signature to outgoing documents. You also can create custom cover sheets and view or search through sent or received faxes.

The eFax Mobile app is free, but you must have a paid eFax account to use it. The monthly $16.95 eFax plan includes a personal fax number (either a toll-free or local phone number). You can send up to 150 pages per month and receive up to 150 pages per month. An extra $0.10 fee applies for additional pages sent or received. To set up an account, visit www.eFax.com.

> **TIP** Once a fax is received and stored as a PDF file, use another app, such as PDFpen, to view, annotate, or digitally sign it, and then use eFax Mobile to re-fax it to others (or back to the original sender). This functionality allows users to receive, review, edit, and return contracts, business documents, and other correspondence digitally via an Internet-connected iPad.

Similar apps available from the App Store: Fax It, iFax Pro, JotNot Fax, FAX, and Pocket Fax

EVERNOTE

If you want to use your iPad for word processing, Apple's own Pages app enables you to create Microsoft Word–compatible documents from scratch on your tablet and then share them with other computers or devices via email or iCloud. You also have the option to import Word or Pages documents created elsewhere into your iPad for use with the Pages app.

The free Evernote app, however, is a powerful note-taking and information organizing tool that's designed to help you compose documents and detailed lists. Within each document, you can record and attach audio clips or digital images (photos). Then, store and organize your documents, lists, and notes into separate virtual notebooks, which can easily be synced with a desktop or notebook computer or other mobile devices using email or a variety of popular cloud-based services.

Versions of Evernote are available for PCs, Macs, all iOS devices, and other mobile operating systems, so regardless of what other equipment you use, your Evernote documents and files can always remain synced and accessible. To learn about or acquire other versions of Evernote, visit www.evernote.com.

Although Evernote does not offer the robust formatting capabilities of a full-featured word processor, it does offer a plethora of tools for organizing, managing, and sharing documents and lists. After you've stored content in Evernote, you can easily search and access it.

TIP If you prefer to write or draw on paper (using a regular pen or pencil) but also want to digitally store, edit, organize, print, or share your notes via your iPad and/or computer, Evernote offers a solution that involves a partnership with Moleskine (www.moleskineus.com/evernote-smart-notebooks.html). Moleskine is a manufacturer of high-quality notebooks.

Priced between $24.95 and $29.95 each, Moleskine offers its Evernote Pocket Notebooks (3.5" × 5.5", 96 sheets) and Evernote Large Notebooks (5" × 8.28", 120 sheets), in which you can write or draw anything on regular paper, using your favorite writing or drawing instruments. Then, at your convenience, using your iPad's built-in camera and the proprietary Page Camera app (free), snap digital photos of your note pages and incorporate them directly into Evernote.

The Moleskine notebook pages have tiny dots imprinted on them to ensure that each page is photo-scanned correctly into the app, so the pages can easily be transferred into Evernote, where they can be viewed, annotated, printed, shared, or archived.

The Moleskine notebooks, combined with the Evernote app running on an iPad, offer a unique blending of "old-school" pad and paper with the high-tech note-taking and file-management capabilities of the iPad. Each Moleskine Evernote Notebook comes with three months' worth of free access to the Evernote Premium service (www.evernote.com/premium), which typically costs $5.00 per month.

NOTE Evernote also offers a special service targeted toward businesses, called Evernote Business (www.evernote.com/business). This is a fee-based service that combines the many features of the Evernote app and Evernote Premium service, with additional functionality that allows for collaboration and the easy exchange of notes between users.

Similar apps available from the App Store: Simplenote, Microsoft OneNote, JotAgent, Note+, Awesome Note HD, Notes Plus, Note Taker HD, Ghostwriter Notes, Note!, Super Note, Penultimate, Easy Note + To Do, and Noteability

FILEMAKER GO FOR iPAD

For many businesses, having an app created (see Chapter 17, "Creating and Distributing Content on the iPad") provides a customized solution for making a wide range of tasks manageable via an iPad. For independent business professionals, entrepreneurs, or small business operators, though, it's too costly to develop a custom app. Fortunately, there are a variety of much more affordable solutions.

FileMaker Pro (and FileMaker Server) continues to be one of the most powerful and robust database management tools on the market. Using this PC, Mac, or network-based software, you can create and deploy highly complex and extremely custom-ized database applications. The FileMaker Go app makes these interactive custom databases accessible from the iPad.

This $39.99 app enables users to access and utilize FileMaker databases from any-where an iPad can connect to the Internet via a Wi-Fi or cellular connection. Using FileMaker Go, signatures can be captured in the field; inventory or customer data can be searched, accessed, viewed, and printed wirelessly; or information can be collected or disseminated between a centralized database and the iPad.

A custom database must be created with FileMaker Pro (or FileMaker Server) before it can be accessed with FileMaker Go for iPad. For many businesses, FileMaker Pro and FileMaker Go provide the perfect tool set for creating the closest thing pos-sible to an custom (proprietary) iPad app, without requiring the time and expense of actually programming, testing, and deploying an app. Using FileMaker Pro, no programming is required.

To learn more about how FileMaker Pro is being used for highly customized mobile applications in a wide range of industries, visit www.filemaker.com/products/filemaker-go.

Similar apps available from the App Store: Things, HanDBase for iPad, FormMobi, Cellica Database for iPad, and MySQL Mobile Database Client

FLIGHTTRACK PRO

Out of all the apps created for travelers, many iPad users who are frequent fliers believe that FlightTrack Pro ($9.99) is the best designed and most feature packed. In addition to helping you manage your travel itinerary, it automatically syncs data with the Calendar app and keeps you informed of flight delays, cancellations, gate changes, and other details pertinent to your trip. FlightTrack Pro (see Figure 15.3) works with every major airline and contains information about virtually all major airports throughout the world.

Using this app, it's possible to track any flight in real time, plus access information based on the flight's past history to determine the chances of it arriving on time. This information is useful if you're picking up someone at the airport or you need to coordinate ground transportation upon your arrival.

If a flight gets canceled, FlightTrack Pro helps you quickly find an alternative flight option online. You can also share your travel itinerary via email, determine at which baggage claim carousel your luggage can be retrieved when you land, and be able to view the extended local weather forecast for your destination.

FIGURE 15.3
FlightTrack Pro handles a wide range of tasks related to flying and helps you more efficiently manage your travel itinerary.

FlightTrack Pro uses the Internet to keep you well informed, plus it's designed to work seamlessly with TripIt.com, so you don't even need to enter your travel itinerary manually. Once you set up your TripIt.com account, simply forward your emailed flight confirmation from any airline to plans@TripIt.com, and your itinerary information is automatically synced with the FlightTrack Pro and the Calendar apps.

This is truly an indispensable app for frequent travelers. It goes well beyond being an organizational tool, and it can actually take some of the stress out of flying on any commercial airline, anywhere in the world.

Similar apps available from the App Store: FlightTrack Live, US Flights, FlightAware Flight Tracker, KAYAK Mobile Pro, TripAssist by Expedia, FlightBoard, TripIt—Travel Organizer, Skyscanner, Flight Update, and Flight Status

GRUBHUB

Whether you're a frequent business traveler who constantly orders room service from hotels, you're often forced to work late at the office, or you're too tired to cook a healthy meal when you get home, the free GrubHub app (shown in Figure 15.4) offers an affordable dining solution. This is an iPhone-specific app that works on the iPad.

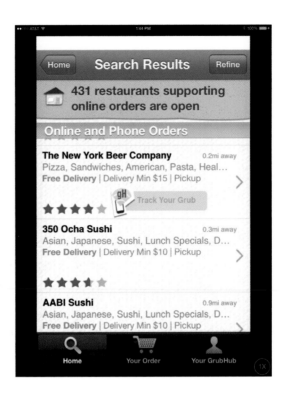

FIGURE 15.4

Have food from your favorite restaurants delivered to your home, office, or hotel room (even if the restaurant doesn't typically deliver) using the GrubHub app.

The GrubHub service has teamed up with more than 20,000 restaurants in major cities to make each restaurant's entire menu available for delivery, often for no extra charge. So, if you live in or are visiting any of more than 500 cities, you can use this app to automatically pinpoint your location and find local participating restaurants; view their menus; place an order; pay by credit card or PayPal; and have your food delivered to your home, office, or hotel room—often within 30–60 minutes.

Instead of being limited to fast food, GrubHub offers delivery from top-rated, fine-dining restaurants (as well as less costly dining options). The choices are not only plentiful; they can be healthy as well.

GrubHub offers a cost-effective alternative to hotel room service, which often features a limited menu and charges a 15%–25% premium to have food delivered.

Similar apps available from the App Store: Many of your favorite chain restaurants, such as Starbucks, McDonald's, Pizza Hut, Chipotle, Papa John's, Ruth's Chris Steakhouse, Outback Steakhouse, The Capital Grille, Subway, and Baja Fresh, have their own custom apps that can help you find the closest location to wherever you happen to be.

> **TIP** To find restaurants to dine at across America and throughout the world, you can utilize the Yelp! functionality that's built in to the Maps app or download and use the free, standalone Yelp! app. The Zagat Restaurants app offers reviews and details about thousands of restaurants, while the Open Table app enables you to find restaurants and then book your reservations directly from the iPad (Internet connectivity is required).

INVOICE2GO FOR iPAD

For small business operators, consultants, and freelancers, the need to generate and send invoices in a timely and efficient manner is essential. Using the Invoice2Go software on a PC or Mac ($99.00 to $149.00 per year), along with the Invoice2Go for iPad app ($14.99), you have the ability to create professional-looking, customized invoices that you can design from scratch or adapt from more than 300 invoice templates offered with the software and app.

A free Invoice2Go Lite for iPad version is available that includes 20 built-in invoice templates. This is a slightly scaled-down version of the paid app, but it is still highly functional and useful.

Finding and generating the perfect invoice to bill a customer or client for your products, services, or time is possible using this app. For invoices sent electronically, you can add an interactive PayPal button, so you can be paid with a click of the mouse by the recipient. As you're generating the invoice, subtotals, sales tax, and totals are automatically calculated.

> **NOTE** Use the Invoice2Go for iPad app to create and generate personalized purchase orders, estimates, and credit memos that can contain all of your company information, including your logo.

In addition to simply generating the invoices, this app generates sales and business reports in 16 different formats, enabling you to email invoices directly to clients or customers from your iPad and track incoming payments. You can print invoices and reports wirelessly from the iPad, or you can transfer all data and sync it with Invoice2Go on your computer. Data from Invoice2go can also be exported for use in Intuit's QuickBooks accounting and bookkeeping software that's running on your primary computer or network.

Invoice2Go can meet all of your customer and client invoicing needs, yet the software and app (either of which you can use as a standalone product) are extremely user friendly and require no:Invoice2Go accounting knowledge to fully utilize. For more information, go to www.Invoice2go.com.

Similar apps available from the App Store: invoiceASAP, Quick Sale for iPad, Invoice Robot, Invoice, iQuote, Simple Invoices—Services, Invoice Studio, Invoice Generator HD, and TapInvoice

INVOICE MANAGER

Unlike other invoice creation and management apps available for the iPad, Invoice Manager ($4.99) has no recurring monthly fees or subscriptions. This app (shown in Figure 15.5) allows users to create an unlimited number of invoices using any of the 10 customizable invoice templates that are built in. Part of the customization process can include displaying a logo, along with a company's address as part of the invoice.

FIGURE 15.5

Create, send, and manage customized invoices directly from your iPad using the Invoice Manager app.

Once an invoice is generated, it can be stored on the iPad, emailed to the recipient, or printed using any AirPrint-compatible printer. With additional in-app purchases ($4.99 each), this one app can also offer functionality for creating and managing time sheets, serve as a receipt and/or inventory tracker, plus can have a built-in cost calculator and currency converter.

Invoices can be exported into PDF format or emailed in an interactive format that allows recipients to pay them online using PayPal or a major credit card (via the sender's credit card merchant account).

The Invoice Manager app includes the ability to generate a wide range of customizable reports using data from the invoices, such as sales reports and tax reports. These reports utilize charts, tables, and graphs.

Similar apps available from the App Store: invoiceASAP, Quick Sale for iPad, Invoice Robot, Invoice, iQuote, Simple Invoices—Services, Invoice Studio, Invoice Generator HD, and TapInvoice

LINE2

Thanks to the Line2 app, your iPad can be transformed into a powerful business telephone as long you're connected to the Internet. The app not only gives you your own telephone number, but it enables you to use VoIP technology to make and receive calls from your tablet wherever you happen to be (including overseas).

Although a free, ad-supported version of Line2 is offered, to fully utilize the app you must subscribe to a monthly service plan, which starts at $9.99. This includes a unique phone number, the ability to make and receive unlimited calls within the United States and Canada, call forwarding, voicemail, the ability to establish conference calls, as well as other useful phone features (such as caller ID, call waiting, and hold).

Line2 (shown in Figure 15.6) integrates nicely with the Contacts app and uses the iPad's built-in microphone and speaker to transform the tablet into a speakerphone. Users can pay for one month at a time; no long-term service contract is required. Using this app, it's not only possible to use the iPad to make and receive calls from an iPad, it's also cost effective and convenient. As long as a good-quality Internet connection is available, calls are crystal clear and you never have to worry about using peak versus off-peak cellular minutes, long distance charges, or (international) roaming charges.

Similar apps available from the App Store: Skype, SecondLine, Takeatone, NorthEast Voip Phone, VOIP, and FreePhoo

FIGURE 15.6

You can use Line2 as a standalone telephone (speakerphone) for making and receiving calls from a unique phone number when your iPad is connected to the Internet.

MICROSOFT ONENOTE FOR iPAD

Based on the Microsoft OneNote software for desktop and notebook computers, this iPad edition of Microsoft OneNote is designed for capturing ideas, taking notes, and managing to-do lists while on-the-go. The free app enables you to create notes that incorporate text, pictures, or bulleted items that are searchable, as well as to-do lists complete with check boxes.

The OneNote app is also Microsoft SkyDrive compatible, so you can back up your documents and notes online, share them with others, or synchronize them with computers or mobile devices also running the OneNote software or app.

By combining elements of a text editor and to-do list manager, but not the full functionality of a word processor, OneNote offers a customizable way to create, manage, and share information and lists. The functionality of the app is somewhat similar to Evernote. This app offers more robust features than the Notes app that comes bundled with iOS 7.

NOTE By exploring the app store and using the search phrase "note taking" or "word processing," you can find a vast selection of third-party iPad-specific apps, some of which are designed specifically for note taking and information organization, while others are geared more toward full-featured word processing and page layout.

Similar apps available from the App Store: Evernote, Text Writer, Note Taker HD, Notes Plus, Noteshelf, iA Writer, and WritePad for iPad

TIP Another app that is ideal for note taking is called Drafts ($2.99). It serves as a versatile text editor that allows you to quickly share your text-based (typed) documents with many popular cloud-based services, or with others via email.

Drafts is an easy-to-use app that allows you to choose from different fonts and font sizes, but it purposely lacks a bunch of page formatting features that would make it more difficult to use. The app was designed specifically for use with iOS 7 on an iPad.

PDFPEN

Simply by visiting the App Store and entering the phrase "PDF" into the Search field, you'll discover dozens of iPad apps that enable you to create, view, annotate, print, organize, store, and share PDF files. Some of these apps have very specific purposes—for example, Adobe Reader simply enables you to view PDF files that are already created and stored on your tablet.

Many apps, such as Pages, Numbers, and Keynote, also enable you to create PDF files that you can share, while iBooks serves as a PDF file viewer. The PDFpen app ($9.99) is one of the more powerful apps for actually working with PDF files because it enables you to view, edit, annotate, print, organize, and share them with ease. It's designed to be a full-featured PDF editor compatible with iCloud, Dropbox, Evernote, and Google Docs. This app (shown in Figure 15.7) makes sharing PDF files with PCs, Macs, and other mobile devices easy.

NOTE Portable Document Format (PDF) files are an industry-standard file type that was originally created by Adobe about two decades ago. With this file format, you can save a file or document that can easily be viewed on any computer, web browser, or mobile device while its appearance, fonts, and formatting remain fully intact. The PDF format provides a convenient way to share information between PCs and Macs or other devices and ensures full compatibility regardless of what software is being used to create or view the PDF file.

For a long time, after a PDF file was created, it could be viewed but not edited or annotated. The PDFpen app for iPad enables PDF files to be edited or annotated after they've been created. Thus, you can add a digital signature to a document or alter the document on your tablet, regardless of where or how it was originally created.

You can export virtually any type of file or document that can be printed—no matter what software it was created with—into the PDF file format using the proper tools (which are built in to some software packages and apps or are available using additional software or apps).

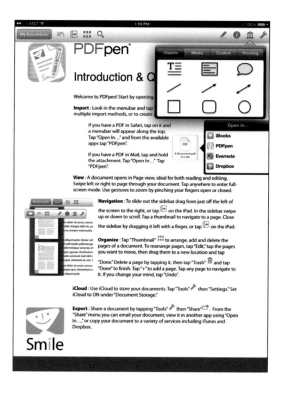

FIGURE 15.7

Using PDFpen, you can mark up or annotate a contract, letter, or document that's transferred to or created on your iPad in PDF format. Then you can email it to others (or upload it to a cloud-based file-sharing service).

The ability to create, view, edit, annotate, print, organize, and share PDF files is a must for most mobile executives. By adding these capabilities to an iPad, it further reduces the need for a notebook computer while you're on-the-go.

Similar apps available from the App Store: Adobe Reader, PDF Reader Pro, SignMyPad, iAnnotate PDF, and UPad

PHOTON FLASH WEB BROWSER

The Safari web browser that comes preinstalled on all iOS mobile devices, including the iPad, is a feature-packed and powerful app used for surfing the Web. Although new features continue to be added to this web browser with each new version of the iOS that Apple releases, one feature that remains absent is the capability to display Adobe Flash animations and graphics.

> **NOTE** An alternative to Safari is Google's Chrome web browser for the iPad (free). While it, too, is feature-packed and it offers some functionality not found in Safari, Chrome also lacks the ability to display Flash animations that are often featured within websites.

Until recently, when surfing the Web, most of the animations on websites were created using an application platform called Adobe Flash. To view these animations, a Flash plug-in for your web browser is required. Apple has never made a Flash plug-in available for the iOS version of Safari. As a result, it's not possible to fully access any websites that utilize Flash programming.

With the ever-growing popularity of iOS devices, many website developers and programmers have turned away from utilizing Flash animations within their sites. However, as an iPad user, if you absolutely need to visit websites that utilize Flash, you have two solutions.

The Photon Flash Web Browser ($4.99) is a full-featured web browser app for the iPad that serves as an alternative to using Safari when surfing the Web. This web browser is compatible with most Flash-based websites and can display their Flash-based animations and graphics.

A second alternative for viewing Flash-based graphics while surfing the Web on an iPad is to use a remote desktop application to access and control a PC or Mac remotely. (See "Splashtop 2—Remote Desktop" later in this chapter.) When your iPad has control over your primary computer via the Internet or a wireless network, you can run any web browser, surf the Web via your computer, and see everything on your tablet's screen (with a slight lag time).

Similar apps available from the App Store: Skyfire Web Browser for iPad, Flash Web Brower, Splashtop Remote Browser, and FlashIE

QUICKBOOKS ONLINE FOR iPAD

One of the most popular bookkeeping and accounting applications in use by small- to mid-size businesses is Intuit's QuickBooks. For companies that utilize the online edition of QuickBooks (a fee applies), the official QuickBooks Online for iPad app (free) gives users complete, secure, and remote access to their financial records from the iPad.

Using QuickBooks Online for iPad, users can generate and send professional-looking invoices from anywhere; instantly capture a customer's electronic signature to approve estimates; track all overdue balances; see a timeline of a customer's transactions; generate customizable sales, income, and expense reports; plus capture and store photos of receipts, for expense tracking purposes.

Using the QuickBooks Online for iPad app is free for existing QuickBooks Online users. However, to utilize all of the app's functionality as a standalone product, a monthly fee of $12.99 per month applies.

Anyone who wants complete, secure, and remote access to their company's financial records can benefit from using QuickBooks Online and this proprietary app.

Similar apps available from the App Store: Instead of using QuickBooks Online, if you utilize QuickBooks software on your PC or Mac, a handful of third-party apps allow you to gather financial data using your tablet and then sync it with your primary computer. For example, there's eBility QuickBooks (a free time-tracking app that is compatible with QuickBooks) and iSlips For QuickBooks ($19.99), which can also be used as a remote data gathering tool for tracking time, expenses, and mileage. The qBooks app ($24.99 to $49.99) allows QuickBooks users to utilize their iPad to remotely connect to their PC or Mac that has QuickBooks installed in order to securely access and work with QuickBooks data.

QUICKVOICE RECORDER

Using the microphone that's built in to your iPad, you can use the tablet as a full-featured digital audio recorder. Use this functionality as a dictation tool or to record meetings, for example. Some digital recording apps, such as Apple's GarageBand, can transform the iPad into a multitrack digital recording studio.

The QuickVoice Recorder is one of the easier-to-use digital recording apps. It is ideal for recording dictation, voice memos, lectures, classes, or meetings. You can play back recordings on the iPad or transfer (sync) them with a computer, cloud-based file-sharing service or another mobile device. A version of QuickVoice is also available for PCs and Macs.

The user interface used by QuickVoice Recorder is very straightforward and simple. To record, simply tap the large red Record button. You can name your recordings and then play them back by tapping the large green Play button. It's also possible to pause and resume a recording.

> **TIP** If the quality of the microphone that's built in to your iPad isn't good enough to meet your needs, several third-party companies offer external microphones that plug into the tablet's headphones jack and offer significantly higher recording quality. For example, Mic-W (www.mic-w.com) offers its i-Series of professional-quality microphones for the iPad, which include a high-sensitivity cardioid microphone, a professional Class 2 microphone, and a lavaliere microphone.

> **NOTE** Audio recording apps like QuickVoice Recorder are designed to capture and create digital audio files from the content that's recorded. These files can be edited, archived, shared, and/or played back. However, these apps do not translate speech to text, which is a function of the Dictation feature that's built in to iOS 7, as well as some third-party apps, like Dragon Dictation (free).

Similar apps available from the App Store: Smart Recorder, Audio Memos, QuickVoice2Text Email, Voice Recorder HD, Voice Memos for iPad, iRecorder Pro, AudioNote, Smart Recorder, Super Note: Voice Recorder, Recorder HD, and Mobile Recorder HD

REMEMBER THE MILK

The Reminders app, which is a to-do list manager, comes bundled with iOS 7. The benefit to using it is that your lists can automatically sync via iCloud with the Reminders app on your Mac and/or iPhone, as well as the online edition of Reminders available from iCloud.com.

For some people, however, Reminders doesn't meet their needs when it comes to managing lists, organizing information, or prioritizing tasks.

The Remember the Milk app (free) offers a feature-packed alternative to the Reminders app. It enables you to easily sync data between this app and Outlook, Calendar, Gmail, Google Calendar, Twitter, and other services, apps, and software.

To fully utilize this app, you should upgrade to the Pro edition, which costs $2.99 per month or $24.99 per year. It allows for unlimited autosyncing with Remember the Milk Online, as well as with multiple mobile devices and computers. It also offers Push Notification reminders and badge updates on your tablet, as well as Notification Center compatibility.

As you'd expect from a to-do list manager, Remember the Milk enables you to create an unlimited number of separate to-do-style lists and then prioritize the lists, as well as each item within each list. Each to-do list item can also be accompanied by notes or photos, and all items are fully searchable.

The user interface and some of the core features of Remember the Milk are different than the Reminders app, although you can use either to successfully manage a vast amount of information in the form of to-do lists.

Similar apps available from the App Store: Post-It PopNotes, Wunderlist HD, To+Do, Errands To-Do List, Toodledo, Task PRO, 2Do, Awesome Lists, Easy Note + To Do, iReminder, and Evernote

SCANNER PRO BY READDLE

Instead of connecting an external scanner to your mobile device, the Scanner Pro app ($6.99) allows you to use the camera that's built in to your iPad in order to snap photos of paper-based documents or photos.

Hold the tablet above the printed page you want to scan, and snap the photo using this app. Scanner Pro automatically detects the borders of the page, straightens the scanned document as needed, and enhances the scanned image in order to make it easier to read in PDF form. Use Scanner Pro to quickly scan receipts, handwritten notes, or other multipage documents and then transform them into PDF files that can be stored on the tablet, printed, or shared.

Once scanned documents are stored as a PDF file, they can also be annotated (using another app, such as PDFpen) or uploaded and synced with Evernote or a cloud-based file sharing service, such as Dropbox or Google Drive.

Available as an in-app purchase, it's also possible to fax a scanned document directly from the iPad. The iPad requires Internet access. The cost is $0.99 per fax.

Similar apps available from the App Store: Genius Scan+—PDF Scanner ($2.99), TinyScan Pro ($4.99), and JotNot Scanner Pro ($0.99)

> **TIP** CamCard HD ($7.99) also uses the iPad's camera to scan paper-based information, but this app is designed exclusively to scan business cards directly into the iPad and then automatically load relevant information from the business card directly into the Contacts app as a new entry.

SPLASHTOP 2—REMOTE DESKTOP

Imagine being able to access and run any software or utilize any files, documents, or data that are stored on your desktop computer (at home or your office) from your iPad—anytime and anywhere. This is possible using a remote desktop app, such as Splashtop 2 ($6.99).

As long as your primary computer is turned on and running free companion software to Splashtop 2, you can use your iPad to remotely access your computer from anywhere and then run software or access files from it. The display on your iPad shows everything on your primary computer's screen and enables you to control PC or Mac software, for example, using the tablet's touch screen.

To make navigating around your primary computer's full-size screen from your iPad's smaller size screen easier, the Splashtop 2 app adds navigational arrow keys to your tablet's virtual keyboard, plus it uses a proprietary interface to reduce the amount of scrolling that would otherwise be necessary.

Instead of using Pages for word processing on your iPad, having to export your Pages document to Microsoft Word format, and then somehow transferring or syncing the document to your computer, with Splashtop 2 you can run the actual PC or Mac version of Microsoft Word (or any software for that matter) directly from your iPad so that you have full control over your primary computer.

In addition to being able to access and utilize files, data, and documents, when you use your iPad to run software from your primary computer, you can also play games, view Flash-based websites, or watch multimedia content that's stored on your computer (without transferring it to your iPad first).

For Splashtop 2 to work, your iPad must have access to a Wi-Fi Internet connection and your primary computer must also be turned on and connected to the Web. Depending on the software you're running, you might experience a slight lag, but for most applications, this is acceptable.

Using a remote desktop solution, such as Splashtop 2, you no longer have to worry about transferring to your tablet the files, documents, or data that you need while you're on-the-go because everything that's stored on your primary computer (as well as external storage devices connected to your computer) is readily available.

Similar apps available from the App Store: Remote Desktop, GoToMyPC, iRemoteDesktop, and Jump Desktop

TIP If you're interested in accessing and taking control over your Windows-based PC directly from your iPad, Microsoft now offers its official Remote Desktop application. It's available for free from the App Store. Using this Remote Desktop app, users can make use of their iOS mobile device's touchscreen in order to actually run and work with Windows applications and/or remotely access files, documents, photos, and data stored on their Windows-based PC via a secure Internet-based connection. Because Microsoft Windows 8.1 also supports a touchscreen interface, remotely running Windows applications from an iOS mobile device is an easier process than it has ever been. The functionality of the official Remote Desktop app is similar to what's possible using Splashtop 2–Remote Desktop, or any of the other remote desktop applications for the iPhone and iPad that also support Windows PCs.

SQUARE REGISTER

Whether you're a small business, consultant, freelancer, or even an artisan showcasing your work at a local crafts show, one of the easiest ways to set up a merchant account and be able to accept credit card payments within a few minutes is to use the Square Register app and credit card processing service.

Begin by visiting http://squareup.com to set up a free account. Next, from the App Store, download the free Square Register app. To use the Square service in order to accept and process credit card transactions, there are no upfront costs, no contracts to sign, no recurring monthly fees, and no hidden charges. You simply pay a flat 2.75% fee per transaction (as long as you swipe the customer's credit card). Without the card swipe, each transaction costs $.15 plus 3.5% of the transaction. For higher-volume small businesses, there's also an option to pay a flat monthly fee ($275.00) but absolutely no per-swipe or percentage of transaction charges.

Square even provides a free, and extremely small, credit card swiper that attaches to the iPad through the unit's headphones jack. Use it to swipe credit cards and process transactions, or you can manually enter credit card information from your customers or clients. For an additional $299.00, the Square Stand (available from Apple Stores and Best Buy, and shown in Figure 15.8) serves as an iPad stand and credit card swiper that's suitable for a retail environment.

The free Square Register app accepts an onscreen signature from your customer, processes each transaction, and promptly emails your customer a detailed receipt. A wireless receipt printer can also be used with the tablet to generate onsite receipts for customers, and a barcode reader can be used to scan in products. For details about optional hardware that the Square Register app is compatible with, visit https://squareup.com/help/en-us/article/5084-supported-hardware.

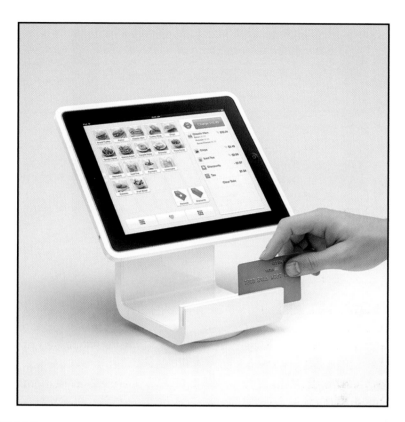

FIGURE 15.8

The optional Square Stand transforms the iPad into a feature-packed cash register and credit card swiper that's suitable for a retail environment.

The proceeds from all transactions are transferred directly to the checking or savings account you have linked to your Square account within 24 hours.

Within minutes of setting up a Square merchant account, you are able to accept Visa, MasterCard, American Express, Discover, and debit card payments using your iPad.

Before using the app for the first time to process credit card transactions, set up the Square Register app to display onscreen icons that represent each item you're selling (shown in Figure 15.9). You can include the item name, price, applicable sales tax, and a brief item description. You also can attach a photo of that item.

FIGURE 15.9

Fully customize the Square Register app to meet the sales needs of your product or service-oriented business. The Square credit card reader is shown sticking out of the right side of the iPad.

When you're ready to accept a credit card payment, simply launch the Square Register app, enter the transaction amount or tap a preprogrammed Item icon (based on what's being purchased), swipe the customer's credit card, and have the customer sign your iPad's screen. The app connects to the Internet and securely processes the transaction within seconds.

Being able to accept major credit cards and debit cards, especially while working offsite, offers a huge advantage to small businesses, consultants, freelancers, and entrepreneurs while also offering added convenience to customers.

Square offers an efficient and low-cost way to be able to handle credit card transactions from any location and automatically maintain detailed records of each transaction that you can later export to bookkeeping or inventory management software on a primary computer.

As a result of the incredible popularity of the Square service, other companies, including Intuit (with its GoPayment service) and PayPal (with its Here service), have made it easy for small businesses and independent professionals to accept credit card payments using their iPads.

Similar apps available from the App Store: Intuit GoPayment Credit Card Terminal, PayPal Here, and Phone Swipe

THE WEATHER CHANNEL

As you're preparing for a trip and deciding what to pack, or determining what to do each day when you arrive at your destination, knowing the local weather forecast is extremely useful. The free Weather Channel for iPad app enables you to pick any city in the world and obtain a detailed current weather report, as well as an extended weather forecast. Plus, you can watch streaming Weather Channel television reports, view animated weather radar maps, and use other features in this colorful app as you monitor the weather in one or more cities.

Use this app as you're packing to figure out the average daily temperature at your destination so you know in advance whether to pack extra sweaters, jackets, hats, and gloves, for example. There are many weather-related apps available for the iPad; however, the Weather Channel app is created specifically for the iPad and offers forecast information and weather reports from a reliable and well-respected source.

Similar apps available from the App Store: Weather+, Weather HD, MyRadar Weather Radar, Weather Live, Nightstand Central for iPad, WeatherBug for iPad, and Fahrenheit Free Weather and Temperature

THINGS FOR iPAD

Things for iPad ($19.99) combines functionality of a basic database manager app with a to-do list manager and scheduling app, enabling it to be used to gather, organize, prioritize, display, and share a wide range of information. By more effectively managing to-do lists, due dates, and data related to projects, it's easier to become more efficient during your workday.

Things for iPad nicely combines functionality found in Calendars, Reminders, and Notification Center into a single customizable app. A version of Things is also available for the Mac and iPhone, so your personalized data can easily be synced and utilized on multiple computers and devices.

Similar apps available from the App Store: FileMaker Go

TIME MASTER + BILLING

If you need to track your time and bill customers or clients for it, the Time Master + Billing app ($9.99) is one of several apps that offer this capability using an iPad. Whether you're a lawyer, accountant, contractor, consultant, or freelancer, the Time Master + Billing app is an easy way to track your time (down to the second, if necessary) and expenses, plus generate invoices from virtually anywhere. The app enables you to run multiple timers simultaneously, start and stop timers as needed, and display or export reports that you can share via email or syncing.

Paid upgrades to the Time Master + Billing app are required to generate invoices from the app, synchronize data, and/or export data to Quickbooks. Using the core version of the app, however, you can export timesheet data to other formats, such as CSV or HTML.

The user interface of this app isn't slick, but the functionality built in to the app is impressive and versatile, making it ideal for use by professionals working in a variety of industries.

Similar apps available from the App Store: eBility Time Tracker for Intuit Quickbooks and TimeTracker—Time Sheet

VIPORBIT

Your iPad that's running iOS 7 comes with the Contacts, Calendar, and Reminders apps preinstalled. Although these apps can work together, they are three separate apps designed for different tasks commonly utilized by businesspeople.

VIPorbit for iPad ($4.99) is a full-featured, mobile contact (or customer) relationship manager (CRM) that's designed for building, managing, and cultivating business relationships. VIPorbit (shown in Figure 15.10) enables you to manage your personalized contacts database, schedule, and to-do lists all from one app that also nicely integrates your data with other iPad apps, plus can sync data with the iPhone version of the app (free) or Mac version of the app (sold separately for $29.99).

FIGURE 15.10

Using VIPorbit, you can look up contacts data, check your schedule, review your Tasklist (to-do list items and pending deadlines), back up your data, and access the app's other main functions.

The VIPorbit app can also utilize the vipSync option (as an in-app purchase for $4.99 per month) to store a secure backup of your data on a cloud-based server, plus make the data accessible using other versions of VIPOrbit on other computers or devices. The Back Up My Stuff option is priced at $4.99 per year.

The goal behind the VIPorbit app is to help business professionals become more efficient when it comes to managing their contacts and building relationships. The premise behind VIPorbit is that in addition to creating a personalized database of your individual contacts (which is what the Contacts app is designed to do), you can categorize your contacts into groups and establish connections between them. Plus, in each contact entry it's possible to include details about the phone number and email address.

The contact management aspect of VIPorbit enables you to customize multiple fields in each entry and attach a digital photo or graphic to each entry as well. In addition, you can add unlimited, free-form notes to each entry over time.

The VIPorbit app greatly differs from the Contacts app and becomes a valuable business tool because with VIPorbit, each time you make contact with someone you've saved in your contact database, it's possible to document details about the interaction and automatically save those notes and activities in chronological order.

Because the app has a built-in scheduling and to-do list manager, as you're speaking or corresponding with a contact, you can quickly schedule a follow-up meeting and set a related alert or alarm, set a reminder to initiate a future call or email, and include detailed notes about what you've already discussed and what you need to discuss during your next communication.

This functionality in VIPorbit enables you to better manage your contacts and build relationships. The app automatically helps you keep track of even the most minute details related to each interaction you have with a contact, so nothing falls through the cracks and you never forget to follow through on tasks or responsibilities related to each contact.

If you need to schedule a meeting for next week, remember to send the contact a follow-up email in a month, or want to remember an important date related to a contact, you can easily handle it with a few taps on the screen in VIPorbit.

Unlike when you use the Contacts, Calendar, and Reminders apps separately, the VIPorbit app enables you to link activities, meetings, and scheduled events directly to contact entries. The app then reminds you of upcoming to-do items or appointments and automatically keeps track of completed activities.

Because you can link contacts or place them into groups within VIPorbit, a single task, to-do item, or scheduled item can also be linked with multiple contact entries or a group. And, because everyone's work habits are slightly different, the calendar/scheduling module of VIPorbit is customizable, so you can view calendars in multiple formats or filter a calendar view by activity type or date range.

> **NOTE** Data already stored in the Contacts and Calendar apps can easily be imported into VIPorbit, eliminating the need for repetitive data entry.

The VIPorbit app also works seamlessly with other apps installed on your iPad and offers email, text messaging (via Messages), Twitter, Facebook, and Skype integration (for Internet-based voice and videoconference calls via your iPad). As a result, you can stay in contact with people in your database with ease without having to manually launch multiple apps or cut and paste information between apps.

As you interact with your contacts, VIPorbit automatically maintains a detailed log of all phone conversations, emails, online communication, and in-person meetings, so you can quickly refer to interactions that have transpired and see alerts for upcoming required actions related to each contact.

VIPorbit is a powerful and highly customizable tool for business executives; salespeople; lawyers; real estate professionals; or anyone who regularly interacts with employees, customers, or clients.

> **TIP** To discover other apps for the iPad that offer similar functionality when it comes to managing contacts, calendars, and/or to-do list management, visit the App Store and enter the phrase "Contact Management," "Scheduling," "CRM" (Contacts Relationship Manager), or "To Do Lists" into the Search field.
>
> If you're a PC user who currently utilizes Microsoft Dynamics CRM (http://crm.dynamics.com/en-us/home) for contact relationship management, a variety of iPad-specific apps give you full access to your Microsoft Dynamics database via your tablet, including Resco Mobil CRM for Microsoft Dynamics CRM, Mobile Client for Microsoft Dynamics CRM, Mobile CRM+ for MS Dynamics, and CWR Mobile CRM for iPad. These apps require Internet access to function.

> **NOTE** VIPorbit was designed and created by the co-creator of ACT! for the PC, which is now owned and distributed by Sage (http://sage.act.com). Although an iPad version of ACT! is not available, you can access the subscription-based ACT! Connect online service from an iPad that's connected to the Web. ACT! Connect gives ACT! users access to their contact details, notes, history, meetings, and activities via a cloud-based service.

XPENSETRACKER

People who are on-the-go, who travel for business, or who entertain or service customers or clients often need to accurately and efficiently keep track of personal or business-related expenses. The XpenseTracker app ($4.99) is one of several available from the App Store designed specifically for this purpose.

Using this app, you can customize how you keep track of expenses—by category or customer, for example—and create as many categories and subcategories as needed. For each expense, you can store details about payment type and include a related time, date, or other notes and details.

In addition to enabling you to create detailed expense reports, the app tracks which expenses have been submitted for reimbursement and which expenses have already been repaid. You can also track vehicle miles and calculate currency exchange rates, as needed.

You can export expense reports and data to Microsoft Excel or Numbers, for example, or synchronize them with your primary computer. In-app add-ons include Dropbox support and OCR scanner support (allowing for printed receipts to be scanned directly into the app using an optional scanner).

> **TIP** The Shoeboxed.com service (www.shoeboxed.com) is also designed for managing expenses. This fee-based service (which starts at $99 per year) offers its own iPad app that is easy to use and powerful, especially when it comes to collecting receipt data while on-the-go and then wirelessly syncing receipts and expense data with your accounting or bookkeeping software that's running on your PC, Mac, or network.

Similar apps available from the App Store: Concur, Expensify, BizXPenseTracker, Expense Tablet for iPad, Visual Budget: Expense Tracker, Office Time—Time & Expense Tracking, and Pocket Expense

YELP! FOR iPAD

Ideal for business travelers, Yelp! (free) helps you quickly locate the businesses, restaurants, or services you want or need, in virtually any city. Although Yelp! functionality is now built in to the Maps app, the standalone Yelp! app (shown in Figure 15.11) offers many additional features and functions. In addition to simply displaying an address and phone number for the desired listing, Yelp! offers customer reviews and ratings, plus directions from your current location.

FIGURE 15.11
Quickly find restaurants, businesses, services, or attractions, when you need them and wherever you happen to be. Yelp! offers detailed reviews, photos, and information—not just an address and contact details.

When it comes to finding restaurants, for example, you can search by geographic region, price, or food type, and it's possible to make reservations for participating restaurants from within the app. You can also use Yelp! to publish where you are and what you're doing on Facebook or Twitter or quickly share your own reviews about a business, restaurant, or bar you're visiting.

Yelp! is an easy-to-use app that provides far more information than a typical Yellow Pages or phone directory app. It works seamlessly with the Maps and Contacts apps, for example, and often showcases photos in business, attraction, and restaurant listings. Using details from your Contacts app and Facebook account (if applicable), Yelp! can share details about who you know that's nearby, as well as the ratings and bookmarked Yelp! listings from others.

Use Yelp! to easily find nearby restaurants, bars, coffee shops, gas stations, drugstores, retail shopping, salons/spas, nightlife, theaters, professional services, hotels, houses of worship, or hospitals, for example, whether you're in your home city or traveling virtually anywhere in the world.

Similar apps available from the App Store: AroundMe!, Zagats To Go, and OpenTable

VERTICAL MARKET APPS ARE ALSO READILY AVAILABLE

Whether you're a doctor, lawyer, contractor, plumber, architect, mechanic, salesperson, public speaker, teacher, manager, artesian, photographer, independent consultant, retail store operator, home business operator, or airline pilot, for example, there are thousands of iPad apps designed to handle very specialized work-related tasks that cater to the needs of specific jobs and work-related responsibilities.

Many of these apps are available within the App Store. Within the Search field of the App Store, enter your occupation or a related keyword. However, industry-specific and vertical market apps are also often reviewed in industry publications and newsletters and are sometimes endorsed by industry-specific associations, which are great resources for finding out about them. These specialized apps are also promoted or demonstrated at industry-specific trade shows.

DISCOVERING WHAT TRAVEL APPS CAN DO FOR YOU

Here's a rundown of the different types of travel-related apps you can find listed under the Travel category of the App Store:

- Apps such as Travelocity, Kayak HD, or Hotwire are designed to help you find and book the best deals on airfares, hotels, and rental cars.

- Just about every major airline (American Airlines, Delta, JetBlue, and Southwest, to name a few), hotel chain, and rental car company has its own proprietary app that enables you to book travel, review your reservations, make last-minute changes to your itinerary, and manage your frequent flier (or customer reward membership) points/miles.

> **TIP**   The AwardWallet app (free) enables you to create and manage a centralized and autoupdating database of your airline frequent flier accounts and easily view balances, recent activity, and other pertinent data. It also can be used for other travel-related hotel or rental car reward programs or to manage credit card-related award points.

NOTE Some of the airline apps even enable you to check in for an upcoming flight via the Internet; choose your seat assignment; precheck your luggage; and generate your boarding pass, which can be scanned by the airline from your iPad's screen as you board the aircraft.

- As you're making travel arrangements, use free apps, such as Trip Advisor: Hotels, Flights, Restaurants, to read detailed reviews of thousands of travel service providers, hotels, airlines, and restaurants that were written by fellow travelers. Discover the best and worst of what a particular travel destination has to offer.

- Use an app, such as FlightTrack Pro (described earlier in this chapter), to manage every aspect of your travel itinerary after you've booked it. For example, you can track flights in real time and have the app alert you of last-minute gate changes, flight cancellations, or other problems. If such problems occur, you can use the app to find alternative flights and notify the people expecting you if your itinerary changes via email or text message. When you land, the app directs you to the correct baggage claim conveyor belt to retrieve your checked luggage, provides a detailed map of the destination airport, and offers a multiday weather forecast for your destination city.

- Instead of using a traditionally printed travel guide to help you navigate your way around a city, most popular travel destinations have interactive travel guide apps. These apps utilize the Location Services (GPS) feature of your tablet to help you navigate your way around a city, as well as share information about the best hotels, attractions, sights, and restaurants. You can also obtain apps for specific cities that contain interactive subway maps and schedules that help you use the city's public transportation system.

- The App Store includes a collection of travel-related apps that pinpoint your exact location and instantly locate a local town car, limousine, or taxi company, enabling you to schedule a pick-up in any city, at any time, with a few taps on your iPad's screen. Call A Taxi, Taxi, and GetLimo are three such apps.

- While traveling, there are also apps that help you find the best restaurants to dine at (such as Yelp!, AroundMe, or Zagat to Go) and other apps that enable you to find a restaurant and then book your restaurant reservation directly from your iPad (such as OpenTable).

- If you're traveling abroad, the Skype app enables you to make Voice over IP phone calls or videoconference with people whenever you're within range of a Wi-Fi hotspot (or willing to use an overseas cellular data connection that typically involves international roaming charges).

■ Many different currency conversion apps are available to help you accurately convert the U.S. dollar to other currencies and quickly figure out how much things actually cost wherever you are in the world. When choosing one of these apps, select one that does not require constant access to the Web; otherwise, you wind up paying high international wireless data roaming charges.

■ When traveling abroad, if you're not fluent speaking the local language, consider using the powerful iTranslate Voice app ($1.99). Simply speak or type into this app (as long as your iPad is connected to the Internet), and the app almost instantly translates what you say or type into the language of your choice and then speaks and displays the translation. Using this app on just one iPad, two people who speak different languages can easily communicate. This app works best using a Wi-Fi Internet connection.

TIP   Don't forget, you can also use your iPad to watch TV shows and movies. Plus, the tablet can serve as an eBook reader or help you pass the time by allowing you to play exciting games. Of course, you can also use your tablet with apps such as Pages, Numbers, Keynote, and FileMaker Go to get work done during a flight or while on-the-go.

TIP   When traveling abroad, if you have a Wi-Fi + cellular iPad model, when you arrive at your destination, purchase a new (prepaid) micro-sim card for the tablet to access the cellular wireless data network in that country from a local service provider, without having to pay outrageously high international data roaming charges. Instead, simply prepay for 1G, 2GB, or one month's worth of online access. Depending on the country, this should cost less than $30.00 (U.S.).

You can swap micro-sim chips in and out of your iPad in minutes using the supplied tool or a bent paperclip. However, do not lose the micro-sim chip for your home country, as you'll need to use it again when you return home.

For help selecting and installing a new micro-sim chip and setting up wireless data service in a foreign country, visit an Apple Store anywhere in the world or visit any local cellular phone store that represents local wireless data service providers that are compatible with the iPad.

ONLINE BANKING MADE EASY ON YOUR iPAD

Many major banks, financial institutions, and credit card issuers, such as Bank of America, Chase, Citibank, Fidelity, Schwab, Capital One, PNC, Citizens Bank, Amex, and TD Bank, now offer specialized apps for handling your online banking and money management from the iPad. You can easily and securely check your balances, transfer money between accounts, pay bills online, manage credit cards, and more using these free, bank-specific iPad apps.

In addition to bank apps that enable you to manage bank accounts (and related credit or debit cards), specific apps are available for managing specific credit cards, like American Express (AmEx).

However, when it comes to managing all aspects of your personal finances while on-the-go, the free Mint.com app makes this process easy and enables you to monitor all of your bank, credit card, investment, and finance-related accounts from one centralized location, for free.

The award-winning Mint.com app is extremely simple to use and takes just minutes to set up. Then, as long as your iPad has access to the Internet, you can keep tabs on all aspects of your personal finances in real time. For example, from a single screen, you can see the balance of your checking and savings accounts, the available credit remaining on your credit card accounts, and what checks you've written or credit card purchases have already cleared.

Your personal financial data is password protected on your iPad but automatically syncs with the Mint.com online service, so you can access your personal finance information from any computer, any time.

SAVING TIME IN YOUR EVERYDAY LIFE

Beyond apps that are strictly for business, you can find a plethora of apps in the App Store that can save you time in your personal life. For example, there's the Walgreen's, CVS, and Rite-Aid apps, which enable you to manage your prescription medications and order refills from anywhere.

> **TIP** If you're a business professional who's constantly on-the-go, the FedEx Mobile app helps you ship and track packages, but it also helps you find the nearest FedEx location wherever you happen to be.
>
> The official USPS Mobile app enables you to find the nearest U.S. post office, look up a ZIP code, determine the price to ship something, track a package, arrange for a package pickup, order shipping supplies, or submit a request to hold your mail (when you're traveling) from a free iPhone app that works fine on the iPad.

Meanwhile, the free UPS Mobile app enables you to track and schedule shipments via the UPS service. To order office supplies or find the closest Staples location, the free Staples app can prove helpful.

If you're in need of a jolt of caffeine, the official Starbucks app (an iPhone app that works on the iPad and that's shown in Figure 15.12) helps you find the nearest Starbucks location and decide what you want to order. You can also use the Starbucks Mobile Pay feature to actually pay for your in-store purchases from your tablet.

If you often make a Starbucks run on behalf of multiple coworkers or employees, there's also the eXpresso Pro! Your Ordering Assistant for Starbucks app ($0.99) that enables you to "write down" and manage each person's complex coffee order to ensure accuracy.

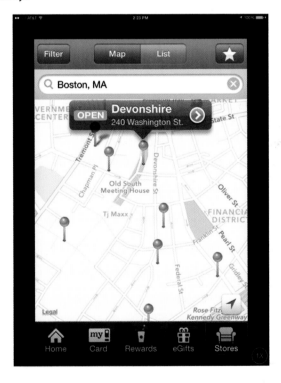

FIGURE 15.12

Find the closest Starbucks and use the Mobile Pay feature to pay for your order directly from your iPad using the official Starbucks app.

16

STAYING INFORMED USING iBOOKS, NEWSSTAND, AND WEB CONTENT

In today's fast-paced business world, keeping up with the latest news headlines, as well as what's happening within the industry you work in is essential. It's also important to constantly be expanding your knowledge and professional skill set. Your iPad can be used as a tool to help educate you and keep you informed in a variety of ways, including:

- ▪ Use the iBooks app to acquire and read eBooks. Apple's iBookstore offers thousands of how-to and self-improvement books, along with all of the latest fiction and non-fiction titles. The iBooks app not only provides access to the online-based iBookstore, it also serves as a feature-packed eBook reader.

- ▪ Use the Newsstand app to acquire and read the latest issues of magazines and newspapers, including *The Wall Street Journal*; *The New York Times*; your city's hometown newspaper; of any of the thousands of consumer-oriented, business, and industry magazines that are available in digital form.

- Use the iTunes U app to participate in thousands of different online classes, seminars, and personal enrichment programs produced by some of the world's most renowned colleges, universities, museums, and philanthropic organizations. All programming is offered for free, and thousands of different subjects are available that incorporate video lectures, audio programming, text, photos, and other multimedia content.

- Use the Podcasts app to subscribe to and enjoy thousands of free audio podcasts produced by news organizations, radio stations, charitable and research organizations, companies, and individuals from around the world.

- Use the proprietary app from a news organization or radio station to access up-to-the-minutes news headlines, plus stream audio or television programming via the Web to your tablet. All of the major news networks, from CNN and NPR, to ABC, CBS, and NBC, offer news-oriented apps.

- Use a customizable news reader app, such as Pulse, Flipboard (shown in Figure 16.1), or News360 to select the types of news and information you're interested in and have only those news stores and related web content automatically gathered from the Internet and displayed on your tablet's screen.

FIGURE 16.1

Flipboard is a customizable app that displays news headlines and content that's of direct interest to you from a wide range of online sources (that you also preselect). This type of app makes it easy to stay up-to-date on the latest news.

> **TIP** The iBooks, iTunes U, and Podcasts apps, developed by Apple, are available for free from the App Store. The Newsstand app comes preinstalled with iOS 7, and the various proprietary apps from news organizations, television networks, and radio stations, as well as the news reader apps, are all available for free from the App Store.

READING EBOOKS AND MANAGING YOUR DIGITAL LIBRARY USING THE iBOOKS APP

Apple's iBooks app offers three main functions. First, it's designed to provide direct access to Apple's online-based iBookstore, from which you can shop for and acquire eBooks. In fact, iBookstore offers one of the largest collection of eBooks in the world, including a vast selection of free eBook titles.

Whether you're looking for a how-to book, reference book, business-related title, or the latest fiction from a bestselling author, it is available from iBookstore. The user interface for the iBookstore is very similar to the App Store. All purchases are made using your Apple ID and are paid for using the credit card or debit card that's linked to your Apple ID account. It's also possible to make eBook purchases using prepaid iTunes gift cards.

Once you acquire eBooks from iBookstore (a process that requires Internet access), the individual eBooks get downloaded to your iPad and also stored within your iCloud account. After its stored in your tablet, an Internet connection is no longer required to read the eBook. It shows up on the Library screen within the iBooks app.

The Library screen within iBooks (shown in Figure 16.2) allows you to manage your eBook collection. From here, tap the Store button to access iBookstore, tap the Edit button to delete eBooks or Move ebooks into customizable folders, or tap an eBook's cover icon to open that eBook and begin reading it.

> **TIP** Once you install the iBooks app, to customize some of its settings, launch Settings, tap on the iBooks option, and then turn on or off the various options displayed within the iBooks submenu screen (shown in Figure 16.3).

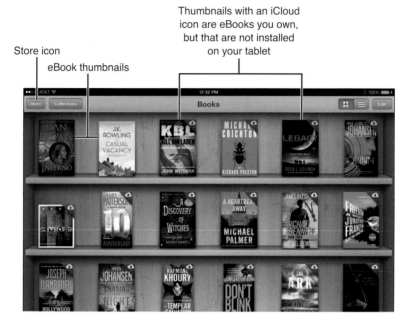

Store icon

eBook thumbnails

Thumbnails with an iCloud
icon are eBooks you own,
but that are not installed
on your tablet

FIGURE 16.2

From the Library screen, it's possible to access iBookstore, manage your eBook collection, open
an eBook and start reading, or load and view a PDF file to read.

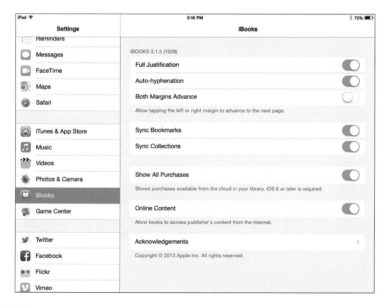

FIGURE 16.3

The iBooks submenu within Settings allows you to customize your eBook reading experience.

CUSTOMIZING YOUR EBOOK READING EXPERIENCE

The second main function of the iBooks app is to serve as a feature-packed and highly customizable eBook reader. Only eBooks acquired from iBookstore (as well as eBooks in the ePub or PDF format) can be read using this app. However, some of the app's functionality for reading eBooks is limited when reading an ePub or PDF formatted eBook.

As you're reading an eBook, it's possible to further customize your reading experience by tapping on the eBook formatting command icon ("aA") that's displayed near the top-right corner of the iBooks screen (shown in Figure 16.4).

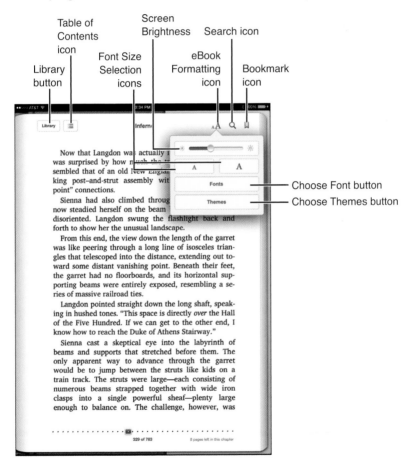

FIGURE 16.4

As you're reading an eBook, tap on the "aA" icon to access the eBook formatting menu within the iBooks app.

When you tap on the "aA" icon to customize your reading experience, the following options are available:

▨ Adjust the screen brightness using the app's brightness slider. You can also adjust the screen's brightness from iOS 7's Control Center or from within Settings.

▨ Increase or decrease the font size of the text displayed within the eBook you're reading. Tap on the "a" icon to decrease the font size or the "A" icon to increase the font size.

▨ Change the font of the text displayed within the eBook you're reading, To do this, tap on the Fonts button, and then choose from the list of fonts displayed by tapping on your selection.

▨ Tap on the Themes button to change the background color of the virtual page. Your options include White, Sepia, or Black. It's also possible to switch between the Book, Full Screen, and Scroll options.

When using the Book option, swipe your finger across the page, from right to left, to advance to the next page or swipe from left to right to move backwards by a page. Full Screen mode eliminates much of the onscreen information, allowing for only the eBook's text to be displayed. Use the Scroll option to reformat the eBook so all of the text scrolls upward as you're reading. This is an alternative to turning the virtual pages.

ADDITIONAL FUNCTIONS ARE AVAILABLE AS YOU'RE READING

As you're reading an eBook using iBooks, tap on the Library button to return to the app's main Library screen. Tap on the Table of Contents button to access the book's interactive Table of Contents, your saved bookmarks, and your eBook-related notes.

Tap on the Search icon (which looks like a magnifying glass) to search the content of the eBook you're reading for a specific word or phase. Tap on the bookmark icon to manually create a bookmark on the page you're currently reading.

Keep in mind, anytime you exit out of the eBook you're reading, the page you're currently on is automatically bookmarked and saved. So, when you reopen the eBook, you can continue reading exactly where you left off. In addition, your saved bookmarks can automatically be synced with iCloud, so you can begin reading an eBook on your iPad, but continue reading it using the iBooks app on your Mac or iPhone.

As you're reading an eBook, hold your finger on a single word. A group of six command tabs appears above that word, labeled Copy, Define, Highlight, Note, Search, and Share.

Use your finger to move the blue dots that appear to the left and right of the word in order to expand the selected text to a phrase, sentence, paragraph, or an entire page.

Tap on the Copy tab to copy the selected text into iOS 7's virtual clipboard. You can then paste that text into another app or into a Note within iBooks.

Tap on the Define tab to look up the definition of a selected word. Tap on the Highlight tab to highlight the selected text. It's possible to choose the color of your highlights or underline the selected text by tapping on the yellow circle icon that's displayed above the word. Tap on the white circle (with a red line through it) to remove highlights, or tap on the Note icon to create a new note. The Share icon also appears above the selected text after you tap on the Highlight option, as do the Copy, Define, and Search options, if you tap on the right-pointing arrow.

If you tap on the Note tab, a virtual sticky note appears on your device's screen, along with the virtual keyboard. Using the keyboard, type notes to yourself about what you're reading. When you're done typing, tap anywhere on the screen outside the sticky note box. A sticky note icon appears in the margin of the eBook. You can later tap on this icon to read your notes or annotations.

When you tap on the Highlight option, you're given the option to choose a highlight color. The last highlight color you selected determines the color of the sticky note that appears when you tap on the Note option. This allows you to easily color-code your highlights and/or notes.

Tap on the Search tab to enter any word or phrase and find it in the eBook. A search window will appear below the Search field. References to each occurrence of your keyword or search phrase will be displayed by chapter and page number. Tap on a reference to jump to that point in the book.

When you tap on the Share option, a Share menu will appear, giving you the option to email, text/instant message, tweet, or send the selected text to your Facebook friends. From the Share menu, you can also copy text to the virtual clipboard and then paste it elsewhere.

The third main function of iBooks is to open and view PDF files. You can create a PDF file using an app, such as Pages, Numbers, or Keynote, and then load it into iBooks to view. As you're using Pages, for example, tap the wrench-shaped icon displayed near the top-right corner of the screen and then select the Open In Another App option. Choose to export the document in PDF format, and then tap on the Choose App button in order to select the Open in iBooks option.

It's also possible to import a PDF file from another source, such as the Internet or via email. This is the third primary use of the iBooks app. Keep in mind, iBooks allows you to view (read) PDF files but offers limited tools for annotating or otherwise working with these documents.

Available from the App Store, there are a wide range of third-party apps, like PDFpen and iAnnotate PDF, for example, that can be used to work with PDF files.

HOW TO FIND A SPECIFIC EBOOK—FAST

While exploring iBookstore, it's possible to use the various command buttons and spend hours browsing through eBook titles, just as you can spend time perusing the shelves of a traditional bookstore. Here are some simple strategies for quickly finding a specific eBook title you're looking for.

As soon as iBookstore loads, use the Search field to enter the eBook title, author's name, subject, or keyword that's associated with what you're looking for. Entering a specific book title will reveal very specific search results. However, entering a keyword relating to a topic or subject matter reveals a selection of eBook suggestions that somehow relate to that keyword.

Tap on any listing to reveal a more detailed description relating to a particular eBook. As you review a description window for an eBook, look carefully at its ratings and its written reviews, especially if it's a paid eBook.

To quickly purchase and download an eBook, tap on the price button displayed within its description window (shown in Figure 16.5). When you tap on a price button, it changes to a Buy Book button. Tap this Buy Book button to confirm your purchase decision. You then need to enter your Apple ID password to begin the download process.

It typically takes between 10 and 30 seconds to download a full-length eBook to your iPad, depending on the speed of your Internet connection and the size of the eBook's digital file. As soon as it's downloaded and ready to read, the book's front cover artwork is displayed as part of the Library screen within the iBooks app.

If you're downloading a free eBook, tap on the Free button that is displayed instead of a price button. Then, instead of a Buy Book button, a Get Book button appears. Tap on it, enter your Apple ID, and download the free eBook. Even though you need to enter your Apple ID, you are not charged to download a free eBook. At the same time it's downloaded to your device, that free eBook is automatically saved to your iCloud account.

FIGURE 16.5
The layout of an eBook's description window is very similar to an app's description window when shopping for apps from the App Store.

> **TIP** Before purchasing an eBook, tap on the Sample button (refer to Figure 16.5) to download and read a free sample.

READING PDF FILES WITH iBOOKS

When you receive an email with a PDF file as an attachment, for example, tap on the PDF thumbnail in that email so the file downloads to your iPad. Next, tap and hold your finger on that same PDF thumbnail for a few seconds, until a menu window appears. The options in this window are Quick Look, Open in iBooks, and (if applicable) Open In…[Compatible App].

The Open in iBooks command automatically launches the iBooks app and allows you to read the PDF document as if you're reading an eBook you downloaded from iBookstore.

> **NOTE** If applicable, the Open In command enables you to open a PDF file using another third-party app. When you tap on this menu option, a list of compatible apps for viewing, printing, sharing, and/or annotating PDF files that are currently installed on your iPad is displayed.

When a PDF file opens in iBooks, you see command icons displayed along the top of the screen, as well as small thumbnails of the PDF document's pages displayed along the bottom of the screen.

Tap on the Library button that's is displayed near the upper-left corner of the screen to return to iBook's main Library screen. When you do this, however, the Bookshelf displays all the PDF files stored on your device—not eBooks downloaded from iBookstore.

To once again access your eBooks, tap on the Collections option and then select the Books option.

> **TIP** As you're viewing a PDF file from within iBooks, next to the Library icon is the Table of Contents icon. Tap on it to display larger thumbnails of each page in your PDF document and then tap on any of the thumbnails to jump to that page. Or tap on the Resume icon to return to the main view of your PDF file.

To the immediate right of the Table of Contents icon (near the upper-left corner of the iBooks screen as you're reading a PDF file) is a Share icon that enables you to email or print the PDF document you're currently viewing. Near the upper-right corner of this screen are three additional command icons. The sun-shaped icon enables you to adjust the brightness of the screen. The magnifying glass–shaped icon enables you to search a PDF file for specific text in the document, and the Bookmark icon enables you to bookmark specific pages in the PDF file for later reference.

> **TIP** As you're viewing a PDF file using iBooks, to zoom in on or out on the page, use a reverse pinch or pinch finger motion on the touchscreen display or double-tap on the area you want to zoom in or out on.

Also, as you're reading a PDF file or eBook, you have the option to hold the device in either a vertical or a horizontal position. If you tap anywhere on the screen (except on a command icon or page thumbnail), the icons and thumbnails on the top and bottom of the screen disappear, giving you more onscreen real estate to view your PDF document or eBook text. Tap near the top or bottom of the screen to make these icons and thumbnails reappear at any time.

ALTERNATIVES TO THE iBOOKS APP

Amazon.com also offers a vast online selection of eBooks which are formatted for its Kindle eBook readers. If you already have a Kindle, or you'd prefer to shop for eBooks from Amazon instead of iBookstore, be sure to download and install the free Kindle app. This app allows you to load (import) and read Kindle-formatted eBooks using your iPad.

Likewise, if you want to shop for eBooks from Barnes and Noble (BN.com) and then read eBooks formatted for the Nook eBook readers on your iPad, download and install the free Nook app.

Thus, if you've already amassed a personal library of Kindle- or Nook-formatted eBooks, it's possible to read these books on your iPad without having to repurchase them from iBookstore.

READING NEWSPAPERS AND MAGAZINES ON YOUR iPAD

Many local, regional, and national newspapers, as well as popular consumer and industry-oriented magazines, are now available in digital form and accessible from your iPad via the Newsstand app. This app comes preinstalled with iOS 7.

WORKING WITH THE NEWSSTAND APP

Not to be confused with the iBooks app (which is used for finding, purchasing, downloading, and reading eBooks), the Newsstand app is used to manage and access all of your digital newspaper and magazine single issues and subscriptions in one place. However, the iBooks and Newsstand apps have a similar user interface, so after you learn how to use one, you should have no trouble using the other.

After you launch Newsstand (shown in Figure 16.6), tap the Store button and browse through the ever-growing selection of digital newspapers and magazines that are available. With the tap of an icon, you can subscribe to any publication, or in most instances, purchase a single current or back issue.

The Newsstand is broken up by publication category. Once you find a publication you're interested in, tap on its listing. This will reveal a detailed description window for that publication, which is very much like what you'd see in the App Store when shopping for apps. This description window has Details, Reviews, and Related tabs that allow you to learn more about a publication.

> **NOTE** The online digital newsstand operated by Apple, which is compatible with the Newsstand app, is actually part of the App Store. Access it either by tapping on the Store button within the Newsstand app or launching the App Store app, tapping on the Featured button (at the bottom of the screen), and then tapping on the Newsstand tab that's displayed near the top of the screen.

FIGURE 16.6
The main Newsstand screen displays thumbnails for all newspaper and magazine issues currently stored on your iPad.

All purchases you make are automatically billed to the credit or debit card you have on file with your Apple ID account, or you can pay using iTunes gift cards. After you purchase a digital newspaper or magazine subscription (or a single issue of a publication), it appears on your Newsstand shelf within the Newsstand app. Tap the publication's cover thumbnail to access the available issue(s).

If you've subscribed to a digital publication, Newsstand automatically downloads the most current issue as soon as it's published (assuming your tablet has a Wi-Fi Internet connection available), so when you wake your iPad from Sleep Mode each morning, the latest edition of your favorite newspaper can be waiting for you.

NOTE Each digital publication has its own proprietary app associated with it. These publication-specific apps are free and are automatically installed on your iOS mobile device when you select a publication from within Newsstand. All of these publication-specific apps are then accessible from within Newsstand, plus have their own unique functionality allowing you access to publication-specific interactive content.

TIP To use a cellular data network to automatically download digital publications, you must turn on this feature from within the Settings app. Launch Settings, select the iTunes & App Stores menu option, and then turn on the virtual switch associated with the Use Cellular Data option.

Keep in mind, downloading digital publications using a cellular data network quickly uses up your monthly data allocation and could ultimately result in additional charges if you're not on an unlimited data plan.

Also from within Settings, tap on the Newsstand option to turn on the virtual switches associated with each specific newspaper or magazine subscription that's listed. After you do this once, your iPad automatically downloads all new publication content when it becomes available, without you having to worry about using up your monthly wireless data allocation.

A Home screen icon badge and/or the Notification Center notifies you immediately whenever a new issue of a digital publication is automatically downloaded to your iOS device and is ready for reading. When you access Newsstand, you also see a thumbnail of that publication's cover on the main Newsstand shelf screen.

READING DIGITAL PUBLICATIONS

Every publisher utilizes the iPad's vibrant Multi-Touch display in a different way in order to transform a traditionally printed newspaper or magazine into an engaging and interactive reading experience. Thus, each publication has its own user interface.

Figure 16.7 shows what a sample issue of *The Wall Street Journal* looks like when being read in its digital form on the iPad.

In most cases, a digital edition of a publication faithfully reproduces the printed edition and features the same content. However, sometimes the digital edition of a publication that's accessible from your iPad also offers bonus content, such as active hyperlinks to websites, video clips, animated slideshows, or interactive elements not offered by the printed edition.

FIGURE 16.7

Digital newspapers and magazines, and their proprietary apps, are accessible from the Newsstand app.

Reading a digital publication is very much like reading an eBook. Use a finger swipe motion to turn the pages or to scroll up or down on a page. Tap the Table of Contents icon to view an interactive table of contents for each issue of the publication. Depending on the publisher, you might be able to access past issues of a publication at any given time in addition to the current issue. (An additional per-issue fee may apply.)

MANAGING YOUR NEWSPAPER AND MAGAZINE SUBSCRIPTIONS

If you opt to subscribe to a digital publication, you often need to select a duration for your subscription, such as one year. However, almost all digital subscriptions acquired through the Newsstand app are autorenewing. Thus, when the subscription ends, unless you manually cancel it, Newsstand automatically renews your subscription and bills your credit or debit card accordingly.

To manage your recurring subscriptions, launch the Newsstand app and tap the Store button. From the Newsstand store, tap the Featured command button that's located near the bottom of the screen. Scroll downward and tap the Apple ID [Your Username] button. When prompted, enter your Apple ID password.

Next, from the Account Settings window, tap the Manage button that's displayed under the Subscriptions heading. Displayed on the Subscriptions screen is a listing of all publications you've subscribed to. Tap any publication's listing to see the expiration date of your subscription, to cancel a subscription, or to renew your subscription.

> **TIP** The publication-specific app related to the digital edition of a newspaper or magazine is free; however, in most cases, you need to pay for individual issues or for a subscription to a publication. From Newsstand, to determine the per-issue or subscription cost, tap on a publication listing, tap on the Details tab, and then scroll toward the bottom of the screen. Tap on the option labeled In-App Purchases.

DOWNLOADING VERSUS STREAMING ONLINE CONTENT

Each type of media you're using with your iPad, such as digital music, video, eBooks, audiobooks, or photos, for example, requires you to utilize a specific app to experience it. However, you also have the option to simply stream certain types of content from the Internet to your iPad. This, too, requires specialized apps.

UNDERSTANDING THE DIFFERENCE BETWEEN DOWNLOADING AND STREAMING CONTENT

Content you download from the Internet is stored in your tablet's internal memory. It then becomes available to you anytime you want to experience it. Keep in mind that when it comes to acquiring media to enjoy on your tablet, you typically must pay a fee to purchase and download it (or rent it, in the case of a movie acquired from the iTunes Store).

The alternative is to stream content from the Internet. In this case, no content is actually saved on your iPad, and you can often stream certain content for free or pay a low monthly fee for unlimited access to content.

CAUTION The ability to stream content from the Internet and experience it on your iPad gives you free access to a wide range of programming. However, whenever you stream audio or video content from the Internet you are transferring a tremendous amount of data to your tablet. Thus, if you use a cellular Internet connection, you can quickly use up your monthly data allocation. So, when streaming web content, it's best to use a Wi-Fi connection.

Not only does a Wi-Fi connection enable data to be transferred to your tablet at much faster speeds, there's also no limit as to how much data you can send or receive. Plus, when streaming video content, you are often able to view it at a higher resolution when you use a Wi-Fi connection and none of your iPad's internal storage space is needed.

WHAT YOU SHOULD KNOW ABOUT DOWNLOADING CONTENT

To download content, you must be connected to the Internet. However, after the content is stored on your tablet, you can enjoy it again and again without having an Internet connection (such as while your iPad is in Airplane mode, when you're out of a Wi-Fi hotspot's radius, or there's no wireless data signal available).

NOTE Depending on the type of media you're downloading, you might need a Wi-Fi connection rather than a cellular data connection. For music, eBooks, and digital editions of newspapers or magazines (which have smaller files), a cellular Internet connection is typically sufficient to download content from the Internet or from the iTunes Store. However, you need a Wi-Fi connection for larger files, such as TV show episodes, movies, or audiobooks.

With the exception of rented movies, legally acquired content you download from the Internet is then owned by you. Thus, you have the right to experience it as often as you'd like on your iPad. Or, if it's iTunes Store content, you can also experience it on your primary computer(s), iPhone, iPod touch, and Apple TV, as long as the devices are linked to the same iCloud account.

NOTE All content you purchase or acquire from the iTunes Store, iBookstore, App Store, or Newsstand is automatically saved in your free iCloud account and becomes accessible from all your computers and iOS mobile devices (and your Apple TV, if applicable) that are linked to the same iCloud account. Apple provides unlimited free online storage space in your iCloud account for content you purchase from its online-based business ventures.

Rented movies from iTunes are temporarily stored on your iPad (and take up internal storage space) and remain there for up to 30 days before they're automatically deleted. However, after you begin playing a rented movie from the iTunes Store, you have 24 hours to watch it as often as you'd like before it is automatically deleted from your tablet.

You pay for content you purchase from the iTunes Store at the time you download it. You pay a one-time fee for unlimited use of that content in terms of how frequently you can experience it. Some content that's available from the iTunes Store, iBookstore, Newsstand, or the App Store is also offered for free. This is treated, however, as purchased content by your iPad, but you are not charged for it.

YOU CAN ALSO STREAM CONTENT FROM THE INTERNET

The alternative to downloading content to experience on your tablet is to stream it directly from the Internet. Content including TV show episodes, videos, music, radio programming, and movies can be streamed from various sources on the Internet, such as Netflix, HuluPlus, or by using a specialized app from a radio station or television network, for example.

When you stream content directly from the Internet, it is not stored on your iPad; instead, a special media player app plays the content on your iPad directly from the Internet. Thus, you need a constant Internet connection to experience the streaming content. If you don't have an Internet connection, you cannot access streaming content.

APPS FOR STREAMING WEB CONTENT

The type of content you want to experience on your iPad determines which apps you use. Using a specialized app that serves as an audio or video player, you can stream a wide range of audio and/or video content directly from the Internet.

Often, streamed content is free of charge. In some cases, you can pay a flat monthly fee to experience unlimited content from a specific online-based content-streaming service, such as Netflix or Sirius/XM.

> **NOTE** Just about every broadcast and cable television network (ABC, CBS, NBC, CNN, etc.), news organization (AP, NPR, etc.), radio station, and radio network (as well as Sirius/XM Satellite Radio) now has its own proprietary iPad app that allows you to stream on-demand (and in some cases live) programming to your tablet directly from the Internet. You'll find these apps within the App Store.

For example, the free NPR News app (shown in Figure 16.8) allows you to stream on-demand and live programming from almost every NPR radio station in the United States for free.

FIGURE 16.8

The NPR News app is one of many proprietary apps available from the various television and radio networks that offer both live and on-demand programming that you can stream from the Internet for free.

There's also another type of app for TV programming that's designed for use while you're watching particular TV shows on a traditional television set. These apps sync up with the show you're watching and offer real-time, interactive content and the opportunity to communicate with other viewers while you're watching. These apps are TV network– or TV series–specific and are available for free from the App Store.

TIP With any app that's used for streaming TV shows and/or movies, you can watch your favorite programming on-demand. You never have to worry about missing the scheduled air time for a show or movie on TV again because you decide what to watch and when it begins. You can also pause, fast forward, or rewind streaming content. With some apps, you can stop the program altogether, use your iPad for something else, and then pick up where you left off later.

Plus, instead of paying $15.00 or more for a pay-per-view movie when staying at a hotel while you're traveling, you can simply stream a movie on your iPad and enjoy a high-definition video experience, with amazing sound quality.

> **NOTE** From the App Store, you can download the free, official YouTube app (from Google) and watch unlimited videos, manage your YouTube subscriptions, and perform any other tasks associated with your YouTube account or YouTube Channel.

If you want to watch TV show episodes without commercials, purchase and download content from the iTunes Store. When you stream TV show content from a free service (or app), the programming typically includes commercials, unless you're accessing it through a premium (paid) service, such as Hulu Plus or Netflix.

A vast amount of timely information is readily available in eBook, digital publication, audiobook, or streaming video/audio format directly from your tablet, allowing you to expand your knowledge or be entertained whenever and wherever you happen to be.

IN THIS CHAPTER

- Self-publishing and distributing interactive eBooks using Apple's iBooks Author software on a Mac
- Creating and selling eBooks using other solutions
- Commissioning a custom iPad app
- Considering developing a mobile website for your business

17

CREATING AND DISTRIBUTING CONTENT ON THE iPAD

Until recently, if you or your company wanted to create an app or distribute proprietary content via the iPad, a costly custom app needed to be created. However, to cater to the needs of businesses and entrepreneurs who want to use the iPad as an interactive tool for disseminating information, Apple has created several low-cost and easy solutions that require no programming skills and that can be used in-house in a fraction of the time needed to create a custom iPad app.

Using any Mac and the free iBooks Author software available from Apple (www.apple.com/ibooks-author), anyone who knows how to use a word processor can create professional-quality and highly interactive eBooks for the iPad that can incorporate text, photos, video clips, audio, other multimedia content, interactive diagrams, 3D objects, voiceovers, and quizzes.

eBooks created using the iBooks Author software can be disseminated to employees, customers, and clients or distributed (sold) to the public via Apple's iBookstore. Using the iBooks Author software, a company can easily adapt any printed materials, such as catalogs, annual reports, user manuals, training guides (and training videos), marketing materials, or other documents into eBooks for viewing on an iPad.

If a company's needs involve gathering data via an iPad, streamlining the process of filling out forms, or accessing database content remotely from a tablet, using the FileMaker Pro database software with the FileMaker Go iPad app serves as a low-cost, extremely customizable option.

In this chapter, discover more about how to utilize the iBooks Author software, learn about other eBook publishing solutions, and learn more about what's involved in having an iPad app created from scratch.

TIP   Does your company have dozens or hundreds of iPads that need to be charged and synchronized simultaneously from a single iTunes source? Parat Solutions (866-647-5976, www.paratsolutions.com) has solved this problem with its ParaSync system, a proprietary docking station that enables up to 10 iPads to be charged and synced from one iTunes library. Using this system, multiple ParaSync docking stations can be linked together, so you can charge and sync 20, 30, 40, or more iPads at the same time. No special software or cable connections are required.

The ParaSync system includes a docking station that connects to a host computer via a USB cable connection for syncing. For charging, a single electrical plug from a wall outlet is needed. The system includes custom-designed iPad cases that not only protect the tablets while they're in use, but also protect the iPad's Dock connector port during the charging process.

Custom solutions for charging and syncing any number of iPads are available. These solutions can include lockable, steel enclosures for the ParaSync charging stations.

CREATING INTERACTIVE EBOOKS FOR iPAD USING iBOOKS AUTHOR

If you use a Mac and know how to use a word processor, you already have the knowledge needed to create visually compelling, professional-quality, and highly interactive eBooks for use with an iPad. When you use Apple's iBooks Author software, any printed materials, as well as photos, graphics, illustrations, video clips, audio, or other multimedia content, can be incorporated into an interactive eBook that also utilizes the touch screen on the iPad.

iBooks Author is a free Mac application that's available from the Mac App Store. Using this software, you can custom create compelling eBook content using templates and a simple-to-learn, drag-and-drop interface.

> **TIP** In addition to the eBook templates that come bundled with the iBooks Author software, a variety of third-party companies have released additional templates for creating specific types of eBooks.
>
> iPresentee has introduced Themes Drawer for iBooks Author ($9.99) that includes 30 original templates designed for use with iBook Author, while Macmanus offers its Templates for iBooks Author 2.0 package ($8.99). It includes 65 professionally designed templates that can be fully customized to create your own, unique eBooks. For $16.99, Graphics Node offers Themes for iBooks Author, which is a compilation of 135 compelling eBook templates into which you can drag and drop or copy and paste your own content.
>
> You'll find additional free and fee-based templates by visiting www.iBookAuthorTemplates.com or by entering the search phrase "iBook Author Templates" into any Internet search engine or the Search field in the Mac App Store.

When you select a template in the iBook Author software, you can import and format content from a word processor (such as Pages or Microsoft Word) and incorporate it into the eBook that's being created. You can then import images or other precreated multimedia content, and the iBooks Author software autoformats the text around the photos or content.

Instead of having to program interactive elements into the eBook, from within iBooks Author, you can import and customize precreated widgets, so it's easy to incorporate an interactive table of contents, glossary, or quiz, for example.

After you've created an eBook using the iBooks Author software, it's possible to easily transfer it to an iPad and read it using the free iBooks app that is available from the App Store. Using this software, publishing your eBook using Apple's iBookstore service and then distributing the eBook for free or selling it online is also straightforward.

Self-published authors, entrepreneurs, small business operators, educators, and public speakers, for example, have discovered a wide range of innovative ways to use iBooks Author to create and distribute compelling iPad content for employees, customers, clients, conference or workshop attendees, or trainees. For example, traditionally printed catalogs and sales materials can become interactive and highly engaging when created as an eBook. Product user manuals can be created for the iPad that utilize more than just text and graphics to teach customers how to use a new product. Boring employee training manuals can be transformed into interactive training tools that can be utilized anywhere. Presentation handouts or reports can be published in eBook form and presented in ways not possible on a traditionally printed page. The possibilities are truly limitless.

iBooks Author runs exclusively on Mac computers and can create eBooks compatible with the latest iPad models.

ADOBE OFFERS HIGHER-END DIGITAL PUBLISHING SOLUTIONS

You'll discover more advanced, professional-level eBook and digital publishing solutions available from Adobe for both the Mac and PC. These solutions, like Adobe Digital Publishing Suite ($395.00, or $49.99 per month for the Creative Cloud edition, www.adobe.com/products/digital-publishing-suite-family.html) enable users to create compelling eBook content, as well as interactive brochures, catalogs, and portfolios, for example, without having to do any programming.

Adobe's digital publishing options are more advanced and powerful solutions; however, they typically require a significant learning curve. If you're already familiar with how to use Adobe's popular InDesign CS6 software (for the PC or Mac), you'll definitely be at an advantage. Adobe and third parties, however, offer printed and online training options.

NOTE Adobe Digital Publishing Suite is also available as a more feature-packed Professional Edition ($495.00) and as an Enterprise Edition (fees vary).

For a flat fee of $49.99 per month, Adobe's Creative Cloud (www.adobe.com/products/creativecloud.html) offers month-by-month access to most of Adobe's software that falls into its Creative Suite category, including the applications available in the Digital Publishing Suite.

PRSS OFFERS A POWERFUL iPAD DIGITAL PUBLISHING SOLUTION FOR BUSINESSES

Another digital publishing solution that allows for the easy creation of interactive eBooks, magazines and digital publications is a comprehensive suite of online-based tools, called Prss (http://www.prss.com). Creating content or publications is free, however, as the content creator, you pay only $0.05 per download when someone downloads and installs your digital publication onto their tablet.

The Prss service then allows you to set your own price for the download that your readers actually pay (although publications can be offered for free). Three of the benefits of using the Prss publishing solution are that up to 30 people can collaborate on the creation of each publication; the publications can be created using almost any computer or device that's connected to the Internet and that has a web browser; and once published, powerful Analytics tools are offered to help you track downloads, reading time, in-app (publication) purchases, ad clicks, engagement time, and the other important behaviors of your publication's readers. These are tools and resources not offered by Apple's iBooks Author software or other digital publishing solutions for the iPad.

Anyone who already knows how to surf the Web using a web browser, such as Safari or Internet Explorer, and who knows how to do word processing, using Microsoft Word or Pages, for example, already possesses the skills needed to create professional-looking and highly interactive digital publications that can be read on an iPad.

SHIFT magazine (available from Newsstand and the App Store for the iPad) is a sample of a digital publication created entirely using the Prss digital publishing platform.

TRANSFORM MICROSOFT WORD DOCUMENTS INTO COMPELLING iPAD EBOOKS

For a flat fee of between $99.00 and $249.00, a handful of companies, including BookBaby (www.bookbaby.com), can take your Microsoft Word document and transform it into a standard eBook that's compatible with the iPad (as well as other eBook readers, including Amazon's Kindles and Barnes and Noble's Nooks). Your eBook is then be made available for sale (at the price you set), on iBookstore, Amazon.com, and BN.com, as well as other popular online-based eBook sellers.

> **NOTE** For an additional $149.00–$279.00, BookBaby will custom-design a full-color cover for your eBook. The company also offers the ability to publish eBooks in traditional printed (softcover) book form in quantities starting at 100 copies.

Using one of the turnkey eBook publishing solutions from BookBaby, you can include up to 50 digital images in your eBook's content, but no interactive elements (like what's possible using Apple's iBook Author software) are available.

> **NOTE** Some word-processing applications and specialized eBook layout and design applications that are available for both PCs and Macs allow users to create eBooks and then export them into the ePub format so that they can be read on an iPad. The Scrivener software for the PC and Mac is an example of this. However, formatting eBooks that have interactive elements can be a bit tricky.

DOES YOUR COMPANY NEED A CUSTOM APP?

There are hundreds of thousands of apps currently available for the iPad from the App Store. If one or more of these apps do not meet the needs of your company, having a custom app created may be a viable option.

Many custom apps have been created by mid-sized to large companies in an effort to better cater to the needs of their customers or to serve as a marketing tool to increase business. Another portion of these apps were custom-designed for specific companies to be used in-house by employees in an effort to streamline or automate specific tasks or give people access to company resources while they're in the field.

Every day, companies in all different industries are discovering innovative ways to utilize the iPad. Some of these uses, however, require a custom app to be created.

NOTE   Before investing the time, money, and resources needed to create a vertical market app or proprietary enterprise solution involving the iPad, see whether a customizable app has already been created. Marketcircle, Inc. (www.marketcircle.com), for example, offers a handful of highly customizable iPad apps for billing, invoicing, time tracking/billing, and scheduling that have been created for use in specific industries, such as film and video, photography, print and design, real estate, sales, legal, recruiting, and software development.

Many entrepreneurs, self-employed professionals, and small businesses use Intuit's QuickBooks software (http://quickbooks.intuit.com) and perhaps a compatible iPad app (such as QBReflex for iPad or eBillity Time Tracker for Intuit QuickBooks) to handle billing, invoicing, time tracking/billing, and other related tasks.

From other app developers, there are countless industry-oriented, vertical market or specialty apps for those working in hundreds of industries, including medical, manufacturing, retail sales, telemarketing, event planning, and education. Be sure to research what's currently available before incurring the cost of re-creating something from scratch that already exists.

WHAT TO CONSIDER FIRST WHEN DEVELOPING AN APP

If you're thinking about having a custom app developed for the iPad, first carefully define the purpose for the app and determine exactly what you want it to do.

Next, sketch out or create a detailed outline for the app. For example, figure out what options should appear on the various screens, and decide what features and functions the app needs to include. This includes determining your target audience for the app. For this step, absolutely no programming knowledge is required, but considering these things gives you, and the programmers you ultimately hire to develop your app, a clear understanding of your goals.

> **TIP** Based on your company's needs, determine whether an iPad-specific app is more appropriate or whether your app development budget is best spent on an app that runs on all iOS devices, including the various iPhones, iPod touches, and iPads. Making an app available to all users of iOS mobile devices dramatically increases the potential audience for an app, which might be important if the app will cater to your customers or clients.

Before proceeding further, visit the App Store to determine whether an iOS app already exists that meets your needs. If similar apps already exist, determine whether you can use one of them or what your intended app needs to do differently or better. It's essential that you understand, from day one, how the app will be used and how it will fit into your company's established workflow and overall business objectives.

> **CAUTION** If you hire an app developer to begin work on a custom app, but you have only a vague idea about what the app should do, how it will be used, and who it will be used by, the result will be a variety of potentially costly problems. At the very least, having a clearly defined one- or two-page summary of what you want the iOS app to do helps a developer dramatically when it comes to designing and programming the app you envision.
>
> Remember, the app developer you hire is most likely an expert at designing apps and programming, but the developer/programmer probably does not understand your business, industry, customers, or the unique needs for the app. Thus, it's your company's responsibility to bring this knowledge to the table and stay active in the development process for your app.
>
> If your app developer doesn't understand your needs or isn't listening to you during development meetings, find a new developer. Otherwise, you'll wind up paying a fortune for a custom app that doesn't meet your needs or expectations, that is confusing to use, and that is actually detrimental to your business because the end result will be an app that does not achieve its objectives.

Next, invest $99.00 (per year) and join Apple's iOS Development Program (http://developer.apple.com) to learn more about what's possible in terms of having a custom app created, plus gain access to the resources and tools available directly from Apple.

HAVING A CUSTOM APP CREATED

After determining that your company does want to pursue developing a custom app, you need to hire experienced and knowledgeable app designers and programmers (unless you already have someone on staff). It's important to understand that developing a custom app is a time-consuming and potentially costly process that requires a clear understanding of what's possible and what you're trying to accomplish.

By hiring an independent iOS app developer, companies are creating innovative, proprietary, and highly specialized apps for use in-house. An app that gives a sales force a streamlined method for entering and processing orders while on the road and grants them full access to an online inventory database or catalog from their mobile devices is an example of a custom app.

In some situations, cutting-edge companies are developing custom apps for their customers and clients as a way to boost sales, distribute marketing or promotional content, improve customer service, increase brand awareness, or build customer loyalty.

Thanks to the Location Services/GPS capabilities and the Maps app that is built in to the iPad, a custom app can determine where a customer is located at any given moment and direct her to a company's nearest retail location. This same customized app can enable a customer to place an order online from her mobile device and have it waiting for her upon her arrival at her destination. In the case of Pizza Hut or GrubHub, for example, a customer can arrange for food delivery with a few taps on her mobile device's screen.

The cost of developing a custom app is becoming far more economical than it was just a year or two ago, in part due to increased competition among independent software and app developers.

One of the biggest challenges you face after you decide to have a custom app developed is not determining what the app should do or how it will be used; it's finding and hiring an independent app developer who is capable of creating an app that perfectly caters to the intended audience by offering the end user value, simplicity, security, and intuitive functionality.

It's important to realize up front that having a custom iOS app created is very much like having customized software developed for any other platform. Having a well-designed, highly functional, and bug-free app developed that includes a slick user interface and the back-end functionality you need is going to be a costly and time-consuming endeavor that should include involvement from various departments in your company.

One problem that many companies encounter is that they hire a low-cost app development company or team of programmers. Companies that do this often wind up with an inferior result that is riddled with problems. It's important to choose an app development company that's stable because you want the same company to be around in the future to support the app and make enhancements or bug fixes.

Speaking of app development problems, to save money, some businesses opt to outsource their work to small, overseas app development companies. Common problems with this solution include dealing with time zone differences, which causes delays in communication, and significant language barriers. If you're unable to easily communicate with your app developer, explain your needs, and closely follow the app's development, the end result will often not be what you anticipated.

Ultimately, your goal should be to establish a long-term relationship with the app developer you hire. Even if you choose not to add new features or functions to the app down the road, as Apple releases new versions of the iOS operating system, you will need to have the app updated to keep it functional.

> **NOTE** As a general rule, when it comes to hiring an app development company, you generally get what you pay for. A single freelancer or a small development company might be able to create the initial app for you, but if you want or need the app to be updated or expanded with new features in the future, that same freelancer or small development company might not be available or might have gone out of business.

Before hiring an app developer, look at the company's portfolio of work. Carefully evaluate the quality of its apps, including each app's user interface and functionality. Also, keep in mind that many different factors go into calculating development costs and the amount of time the development process will take.

Development costs for most good-quality apps, created by an experienced and competent development company, run between $5,000 and $50,000 (or more). Realistically, the development, programming, and testing process typically takes between 12 and 16 weeks, so plan accordingly.

The more detailed your company's initial outline or plan for the app is, the easier it is for the app development company you hire to offer you a reliable price quote. How much you wind up paying for the app's development is in part based on the complexity of the app itself.

TIP   As you're sketching your app on paper and brainstorming about what the app should be able to do, start with what you envision the app's home screen and main menu will look like. Then work your way out from there, focusing on one page or screen of the proposed app at a time. This helps you create a more comprehensive plan for your app.

To keep things simple, start by developing an app with the core features and functionality you want or need. Work with your app development team to get the core app up and running so you can release it to your workforce or customers. You can later revise the app to add new features and functions after the initial app has proven itself to be a success. After launching your app, solicit feedback from its audience to discover ways to improve upon its interface, features, and functionality.

Hiring a programmer, as opposed to a full-service app development company, is a low-cost option for small to mid-size businesses. You can find iOS app programmers using an online service, such as eLance.com or guru.com. Alternatively, use a search engine to enter the search phrase "iOS app developer" or "custom iPad app development" to find links to app developer websites.

Another method for finding a well-qualified developer is to search the App Store for apps you like and then contact those developers. Part of every app's description in the App Store includes the developer's name and a link to the developer's website.

TIP   It's a good idea to have a lawyer who represents your company create a contract between your organization and the app developer. The contract should clearly state who will ultimately own the programming code and indicate that your company will also receive the source code associated with the app, not just the finished app.

In addition to indicating who owns the code, the contract should give you the right to modify the code as needed in the future and ensure that the code contains no backdoor access that could later be used by the app developer for unauthorized purposes.

Also, if your company will own the code, by purchasing it outright from the developer, the contract should stipulate what rights the developer has to reuse or resell the source code (or portions of it) to develop future applications.

OTHER POTENTIAL LOW-COST CUSTOM APP SOLUTIONS

If you're thinking about having a proprietary app developed for in-house use to handle specialized tasks, determine whether it would be less expensive to have a developer create a mobile website that your iPad-using employees could access. Another alternative might be to have a custom database application created using FileMaker Pro and then use the FileMaker Go app for iPad to allow for remote access to that custom database.

Often, having a custom FileMaker Pro database created is significantly less expensive and much faster than having an iOS custom app developed, yet the functionality could be similar, depending on your company's needs. To learn more about the FileMaker Pro and FileMaker Go options, visit www.filemaker.com/products/filemaker-go.

TIP To learn more about having a custom iOS app developed for your business, visit Apple's iOS In Business website at www.apple.com/business/accelerator.

iPAD CUSTOM APP DEVELOPMENT STRATEGIES

When you decide to move forward with a custom app, follow these strategies to help ensure the successful planning, development, and deployment of the app:

- Do your research to determine what's possible, and then decide exactly what you want your custom app to do. As you do this, put yourself in the app user's shoes. Determine their wants, needs, and level of expertise using the iPad, and then cater to the intended user every step of the way.

- Develop a specific plan for your app, outlining the overall goal or objective of the app, as well as each feature or function you want to include in it.

- Plan the development process in a realistic way, making sure you have the budget and resources in place to handle the process appropriately. The main stages of an app's development include Planning, Design, Coding/Programming, Debugging, Testing, and Deployment/Implementation. Each of these steps requires planning, time, resources, and money. Cutting corners during any of these steps could result in costly problems, development delays, or unanticipated results.

- Be sure to put together the most knowledgeable and experienced app development team possible, starting with people within your business or organization who clearly understand how your business operates, the needs of those who will ultimately be using the app, and the ultimate goal for the app itself. Pair this in-house team with skilled and experienced programmers and app testers.

■ For apps being developed from scratch, start by incorporating the core functionality that's wanted and needed, and make sure that it works properly and has an intuitive user interface. Then, over time, add additional features and functions. Not only will this save time and money, it will also keep the app's development easier to manage.

■ Before releasing the app to your employees, customers, or clients, be sure it has been properly tested, is 100 percent bug-free, and functions exactly how it should. The easiest way to alienate your customers or annoy those who will ultimately be using the app is to release an app that contains bugs, is unstable and crashes, that doesn't handle the intended objectives properly, or that is unintuitive to use.

■ The app should also function using the latest version of the iOS operating system and fully utilize the capabilities of the iPad. If the app ultimately doesn't serve a defined purpose, successfully address a need, solve a problem, or provide value to the user, it will not be embraced and adopted by its intended users.

> **NOTE** After your custom app is created and ready for distribution, you have several options, based on the target audience for your app. An iPad app can be distributed through the App Store and made available to the general public, or your company can work with Apple to utilize other enterprise solutions for distributing an app in-house. To learn more about custom app development and distribution (deployment) options, visit www.apple.com/business/accelerator.

ALSO CONSIDER A MOBILE WEBSITE TO REACH iPAD USERS

A much lower-cost alternative to having a custom iPad app developed from scratch is to have a mobile website developed that's formatted for the iPad's screen. A mobile website can be developed much faster and more economically than a custom app, but iPads (and other wireless mobile devices) must have a Wi-Fi or cellular Internet connection to access and use it.

> **TIP** Depending on how you develop your mobile website, it could use Safari's Reading List feature that allows for web page content to be downloaded to the iPad and read offline.

It has been predicted that online mobile use will surpass people using their desktop computers to access the Internet by 2015. Knowing that your company's clients, customers, and employees, for example, will be accessing the Web from their mobile devices, including the iPad, consider offering your company's websites and other online content in a format that's conducive to being accessed by these devices.

To find website designers that specialize in the creation of mobile websites, using any Internet search engine, enter the search phrase "mobile website development."

Google, for example, offers free, online-based tools called Go Mo for designing a mobile website (http://www.google.com/think/collections/make-website-work-across-multiple-devices.html). From this website, you can also download free case studies that explain why a mobile website can be useful to your small, medium, or large company, regardless of what business or industry you're in.

The WordPress website/blogging platform (www.wordpress.org) also offers tools for developing websites and blogs that utilize professionally designed custom templates that adapt to the screen size someone is using to view the site/blog.

> **NOTE** Using research gathered in 2013, Google has published a free report, called *Our Mobile Planet: United States*, which explains how Americans are using their mobile devices (including their tablets) now and how they're projected to use them in the near future. By understanding how your customers, clients, and employees currently use their iPads, for example, you can better cater to their needs by addressing them with a custom app and/or a mobile website.
>
> To download and read this report, visit http://services.google.com/fh/files/misc/omp-2013-us-en.pdf. To access Google's interactive website targeted toward businesses that covers how to create and utilize a mobile website, visit www.thinkwithgoogle.com/mobileplanet/en.

18

MUST-HAVE iPAD ACCESSORIES

By adding optional accessories to your tablet, you can further personalize the device and, at the same time, enhance its capabilities to broaden its functionality.

The majority of the accessories showcased within this chapter work with the full-size iPads as well as the iPad mini models. However, when purchasing an accessory, it may be necessary to choose the version that's compatible with your tablet and its 30-pin Dock Connector port or Lightning port (based on which iPad model you're using).

THREE WAYS YOU SHOULD PROTECT YOUR TABLET

The first of the three options for your iPad you should seriously consider investing in is AppleCare+ ($99.00). This service provides technical support as well as repair services for the tablet for a two-year period.

Second, to help protect your iPad, seriously consider purchasing a protective Apple Smart Cover ($39.00–$69.00) or Smart Case ($49.99), or another type of case that can be used whenever the tablet is not in use. Saddleback Leather Company ($88.00–$111.00, www.saddlebackleather.com), for example, offers a really nice, handcrafted leather case for the iPad or iPad mini. Many other companies also offer a vast selection of iPad cases to choose from in many different styles.

Third, consider applying a thin, clear protective film over the tablet's screen. This helps to keep the screen clean and prevents scratches or cracks. Plus, some of these optional films help to prevent glare or serve as a privacy screen. Visit almost any mall to find a kiosk-based business that can professionally apply a protective film on your tablet, or purchase just the protective film from any consumer electronics store and apply it yourself. Plan on spending between $20.00 and $50.00 for a protective, ultra-thin, clear, and durable film that covers just the iPad's screen or the entire tablet.

EXTERNAL KEYBOARDS FOR YOUR TABLET

Many iPad users have discovered that the tablet's onscreen virtual keyboard and its Dictation feature are ideal for composing short email messages or performing a limited amount of data entry but not ideal for touch-typing and creating long documents. By adding an external keyboard to your iPad, you can utilize a full-size keyboard or a portable keyboard that has tactile keys (as opposed to flat icons displayed on the tablet's flat screen).

> **TIP** Some iPad cases have external Bluetooth keyboards built in to them. These also protect the tablet while it's being transported and serve as a tablet stand while it's in use.

A handful of companies offer iPad-compatible keyboards. Some connect to the tablet via its 30-pin Dock Connector or Lightning port (depending on the iPad model), whereas others utilize a Bluetooth wireless connection. Some optional external keyboards are full size, and others are more compact and designed with portability in mind.

The Apple Wireless Keyboard ($69.00 USD) is a full-size keyboard for the iPad that uses a Bluetooth connection. This keyboard is ideal for touch-typing or data entry and is the same keyboard that comes with most iMac computers, so it can serve double duty, depending on which device you're using. The keyboard operates using two AA batteries. It's ideal for working with your iPad at a desk when portability is not important.

The TacType keyboard ($35.00, www.redtreegear.com/tactype) is an overlay accessory that you place directly over a full-size iPad's virtual keyboard in order to give the keys a more tactile feel (see Figure 18.1).

FIGURE 18.1

The TacType transforms the virtual keyboard of a full-size iPad into one with simulated tactile keys, which makes it easier to type.

The TacType keyboard accessory adds practically no thickness to the tablet, so you can use it with most covers and cases, but it helps improve your ability to accurately touch-type using the iPad's virtual keyboard. TacType is made from a durable plastic and has an everlasting sticky backing that allows it to be stuck on and removed from the tablet's screen thousands of times with no residue left on the iPad. It's available in black or white and, unlike other keyboards, it requires no batteries.

For people on-the-go, Zagg.com (www.zagg.com/keyboard-cases/index.php) offers several traditional style, wireless (Bluetooth) keyboards that are slightly more compact than a full-size keyboard but offer real (tactile) keyboard keys that enable touch-typing and quick data entry. Some of their keyboards double as iPad stands and cases for either a full-size iPad or an iPad mini, depending on which version of the keyboard/case combo that you purchase.

The Brookstone Roll-Up Keyboard ($29.99, www.brookstone.com) offers a full-size keyboard that's compatible with any iPad model. It's made from silicon rubber and actually rolls up into a compact package for easy transport. When you place it on a flat surface, you can utilize the full-size keyboard, but then you can roll it up and store it while you're on-the-go. The keyboard offers a wireless connection and full-size, "comfort-touch" keys, which make no clicking noise as you're typing. The keyboard is available in black, blue, green, or pink.

Brookstone also offers a growing selection of other iPad external keyboards, as well as cases, external speakers, headphones, desktop stands, external battery packs, and chargers. These accessories are available from the company's chain of retail stores, via mail order, or from Brookstone's website (www.brookstone.com).

The Verbatim Bluetooth Mobile Keyboard ($104.00, www.verbatim.com/prod/accessories/keyboards/wireless-mobile-keyboard) is a durable plastic keyboard that folds into a compact design for easy transport but unfolds into a near-full-size wireless keyboard that you can use on any flat surface. The keyboard operates using two AAA batteries and includes directional arrow keys, a full QWERTY keyboard layout, and additional function keys. It comes with its own case.

For any full-size iPad model, the Props Power and Keyboard Case ($109.95, www.digitaltreasures.com) not only offers a near full-size tactile keyboard, it also serves as a case and stand for the tablet. Plus, it has a built-in rechargeable 8000 mAh battery pack that dramatically extends the life of the iPad, while also allowing you to charge your iPhone, for example.

Yes, the Props Power and Keyboard Case adds thickness and weight to the tablet, but in this case, the added benefit of the keyboard, protective casing, adjustable stand, and battery pack make it ideal for mobile businesspeople who rely on their tablets during long flights, for example.

REPLACING FINGER MOTIONS WITH A STYLUS

Some apps enable you to write or draw directly on the iPad's screen, and others require precision tapping. Instead of using your finger, you can purchase a pen-shaped stylus.

NOTE A stylus is a pen-shaped device that has a soft tip that does not scratch or smudge the iPad's screen but offers a greater level of precision than your finger when writing or drawing on your iPad.

You can also use a stylus to interact with your tablet's touch screen when you're wearing gloves. (The tablet's touch screen will not otherwise recognize glove-covered fingers.) A basic stylus costs anywhere between $15.00 and $30.00; however, more costly pressure-sensitive devices, such as the Hex3 Jaja Stylus ($89.99, www.hex3.co/products/jaja), are also available.

The Hex3 Jaja Stylus (shown in Figure 18.2) links wirelessly to the iPad and allows compatible apps to react based on how hard you press down on the tablet's screen when writing or drawing. This stylus is compatible with more than 25 third-party apps and is ideally suited for digital artists and photo editors, for example.

FIGURE 18.2

The Hex3 Jaja stylus is pressure sensitive and communicates wirelessly with compatible writing, drawing, and photo-editing iPad apps.

Other stylus devices are more low-tech and work with any iPad app. For example, there's the Bamboo Stylus Feel from Wacom ($39.95, www.wacom.com/us/en/everyday/bamboo-stylus-feel).

This stylus feels like a pen in your hand, but it offers an interchangeable, soft tip that's ideal for use with any apps that enable you to handwrite or draw on the tablet's screen. This stylus offers much greater precision than using your finger with a writing, drawing, or photo-editing app.

The L-Tech Plus Twist Ballpoint with Stylus ($69.00) from Levenger (www.levenger.com) is a high-quality, brass barrel ball point pen that also features a silicone rubber stylus head which is ideal for use with an iPad. The L-Tech stylus also comes in a rollerball and fountain pen design, each of which is modern looking; fits nicely within the hand; and allows for added precision when using any iPad apps, particularly those designed for handwriting or drawing.

Many business professionals find it helpful to use an app that transforms their iPads into a traditional notepad so that they can handwrite notes directly on the screen as opposed to typing them using the iPad's virtual keyboard. This is just one type of application where using a stylus, instead of your finger, is helpful.

> **NOTE**   Some of the apps that are ideal for note-taking, sketching, handwriting, or drawing on the iPad's screen, including: Paper by FiftyThree, Penultimate, Notes Plus, GoodReader for iPad, Draw Pad Pro, OmicronNotes Interactive Notepad, and LooseLeaf Notes.

POWER OPTIONS

Depending on how it's being used, your iPad has an average battery life of 10 hours (less if you're doing a lot of web surfing via a cellular data connection). Unfortunately, it's not always convenient to recharge your tablet by plugging it into an electrical outlet. Fortunately, you can purchase optional battery packs and battery chargers to help you keep your iPad sufficiently powered.

BATTERY PACKS

A handful of companies offer external, rechargeable battery packs for the iPad that plug into the tablet via a cable that connects to its 30-pin Dock Connector port or Lightning port. These optional battery packs come in different configurations and sizes, but most of them are smaller than a deck of cards.

The RichardSolo 9000 mAh Universal Mobile Charger ($69.95, www.RichardSolo.com) connects to your iPad via the supplied USB cable. It can dramatically extend the life of your tablet's battery power in between charges. Shown in Figure 18.3, this particular external rechargeable battery pack measures 3.76″ × 1.57″ × 1.57″ and doubles the battery life of your iPad to about 20 hours per charge. It can also be used to recharge your iPhone or other battery-powered devices with a USB port.

FIGURE 18.3

The RichardSolo 9000 is one of many external battery packs available for the iPad that can dramatically extend its battery life in between charges.

BATTERY CHARGERS

Your iPad comes with a white USB cable that you use to connect the tablet to your primary computer (unless you have an older computer that doesn't have a USB port that supplies ample power). The tablet uses the USB connection to charge its batteries while it's connected to the computer.

It's also possible to attach the AC adapter that comes with your iPad to the USB cable in order to charge your tablet by plugging in the adapter to an electrical outlet. For those times when neither your primary computer or an electrical outlet is available, you can purchase and use an optional car charger to plug in the iPad into your car's 12v power outlet/cigarette lighter.

Car charger accessories are readily available from consumer electronics stores, mass market retailers, and office supply stores (such as Best Buy, Radio Shack, Staples, Wal-Mart, and Target), as well as Apple Stores and Brookstone.

When choosing a car charger adapter, make sure it has been approved to work with your iPad model and not only an iPhone (which uses the same 30-pin Dock

Connector or Lightning port, depending on the model). You also have the option of choosing a car power adapter with a USB jack, which you can then plug the white cable that came with your tablet into in order to charge it from your vehicle. This is an easy solution if you have various multiple iOS mobile devices, but one has a 30-pin Dock port and the other has a Lightning port, for example.

> **TIP** While driving in your car, you can use a car charger adapter to recharge the tablet's battery while it's also in use. Depending on your vehicle, however, the engine might need to be running for its 12v power outlet to operate.

DESKTOP STANDS FOR EASIER iPAD ACCESS

While you're sitting at your desk, there are a variety of ways to prop up your iPad for easy access and viewing. These desktop stands come in a range of styles. Some are designed exclusively to hold your tablet in only a portrait or landscape direction, whereas others are more flexible. Ideally, you want a stand that's stylish and sturdy. It should also be able to hold your iPad in portrait or landscape mode, and potentially in a position that's conducive to typing.

Dozens of companies offer hundreds of general-use and specialty iPad stands (designed for use in specific situations). For example, there are stands that attach to a refrigerator door or kitchen cabinets, music or microphone stands, car dashboards, or that are designed for use in a high-traffic retail setting.

The easiest way to find a stand that best suits your needs is to use Google or Yahoo!, for example, and enter the search phrase "iPad Stand." The following are some companies that specialize in iPad stands in a variety of designs:

- Belkin (www.belkin.com)
- Blue Lounge (www.bluelounge.com)
- Brookstone (www.brookstone.com)
- Griffin Technology (www.griffintechnology.com)
- HyperJuice (www.hypershop.com)
- IK Multimedia (www.ikmultimedia.com)
- Incase (www.goincase.com)
- Joby (www.joby.com)
- Levenger (www.levenger.com)
- Logitech (www.logitech.com)

- SwingHolder (www.standforstuff.com)
- Targus (www.targus.com)
- Twelve South (www.twelvesouth.com)

TIP Villa ProCtrl (http://pro-ipad-stand.com/1/apple-ipad-floor-stand-wall-mount-counter-stand) offers a handful of ultra-contemporary-looking, extremely durable iPad stands designed in Holland that are for use in high-traffic retail or trade show environments. The company's offerings include a stainless steel floor stand, wall-mount, and countertop stand. These stands include anti-theft locks and can be used with an iPad for digital signage, interactive kiosks, touch panels, and tradeshow displays.

iPAD CAMERA CONNECTION KIT

If you have a separate digital camera (aside from what's built in to to your iPad), it's possible to connect it directly to your tablet via a USB cable and Apple's iPad Camera Connection Kit ($29.00). With the connection kit, you can quickly transfer your digital images from the camera's memory card to your tablet in order to view, edit, and share your photos.

Available from Apple Stores, Apple.com, or wherever Apple products are sold, the iPad Camera Connection Kit comes with two adapters that connect to the bottom of your iPad via the 30-pin Dock Connector port.

NOTE To use the original iPad Camera Connection Kit and some other accessories with a newer iPad model that features a Lightning port, instead of a 30-pin Dock Connector port, you'll also need the Apple Lightning to 30-pin Adapter ($29.00), which is available from the Apple Store and Apple.com.

Sold separately are the Lighting to USB Camera Adapter cable ($29.00) and Lightning to SD Card Camera Reader cable ($29.99) that are designed for the newer iPad and iPad mini models that feature a Lightning port connector.

NOTE If your digital camera also shoots digital video, you can transfer videos to your iPad using the iPad Camera Connection Kit.

YOUR iPAD AT WORK

ENHANCING THE RECORDING CAPABILITIES OF YOUR iPAD

Whether you want to use your tablet to record dictation, meetings, lectures, workshops, or classes; you're a musician or singer who uses your tablet as a portable multi-track recording studio; or you have other work-related tasks that require high-quality digital recordings to be created, sometimes the microphone that's built in to your iPad does not offer the recording quality that's needed.

Mic-W (www.mic-w.com) is one company that offers professional-quality, external microphones for the iPad that attach directly to the tablet's headphones jack. The company's iSeries of microphones are each priced below $200.00, and each offers exceptional performance for audio measurement applications, recording, or even broadcast use. These mics require no additional power source.

HEADPHONES AND EXTERNAL SPEAKERS

Whether you're listening to music, watching TV shows or movies, recording and then listening to important meetings, or streaming content from the Internet, the speaker built in to your iPad has decent quality, but it's not good enough to satisfy a true audiophile. It's possible to dramatically improve the sound output of your tablet simply by plugging in decent-quality stereo headphones to the iPad's headphone jack or by using good-quality external and wireless (Bluetooth or AirPlay) speakers.

When it comes to adding external speakers to your iPad, the choices are plentiful and the price range is dramatic. You can spend between $25.00 and $100.00 for some decent external speakers, or you can invest hundreds in some top-of-the-line speakers from companies such as Bose (www.bose.com) or Bang & Olufsen (www.bang-olufsen.com).

> **NOTE** External speakers can connect to your iPad in a variety of ways: via the headphone jack, the 30-pin Dock Connector port (or Lightning port, depending on your iPad model), or a wireless Bluetooth connection (so no cables are required). There are also a handful of AirPlay-compatible wireless speakers from Demon, Creative, Marantz, Bowers & Wilkins, JBL, and iHome that work nicely with the iPad. Visit www.apple.com/itunes/airplay for details on AirPlay-compatible speakers.

If you want awesome-quality sound from an external speaker, but portability is important, Jawbone's Jambox Wireless Speaker ($199.99, www.jawbone.com) is the perfect companion for your tablet. This battery-powered speaker has an output capacity of 85 decibels and measures 6" × 1.5" × 2.25". It truly offers the power and sound quality you'd expect from an expensive home theater system. Because it's portable, battery-powered, and wireless (shown in Figure 18.4), you can use it virtually anywhere.

The larger and more powerful Big Jambox ($299.99) is also available. It offers Bluetooth connectivity, a 15-hour battery life, and enough power to fill an entire room with high-quality sound.

FIGURE 18.4

The Jawbone Jambox is the ideal portable speaker for the iPad.

The iHome product line (www.ihomeaudio.com) from SDI Technologies includes a selection of external speakers with built-in connectors or docks for an iPad. These speakers are mid-priced and are ideal for at-home or office use.

If you prefer to listen to high-quality audio in private, such as when you're on an airplane, consider investing in a pair of high-quality, noise-reduction stereo headphones. These range in price from $100.00 to $300.00, and are available from companies such as Bose, Monster Beats, Audio-Technical, Sony, and JVC.

In addition to full-size headphones that fit over your ears, you can achieve true portability and convenience without compromising sound quality with a pair of in-ear headphones. The Bose MIE2i mobile headset ($129.95, www.bose.com) is ideal for listening to audio or watching TV shows or movies in private via your iPad.

> **NOTE** If you've already invested in a high-quality home theater system, there are multiple ways to connect your iPad to it using either cables or a wireless connection. Connecting to your home theater system enables you to view content stored on your tablet on an HD television or listen to audio using your stereo surround-sound speakers.

EXTERNAL WIRELESS STORAGE FOR YOUR iPAD

Seagate, a well-known manufacturer of computer hard drives, offers its GoFlex Satellite mobile wireless storage drive that's designed to work with the iPad ($119.99, www.seagate.com/www/en-us/products/external/external-hard-drive/goflex-satellite).

Instead of utilizing your tablet's limited internal storage space to store multimedia content, including photos, music, movies, and TV show episodes, the GoFlex Satellite (shown in Figure 18.5) is a highly portable, 500GB external hard drive that can be accessed wirelessly via Wi-Fi from an iPad.

FIGURE 18.5

Use the GoFlex wireless hard drive to store a vast amount of multimedia content and data that you can access using your iPad.

The content stored on the GoFlex Satellite from your primary computer (a PC or Mac) can then be accessed simultaneously by up to three different devices wirelessly, and the drive itself can hold more than 300 full-length movies.

The GoFlex Satellite is ideal for storing a vast amount of data, documents, or files that you want with you while on-the-go. The hard drive is battery powered (offering up to 5 hours of continuous data streaming or 25 hours of standby). It weighs less than .6 pounds and measures 4.72" × 3.54" × .87".

CONNECTION OPTIONS: HD, VGA, HOME THEATER

When it comes to giving presentations or sharing multimedia content on your iPad with groups of people, you can easily connect your tablet to an HD television set or LCD projector using the right cables or adapters. Thanks to the AirPlay feature built in to the iOS 7 operating system, you can also wirelessly stream content (movies, TV show episodes, photos, digital slide presentations, and so on) from your iPad to your HD television via an Apple TV device ($99.00, www.apple.com/appletv).

CONNECTING TO AN HD MONITOR OR AN HDTV

If you have a high-definition television (HDTV) or monitor with an HDMI input, use Apple's Digital AV Adapter ($39.00) or Lightning Digital AV Adapter ($49.99), depending on your iPad model, to connect your iPad to that monitor. After connecting, use the iOS's built-in video mirroring feature so everything you see on your iPad's screen is also displayed on the monitor or television set.

This is a great way to showcase your Keynote presentations to groups of people in a meeting or display your digital photos on your television at home. In addition to this adapter, you need a standard HDMI cable (sold separately) that's long enough to connect your iPad to your monitor.

> **CAUTION**   The Apple Digital Video Adapter or Lightning Digital AV Adapter enables you to display whatever appears on your tablet's screen simultaneously on an HD monitor or television set that has an HDMI input. Keep in mind, however, that certain apps that play copyrighted video content, such as television episodes or movies downloaded from the iTunes Store or content streamed using Netflix or a similar content streaming app from a television network, for example, cannot be displayed on a monitor using this adapter.

CONNECTING TO A VGA MONITOR

The Apple VGA Adapter ($29.00) connects from your iPad's 30-pin Dock Connector port to a monitor cable (sold separately) that then attaches to a standard VGA computer monitor. For iPads equipped with a Lightning port, the Lightning to VGA

Adapter ($49.00) is available. Either adapter enables you to display content from your tablet on a computer monitor as you give presentations or demonstrations using content, data, drawings, or animations from your iPad, for example. This type of connection works with most LCD projectors as well.

CONNECTING TO A SOUND SYSTEM OR HOME THEATER SYSTEM

There are several ways to give your iPad a louder voice. The method that gives you the most flexibility to wirelessly stream audio and video content, as well as photos, between your tablet and television set is to connect an Apple TV device to your home theater system and have a Wi-Fi hotspot set up in your home. With this equipment, you can fully use your iPad's AirPlay feature. Keep in mind, however, that Apple TV and other home theater equipment can just as easily be used in a work environment, office, conference room, or auditorium, enabling you to stream content from your tablet and share it with others on large-screen TVs and monitors that are connected to high-end audio systems.

You can also connect your iPad directly to your home theater system using the Apple Composite AV Cable ($39.00 USD), which enables you to watch iPad video on a big screen with stereo sound. Depending on the input connections available as part of your system, the Apple Component AV cable (which serves the same purpose as the Apple Composite AV cable but offers different connectors) is also available.

If you want to give a presentation or transform a blank wall in your home or office into a 60-inch diagonal screen, the HDMI Pocket Projector from Brookstone ($299.99, plus $39.00 for the apple Digital AD Adapter, sold separately) is an extremely portable, battery-powered projector that connects directly to your iPad. Using this device, you can give presentations, watch video media, or project digital photos on any wall or screen without needing a television, speaker system, or cables. The built-in LED lamp projects up to 85 lumens at 1080p HD resolution. The built-in rechargeable battery lasts for about two hours, or the projector can be plugged in to an electrical outlet. The HDMI Pocket Projector (product #802485) is sold at all Brookstone retail stores or can be ordered from www.Brookstone.com.

NOTE   When using the Brookstone HDMI Pocket Projector, you'll probably want to also use external wireless speakers with your iPad when projecting video or multimedia content that includes sound.

AUTOMATING YOUR HOME OR OFFICE LIGHTING WITH PHILIPS HUE

The cutting-edge Hue LED lighting system from Philips (www.meethue.com) offers color-changing light bulbs and lighting fixtures and lighting strips that allow you to create fully programmable ambient lighting "scenes" within your home or office, and control them wirelessly from your tablet.

The Hue three-bulb Starter Kit (shown in Figure 18.6) is priced at $199.99. Additional standard LED bulbs are priced at $59.99 each, the Philips Friends of Hue Bloom Lamp is available for $79.95, and the Philips Friends of Hue LightStrips (6.56 feet long) cost $89.95.

FIGURE 18.6

The Philips Hue lighting system uses programmable, color-changing LED lights in an innovative way to create customizable ambient lighting in any home or office.

All of the Hue products are capable of displaying more than 16 million colors at up to 600 lumens (for the light bulbs) or 120 lumens (for the Bloom Lamp lighting fixtures and light strips, which are sold separately). The Philips Hue lighting system is available exclusively from the Apple Store or Apple.com.

USING A WIRELESS CAMERA TO TRANSFORM YOUR iPAD INTO A REMOTE SECURITY CAMERA OR BABY MONITOR

Several companies have developed extremely portable and wireless cameras that can stream full-color video and sound via the Internet to your iPad. Using specialized apps, these cameras can be used as a remote security camera within a home, office, or hotel room. As a baby monitor, it can be used to watch an infant from whichever room you're in or used remotely to keep tabs on your infant (and their caretaker) while you're at work.

As long as you have a wireless network, any of these cameras can be set up in minutes and begin streaming a live video feed to your iOS mobile device using the Internet.

Priced at $129.95, the iZon Remote Room Monitor from Stem Innovation (www.steminnovation.com) is an app-controlled video camera. It offers live and full-color video and accompanying audio that can be watched in real time and/or automatically recorded and stored online using a private (password-protected) online service.

FINDING LOST ITEMS FAST USING TILE

Thanks to the Find My iPad feature of iCloud, it's easy to track the whereabouts of your iPad if it gets lost or stolen. Thanks to the new Tile accessory that works with the iPad or iPhone ($18.95 each, www.thetileapp.com), it's possible to attach a tiny plastic tag to your computer, keys, purse, briefcase, backpack, or any other item and then track its location from your iOS mobile device that's connected to the Internet.

Each Tile device has a built-in battery that lasts about one year. Using the Tile app, you can then track your device that's within 50–150 feet of your location. However, once you "report" your item missing (via the Tile app), all other Tile users in the world can also help you pinpoint the location of your lost item.

STAYING IN SHAPE USING THE NIKE+ FUELBAND

If you're a fitness buff, several iOS mobile device accessories are available to help you monitor and track your workouts and progress. For example, there's the Nike+ FuelBand ($149.95, www.nike.com/cdp/fuelband) that's worn on your wrist (shown in Figure 18.7). It tracks your steps, calories burned, distance traveled, and time and transmits this information to a specialized app.

FIGURE 18.7

The Nike+ FuelBand can communicate wirelessly with your iOS mobile device throughout the day and during your workouts.

A handful of other companies offer similar fitness accessories that work with the iPad.

A SMART WATCH IS THE PERFECT COMPANION TO YOUR TABLET AND SMARTPHONE

Just as the iPhone has become the world's most popular smartphone, and Apple's iPad is the world's best-selling tablet, the next "must-have" device is quickly becoming a smart watch.

The Pebble Smart Watch ($150.00, www.getpebble.com), shown in Figure 18.8, is available right now. However, Apple is also hard at work developing the iWatch for release most likely in 2014.

A smart watch is a digital watch worn on your wrist that can display the time and date, just like any watch. However, it can also communicate wirelessly with your Smartphone or tablet and display details about incoming emails and text/instant messages, as well as inform you of alerts, alarms, or notifications generated by various apps running on your iOS mobile device.

FIGURE 18.8

The Pebble Smart Watch communicates wirelessly with the iPad.

Many of the smart watches already on the market are also able to run their own apps, allowing them to collect data and transmit that information wirelessly to an iOS mobile device. Thus, the screen of your wristwatch has become another viable way to interact wirelessly with your iPad.

Index

U

V

X-Z

FREE
Online Edition

Safari
Books Online

Your purchase of **Your iPad at Work** includes access to a free online edition for 45 days through the **Safari Books Online** subscription service. Nearly every Que book is available online through **Safari Books Online**, along with thousands of books and videos from publishers such as Addison-Wesley Professional, Cisco Press, Exam Cram, IBM Press, O'Reilly Media, Prentice Hall, Sams, and VMware Press.

Safari Books Online is a digital library providing searchable, on-demand access to thousands of technology, digital media, and professional development books and videos from leading publishers. With one monthly or yearly subscription price, you get unlimited access to learning tools and information on topics including mobile app and software development, tips and tricks on using your favorite gadgets, networking, project management, graphic design, and much more.

Activate your FREE Online Edition at
informit.com/safarifree

STEP 1: Enter the coupon code: KCAJDDB.

STEP 2: New Safari users, complete the brief registration form.
Safari subscribers, just log in.

If you have difficulty registering on Safari or accessing the online edition,
please e-mail customer-service@safaribooksonline.com